The Explanation of

FAMILY, SEXUALITY AND SOCIAL RELATIONS IN PAST TIMES

GENERAL EDITORS:
Peter Laslett, Michael Anderson and Keith Wrightson

Western Sexuality: Practice and Precept in Past and Present Times
Edited by Philippe Ariès and André Béjin
Translated by Anthony Forster

The Explanation of Ideology: Family Structures and Social Systems
Emmanuel Todd
Translated by David Garrioch

The Explanation of Ideology

Family Structures and Social Systems

Emmanuel Todd

Translated by
David Garrioch

Basil Blackwell

English translation © Basil Blackwell Ltd 1985

First published in French as *La troisième planète, structures familiales et systèmes idéologiques*
© Editions du Seuil, Paris

English translation first published 1985

First published in paperback 1988

Basil Blackwell Ltd
108 Cowley Road, Oxford OX4 1JF, UK

Basil Blackwell Inc.
432 Park Avenue South, Suite 1503,
New York, NY 10016, USA

British Library Cataloguing in Publication Data

Todd, Emmanuel
  The explanation of ideology: family structures
  and social systems. — (Family, sexuality and
  social relations in past times)
  1. Religion 2. Ideology 3. Family
  I. Title II. La Troisième planète. *English*
  III. Series
  306   BL48

ISBN 0-631-13724-6
ISBN 0-631-15491-4 Pbk

Library of Congress Cataloging in Publication Data

Todd, Emmanuel, 1951–
  The explanation of ideology.

  Translation of: La troisième planète.
  Bibliography: p.
  Includes index.
  1. Family.   2. Social structure.   I. Title.
  HQ737.T63513 1985   306.8′ 5   85–756
  ISBN 0-631-13724-6
  ISBN 0-631-15491-4 (pbk.)

Typeset by Cambrian Typesetters, Frimley, Surrey
Printed in Great Britain by The Bath Press Ltd, Bath

Contents

Preface to the English edition

This book, although first published in France, owes a great deal to research carried out in association with the *Cambridge Group for the History of Population and Social Structure*. It was in Cambridge, as a research student at Trinity College, that I began working on the comparative analysis of French, Italian and Swedish family systems in the eighteenth and nineteenth centuries. At the time, I was deeply impressed by the extraordinary diversity of household forms and family structures in pre-industrial Europe. My PhD thesis was not, however, at all concerned with the interpretation of ideological phenomena.

The Explanation of Ideology takes as a logical starting-point a hypothesis formulated by Peter Laslett, further developed by Alan Macfarlane, on the relative constancy of family forms and anthropological structures in England during the last five centuries. It considers as valid and verified the idea that the nuclear family is an ancient and stable feature of the English social system, an anthropological rather than a historical trait. Here, this hypothesis is generalized and extended to peasant societies throughout the world, and to the corresponding variety of family forms. In this wider context, the English nuclear family appears as a minority type. Seven main family types are defined, three nuclear and four complex, all considered to be fairly stable between 1600 and 1900.

On the other hand, the emphasis on the geographical stability of political attitudes — a stability which reflects on the ideological plane the stability of family types on the anthropological level — is taken from the French tradition of electoral sociology. As early as the beginning of this century, André Siegfried showed the almost perfect inertia of political attitudes, whether monarchist or republican, throughout the various French provinces. Since then the existence of geographically stable ideologies has remained one of the classic questions in French political science.

In short, the argument of this book combines French traditions with recent British findings.

Emmanuel Todd

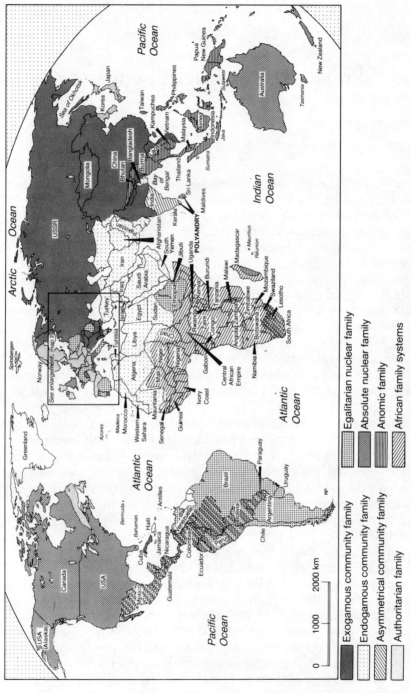

Map 1 Family types throughout the world: main anthropological regions only

Legend:

- Exogamous community family
- Endogamous community family
- Asymmetrical community family
- Authoritarian family
- Egalitarian nuclear family
- Absolute nuclear family
- Anomic family
- African family systems

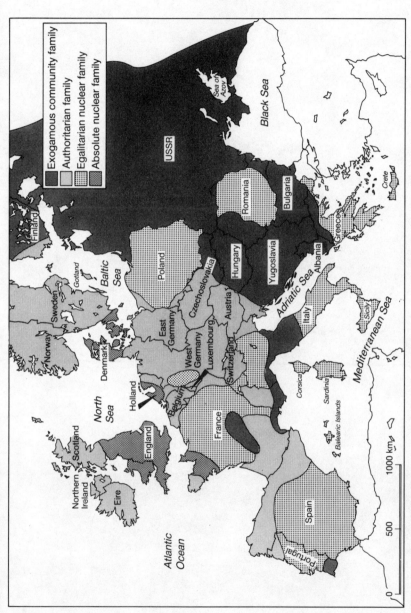

Map 2 Family types in Europe: main anthropological regions only

Introduction:
democracy and anthropology

No theory has so far succeeded in explaining the distribution of political ideologies, systems and forces on our planet. No one knows why certain regions of the world are dominated by liberal doctrines, others by social democracy or Catholicism, by Islam or by the Indian caste system, and others again by concepts which defy classification or description, like Buddhist socialism.

No one knows why communism has triumphed after a revolutionary struggle in Russia, China and Yugoslavia, in Vietnam and Cuba. No one knows why in other places it has failed – sometimes honourably, for in certain countries it plays an important although not dominant role in political life. In France, Italy, Finland and Portugal, in Chile before the coup in 1974, in the Sudan before the elimination of the communists by the army in 1971, and in certain Indian states such as West Bengal or Kerala, communism has a stable electoral position and traditionally enjoys the interest and support of many intellectuals.

In some areas of the world communism has made a brief but conspicuous appearance. In Indonesia it once seemed set for a brilliant future but evaporated after a military take-over and a brutal massacre. In Cambodia, a near neighbour in global terms, its performance was still more striking, rapidly developing to such murderous intensity that it destroyed itself within a very few years. One suspects, however, that these last two examples, spectacular in their power and instability, are not representative of conventional types of communism.

Elsewhere we find that Marxist-Leninist organization, while not entirely absent, is very weak and of almost no political importance: for example, in Japan, Sweden, Germany, Spain and Greece. Throughout much of the world the conquering and would-be universal ideology of the twentieth century has no real influence and is represented only by tiny fringe groups. Communism, which in Russia and China has produced Titans, in the Arab world has given birth to no more than a few martyrs and in the English-speaking world to a number of eccentrics. In most of Latin America — if we exclude Cuba and Chile — in Africa, Thailand, Burma and the Philippines, Marxist-Leninist influence is insignificant.

The history of communism is similar to that of other universal creeds: Buddhism, Christianity, Islam. It has proved rapidly successful in certain societies with which it has a mysterious affinity, only to be stopped after this initial expansion by barriers which remain invisible.

The failure of political science

A simple enumeration, worthy of Ionesco, of the regions and countries where communism is strong illustrates the failure of a political science at present largely dominated by utilitarian and materialist ideas. Liberals and Marxists alike now agree on the importance of economic factors in history: the public or private nature of the means of production and exchange, the level of industrial development, the efficiency of agriculture, the numerical importance of different socio-professional groups. But could one hope to find any economic characteristic which was shared by all the regions where Marxism-Leninism is strong: by Finland and Kerala, Vietnam and Cuba, Tuscany and the Chilean province of Arauco, Limousin and West Bengal, Serbia and southern Portugal, or even for that matter by Russia and China before their revolutions?

On the eve of 1917, Russia was overwhelmingly rural but had sufficient agricultural surplus and enough mineral resources to finance rapid industrial growth. China in the first half of the twentieth century was even more strongly rural, but would have had the greatest difficulty in producing any agricultural surplus at all. Even in good years she could hardly feed her population. So sparse was her industrial development that even the most hard-line Marxist would not dare to accord responsibility for the 1949 Revolution to the proletariat of the Celestial Empire. From a Marxist point of view, the China of 1949 differed from the Russia of 1917 in one vital respect: the peasants had a much clearer idea of private property than did their Russian counterparts, among whom a sort of agrarian communism, the periodical redistribution of land according to family size, was widely practised. But this difference does not really help explain these events because it invalidates the most convincing of the 'economic' interpretations of communism: that which portrays it as a more modern industrial version of a traditional agricultural system.

For we find Russia and China, entirely different countries from an economic point of view, plunging with similar enthusiasm into the same political adventure only thirty years apart and with surprisingly similar results. They shared, to begin with, a single characteristic — their rural economy — which explains nothing: in 1848 when Marx called on the workers of the world to break their chains, 95 per cent of the inhabitants of the world were peasants. Ireland, Sweden, Greece, Japan, Thailand, Turkey, Mexico, all nations where communism was to remain weak, were no more developed industrially than Russia or China. The one major exception was Britain, whose working class was to remain impermeable to communist ideology for 200 years.

Theories of class struggle explain nothing. Some working classes are attracted by Marxism-Leninism and others are not. The same applies to the rural population which in some countries is open to communism, in others not. Even normally conservative bourgeois intellectuals in many countries betray the most elementary rules of class warfare and allow themselves to be seduced by Bolshevism.

Social democracy, Islam, Hinduism, and the rest

As the most crucial ideology of the twentieth century, communism has been widely studied. Traditional political science, although unable to explain its appearance in a particular country, has nevertheless managed to give a good description of it, one which also serves to define, negatively but with equal precision, its economic and political antithesis and its world-wide enemy, Anglo-Saxon liberalism. The characteristics of communism are therefore absence of elementary political, religious and economic freedoms; egalitarian subjection of the individual to the state; and a single permanent ruling party. The features of liberalism, on the other hand, are seen to be free exercise of political, economic and religious rights by the individual; abhorrence of the state, which is perceived as an administrative necessity but also as a threat; and rapid changes of the party in power as a result of the workings of an electoral system.

4 INTRODUCTION

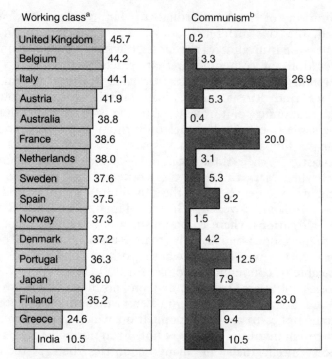

Working class[a]   Communism[b]

	Working class		Communism
United Kingdom	45.7		0.2
Belgium	44.2		3.3
Italy	44.1		26.9
Austria	41.9		5.3
Australia	38.8		0.4
France	38.6		20.0
Netherlands	38.0		3.1
Sweden	37.6		5.3
Spain	37.5		9.2
Norway	37.3		1.5
Denmark	37.2		4.2
Portugal	36.3		12.5
Japan	36.0		7.9
Finland	35.2		23.0
Greece	24.6		9.4
India	10.5		10.5

[a] percentage of the active population employed in industry in 1972.
[b] percentage of communist votes in the late 1960s (the exact dates
are given on p. 51)

Figure 1 The working class without communism. The coefficient of
correlation between the percentage of the active population which is
working class and the communist vote expressed as a percentage of votes
cast is practically nil: −0.09. The coefficient of correlation varies between
−1 and +1. It is higher when its absolute value approaches 1, and lower as the
absolute value approaches 0. It shows a positive correlation between two
variables when it is positive, a negative one when it is negative.

Anything beyond these two poles is heresy. Yet the nations
which subscribe to one or other of these ideologies, to liberalism
or to communism, account for only 40 per cent of the world's
population. The remaining 60 per cent have not received nearly
the same attention from political scientists, and are considered
conceptually irrelevant. Their ideologies and political systems
are at best treated as imperfect forms, somewhere in between
communism and liberalism according to the degree of economic,
religious or political authoritarianism. At worst, they appear to

social scientists as legal or religious monstrosities, aberrations of the human imagination that cannot be registered on the scale dictated by European political conventions whose linear structure is like a thermometer, capable of measuring only hot or cold, the degree of liberty or of totalitarianism.

Putting together all these misfits, all the ideologies which are neither 'communist' nor 'liberal', gives another of those comical lists which political science is capable of producing: social democracy, libertarian socialism, Christian democracy, Latin-American, Thai or Indonesian military regimes, the Buddhist socialism of Burma or of Sri Lanka, Japanese parliamentarianism, technically perfect but with the sole flaw of never changing its ruling party, Islamic fundamentalism and socialism, Ethiopian militarist Marxism, and the Indian regime which combines parliamentary and caste systems and whose 700 million subjects have in one swoop been disqualified by 'modern' political science.

Social science has found a justification for refusing to fit these exotic systems and ways of thinking into its conceptual framework: is it reasonable to hope to understand them when the principal mystery, that of the liberal/communist conflict, has yet to be resolved? But this argument is easily refuted: it is precisely because of the refusal to look on all political forms – whether European or not – as normal and theoretically significant that communism has never been fully understood, and nor, as a direct result, has its liberal 'antithesis'.

Furthermore, if we move from a politico-economic definition of ideological systems to a religious one, the opposite of communism is no longer liberalism but the whole group of doctrines which proclaim the existence of a spiritual realm. For communism alone declares that God does not exist and is prepared to impose this belief on humanity. Here the liberal, pluralist systems, tolerant or agnostic on religious questions, are out of the picture. They cannot provide a conceptual framework for the increasingly violent conflict between communism and Islam in Afghanistan, or between communism and the Catholic church in Poland.

Is it, then, too much to allow that the range of political and religious ideologies spread around the world does not divide into two camps, but forms a system with many poles, and that all these poles – communist, liberal, Catholic, social democratic, Hindu, Islamic, Buddhist – are equally normal, legitimate and worthy of analysis?

A satisfactory explanation of communism must also provide

the key to other world-wide ideologies. The situation is precisely that which is encountered in the natural sciences: one cannot *partly* understand the principle of the attractive force of matter, that of the circulation of the blood or of the classification of the elements in chemistry. To take the whole world as the field of study, therefore, is simply to apply to social science the minimum of intellectual rigour which the natural sciences take for granted. Any hypothesis must take all the forms observed into account.

A hypothesis: family structure

There is one ubiquitous theory which may be detected in political thought all over the world from Confucius to Rousseau, from Aristotle to Freud. It is the idea that family relations — those between parents and children, between husband and wife — provide a model for political systems and serve to define the relationship between the individual and authority. It is a theory which until recently was as unusable as it was indestructible, for the embryonic state of social anthropology (which is concerned with studying and classifying family forms) has never before allowed any systematic comparison between family models and political structures.

For political scientists in the past, in any case, there existed only one family form, that of their immediate social environment, which determined the political structure. And it is not easy to see how this single form could give rise to the baffling variety of systems, forces and ideologies which exist throughout the world. This ideal family, of course, is not the same for all scholars: implicitly Confucius refers to a Chinese type, Rousseau to that dominant in and around Paris or in certain parts of Switzerland, Freud to the German model, and Aristotle to the Athenian version.

With Frédéric Le Play (1806—82), sociologist, Catholic, reactionary, as successful in empirical research as he was hopeless in political theory, the anthropological study of the family took a decisive step. It abandoned its universalist approach and began to analyse local variations. Le Play set out a typology which included three family forms, and studied their distribution throughout Europe, from Tangiers to the Urals. One is still surprised today by the quality of the monographs which this product of the Ecole Polytechnique, and his team, produced.

Not one has been invalidated or even weakened by the most recent research, whether on England, Russia, Scandinavia, Italy, France or Hungary.

Liberty and equality

The analytical strength of this first typology arises from the fact that Le Play, hostile to the principles of 1789, picked out within family structures themselves the working of the ideas of liberty and equality which sum up the French Revolution and mark, for the whole of the world, the beginning of modern politics.

According to Le Play, relations between father and son determine people's concept of liberty or its opposite; the bond between brothers creates an idea of equality or of inequality.

Liberty The child who continues to live with his parents after marriage, forming a 'vertical' relationship within an extended family group, is conforming to an authoritarian model of family relations. If, on the other hand, he leaves his parents after adolescence to form an independent household through marriage, then the model is a liberal one which puts the emphasis on individual independence.

Equality Inheritance may work in one of two ways: if parental property is divided up, the process expresses an egalitarian relationship between brothers; if the inheritance system is based on the indivisibility of the succession and excludes all but one of the brothers, then it embodies an ideal of inequality.

Logically, the application of these two principles of liberty and equality together with their opposites (liberty/authority, equality/inequality) should produce four possible types of family system, as follows:

1 liberal and inegalitarian;
2 liberal and egalitarian;
3 authoritarian and inegalitarian;
4 authoritarian and egalitarian.

However, only types 2, 3 and 4 are to be found in Le Play's typology. A detailed examination of the way in which the principles of liberty and equality work together in family life indicates the reason for Le Play's hesitation and for the only error in his typology.

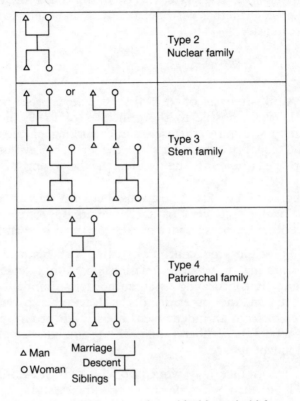

Figure 2   Le Play's typology: ideal household forms

Type 4, authoritarian and egalitarian, produces the densest family forms. All the sons have an equal right to their father's succession. But all of them continue as married adults to live with the elder generation, producing an 'undivided' family community which Le Play calls patriarchal. Each brother brings his wife and children into this group and all of them remain under the authority of the father, a proper patriarch. On the death of the head of the community, each of the brothers may, if he so wishes, claim his share of the succession and found his own household, which as it grows will in turn make him a patriarch. This model combines vertical characteristics – a close father/son relationship – with horizontal ones – strong ties between brothers.

Type 3, authoritarian and inegalitarian, maintains a close vertical association only between the father and the one son who will succeed him as head of the family. The other brothers must leave what Le Play called the 'stem family', or if they stay must remain unmarried. In this system the heir may be the eldest son (primogeniture), the youngest (ultimogeniture), or even one of the other children chosen by the father.

Type 2, liberal and egalitarian, is the exact opposite of type 3. It requires rapid separation of father and sons and equal division of the succession between the children. Le Play calls this type the 'unstable family'. The principles of liberty and equality (or their opposites) are quite compatible in types 2, 3 and 4 – the components of Le Play's typology.

Type 1, liberal and inegalitarian, which Le Play rejects as a practical possibility, combines apparently contradictory concepts. If none of the adult children is required to live with the father what purpose is served by the inegalitarian principle of indivisible succession? The liberal family has no interest in household continuity, in the permanence of the family group over time. If the original household is going to disappear anyway, why not practice a simple division of spoils? Such reasoning refuses to see the ideas of liberty and equality as first principles (part of a way of thinking) which are not necessarily tied to a particular social and economic environment.

In practice a liberal family system (excluding cohabitation between parents and adult children) which is indifferent to the concept of equality can be observed, in Le Play's own work, in England and Holland and, according to recent work in historical anthropology, in Denmark. The father expects his children to found their own households, but sets about dividing his property in his will without being bound by precise conventions of inheritance. While not systematically inegalitarian like the stem family, this type is not egalitarian. Not knowing what to make of this family model, which he observed in England, Le Play concluded that it was a degenerate form of stem family – authoritarian and inegalitarian – thus introducing into his model an evolutionary tendency very much in line with the ideas of his time, but which diminishes the force and originality of an approach which would later be called structuralist.

But both deduction and observation reveal the existence of two liberal models, two forms of what Le Play called the 'unstable' family: the 'nuclear' family in the language of modern sociology. It is in fact found in its purest form when the egalitarian ideal is rejected and the father is free to disinherit some of the children. The resulting uncertainty about succession is at first sight a formidable weapon in the service of parental authority. But looked at from the point of view of the values which underlie an anthropological system, its significance is quite different. Disinheriting a child means accepting an absolute break between the generations and allows that there may be no tie between father and son. It amounts to denying the strength of the biological relationship.

In the egalitarian model, however, father and son are bound together legally, unable to escape an apparently natural determinism. An egalitarian inheritance system undermines the basic principle of the nuclear family: the separation of father and son.

I will therefore use the term 'absolute nuclear family' to mean a nuclear family which admits the possibility of disinheritance and the right of the generations to have nothing to do with each other. When, on the other hand, refusal to cohabit is nevertheless

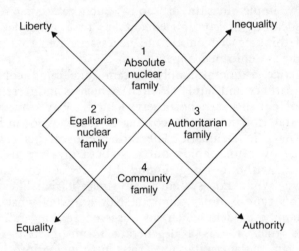

Figure 3 Values underlying family types within Europe. A diagramatic depiction along two axes (liberty/authority and equality/inequality) gives a squared figure with four boxes, each one representing one family type. It shows at a glance the differences and similarities between the types. The two family models on any side of the square have one shared characteristic: liberty or equality. The two diametrically opposed models, which touch only at the centre point, differ in every sense, both in their attitude towards liberty and in that towards equality. The egalitarian nuclear family and the authoritarian family lie directly opposite each other, as do the absolute nuclear family and the community family.

accompanied by the principle of equal inheritance I will use the term 'egalitarian nuclear family'.

Like the three musketeers, Le Play's families now number four. To avoid confusion and to emphasize the fundamental values which underlie each family model, I will also rename types 3 and 4, the stem family and the patriarchal family. The stem family, which is organized around strict interdependence between father and son, will be termed the 'authoritarian family'. The patriarchal family — an imperfect term because it neglects the solidarity between brothers and evokes only the father—son relationship — I will henceforth call the 'community family'.

The contribution of psychoanalysis

Having recognized the demoniacal principles of the French Revolution, or their negation, in the structure of the family, Frédéric Le Play then succumbed to the great illusion of revolutionary philosophy, the belief that politics shape society and not the reverse. He thought that conscious action on the part of reformers could modify family structure. He accused the French Civil Code of encouraging the fragmentation of inherited property, of undermining paternal authority, and of destroying the community and authoritarian families (patriarchal and stem families in his terminology). He proposed the reintroduction of the anti-egalitarian principle of indivisible inheritances. This man who had devoted his life to the study of the family did not believe in its solidity. He saw it as something essentially malleable, not perceiving it as a basic, fundamental sociological phenomenon. Le Play did recognize that political and religious ideologies and ideas of family relations in some sense mirror each other, but implicitly he made ideology the solid object — the family its faithful but fragile reflection.

It was only with Freud and the psychoanalytic school that the autonomy and the primordial importance of the family were recognized, and that ideology in turn appeared as a simple reflection of concepts of the family. The definitive step is taken in Freud's *The Future of an Illusion* (1928), a treatise which finds in the family the unconscious origins of metaphysical ideas and which portrays God as no more than a father-image. Ideology, in this case religion, is now no more than the complex and often pathogenic web of normal family relations put into intellectual form.

The forgotten brother

The great weakness of the psychoanalytic approach is that it postulates the existence of a single, universal family structure, and it is not clear how this could engender all the various ideological products of the human imagination. How could the very same family structure produce the stern Protestant Creator, the merciful Allah of the Muslims, the Hindu pantheon, and Buddhist uncertainty about the nature of the spiritual? Psychoanalysis has little to learn from political science as regards Eurocentricity.

Above all, Freud and his disciples chose largely to ignore the sibling relationship, despite the fact that just as much as vertical relations — father/son, father/daughter, mother/son, mother/daughter — it helps to determine unconscious feelings. Why? Simply because the family system in Germany, the birthplace of psychoanalytic thought, is hostile to the concept of brotherhood. Likewise, the new discipline was to be most enthusiastically received in another anthropological system which favours distance between brothers, that of Anglo-Saxon America. Elsewhere, where the ideal of an equal and united brotherhood dominated — in Russia, China and still more in Muslim areas — a refractory mentality offered few openings for Freud's ideas.

Self-perpetuation of the family

Anthropological structure, unlike an ideological system, is self-perpetuating. The family by definition reproduces people and values. Unconsciously but inevitably, each generation absorbs those parental values which define elementary human relationships: between parents and children, between siblings, between husband and wife. The power of the reproductive mechanism springs from the fact that it does not need to be conscious or expressed: it is automatic and has its own internal logic.

For ideology to be passed on from one generation to the next, it must be embodied in a complex process of highly organized intellectual apprenticeship, in practice in the schools. It is more difficult to absorb ideas about the republic, communism, racism, anti-Semitism, the existence of God or of castes, or about metempsychosis, than to assimilate by instinct or imitation the stereotyped norms which govern relations between individuals belonging to the same elementary unit, the reproductive family.

In practice each generation whose fundamental values are formed in the crucible of the family has the capacity to re-create in adolescence the dominant ideology of its own social world without being indoctrinated. To do so appears just and above all natural. Two brothers who have always been accustomed to receiving the same punishments and the same toys, meticulously evenly distributed, will in puberty irreversibly adopt egalitarian values. The left-wing parents of these children, who nevertheless have never wanted to talk politics with their children and have never tried to indoctrinate them, are amazed and delighted to find that by some physiological miracle they have produced left-wing offspring.

But it would be a mistake to restrict the idea of equality to material or economic things. Toys and punishments are simply, among a host of other feelings and emotions, a manifestation of affection. An equitable distribution of inheritance, of gifts and of punishments is the outward sign of a homogeneous, symmetrical emotional system in which parents display their feelings for all their children in equal measure. For adult children equality is not simply expressed in the equitable division of goods but by the equal right of all of them to marry; conversely, inegalitarian principles allow only some of them to have a sex life, at least within marriage. Thus equality is not an economic ideal but an intuitive, mathematical concept, as applicable to the emotions as it is to the weighing of potatoes.

Human relations and social relations

The opposition ideology/anthropology is based on the existence of two types of interaction between individuals. The first is interaction with the immediate environment, a network of basic relationships which has its own laws but whose norms are learnt unconsciously through first-hand experience, in day-to-day contact with individuals of flesh and blood. These may be called 'human relations'. The other type is secondary interaction, determined by sets of attitudes which govern relations between individuals who do not know each other directly. Learning the rules of such impersonal relations is an artificial, conscious process conducted in ideological terms. These may be termed 'social relations'.

Belief in equality between brothers belongs to the first type (human relations) and its reflection, the idea of equality before the law, to the second (social relations).

The dress rehearsal: the French Revolution

At this point we can suggest a new interpretation of the French Revolution, one which shows the interaction between the anthropological and the political spheres and the way in which ideology is determined by family structure.

Revolution came to France at the end of a period of rapid cultural development during which half the country, to the north of a line drawn between Saint-Malo and Geneva came to enjoy the benefits of reading and writing. Ideological ferment followed intellectual agitation, and the indoctrination of the people accompanied the spread of literacy.

But the great ideas of the eighteenth-century French philosophers and revolutionaries — liberty and equality — which seemed to them to be natural laws and direct products of pure reason, were in fact only an elegant transcription of a latent anthropological structure which had existed at least since the Middle Ages. Liberty and equality are the characteristic features of the family model which traditionally occupies northern France. The egalitarian nuclear family (type 2) is found throughout the Paris region and its periphery: north of the Saint-Malo—Geneva line the only exceptions are Alsace and parts of Normandy and of the Nord-Pas-de-Calais region. These educators and teachers, who thought they were modelling the people according to their idea of progress, were simply expressing aspirations and sentiments of anthropological origin. At the very moment when the modern world thought it was gaining control of the French countryside and destroying its traditions it was itself overtaken by anthropology.

De Tocqueville's error

The French Revolution saw the birth of a conceptual error which continues to dog political science: the confusion of mass politics with individualistic egalitarianism. 'Mass politics' refers to the development of political consciousness and activity among the people, both urban and rural; 'individualistic egalitarianism' to the adoption by the people of an egalitarian mentality. The events of the French Revolution brought together mass politics and individualistic egalitarianism. De Tocqueville, who better than anyone saw in the events of 1789—1848 a crucial question of *mentalités*, confused the two as 'democracy'. Looking to the

future, he believed the process of democratization to be universal
and inevitable: France was affected first, but all of Europe would
follow.

However, if one divides democratization into its two components
— mass politics and individualistic egalitarianism — it is clear
that only the former is universal. Between the year 1000 and the
year 2000 all the peoples of the world have been or will be
affected by the uprooting of traditional peasant society. The
process today is almost complete in the Third World where
unrestrained urbanization and the spread of literacy are proceeding
at an even faster rate than in Europe from 1600 to 1900.

The diversity of nations

Nevertheless, in those societies where the anthropological base
— that is to say the family system — is not egalitarian and liberal,
the advent of mass politics has not produced ideologies of the
French kind. In England, Germany and Russia, the spread of
literacy has produced fervent doctrines which have little to do
with the ideology of 1789, apart from the fact that they also
seized the imagination of the people and galvanized them into
action. Until 1848, France (and, within the country, the Paris
region) dominated the continent demographically and militarily
and succeeded in imposing her political ideals on Europe. After
this, each nation began to speak its own language and to put
its own dreams into practice. England embraced the idea of
liberty but not that of equality. Germany produced authoritarian,
inegalitarian doctrines, preaching submission to the state and
affirming the inequality of men and of races. Russia invented the
modern form of authoritarian, egalitarian communism which
proclaims itself universal.

This diversity arose from the fact that these nations, each one
constructed on a particular anthropological foundation, set its
own family values into ideological form. In England the absolute
nuclear family requires its children to be independent but not
equal. The German family, essentially authoritarian and based
on the submission of children to their father's will and on the
indivisibility of inheritance, exalts discipline but is indifferent
to equality. The Russian community family combines equality
and discipline, parity between brothers and obedience to the
father.

It is mere anthropological coincidence that each of the four

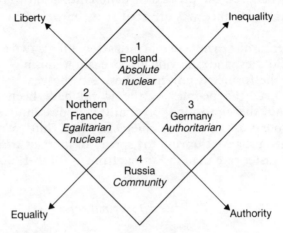

Figure 4   Regions of family types within Europe

family categories derived from Le Play's model dominates one of the European powers, and that each of the great nations of the continent embodies one typological possibility.

At this point one could illustrate the correspondence in Europe between the political system and the anthropological base — but only in Europe. For Le Play's typology, even with the addition of a further category, does not permit analysis of family structure on a world-wide scale. However, one must go beyond a European interpretation of communism, 70 per cent of whose demographic and ideological weight lies outside Europe, principally in Asia. Above all, if there really is a general connection between anthropology and ideology then one would not expect European-type family structures to give rise to ideologies which do not exist in Europe: most notably Islam and the caste system (these two socio-religious systems alone cover one-third of the world's population). It must also be remembered that the existence of communism in Asia suggests that communism's underlying family structure is not exclusively European.

General methodology

The oppositions ideology/anthropology and social relations/human relations are particularly useful outside Europe when attempting to trace the origins of religious ideological systems. They are indispensable if one is accurately to describe ideologies which are based on ideas about family ties.

The Indian caste system is a family ideology which places each individual in an abstract and impersonal social network, the caste (or to be more precise the sub-caste), which is defined by ties of descent outside which he or she cannot marry. But the sub-caste is composed largely of people who do not know each other and who live in different places. Beneath this intellectual edifice can be seen a particular family structure, a model of interpersonal relations which produces the concept of and the need for social segregation. These two levels — social and human, ideological and familial — must be clearly distinguished if the caste system is to be placed with any precision among the various political and religious ideologies — communism, Islam, social democracy, the various forms of Christianity — which likewise define social relations between people who do not know each other directly.

A universal hypothesis is possible: the ideological system is everywhere the intellectual embodiment of family structure, a transposition into social relations of the fundamental values which govern elementary human relations: liberty or equality, and their opposites, are examples. One ideological category and only one, corresponds to each family type.

Ignoring all the accepted procedures of present-day social science and at the risk of being branded a positivist, I am going to test this theory and prove it in the same way as in any exact science: by exhaustively comparing the hypothesis and the evidence, that is by a complete examination of the familial and ideological systems experienced by the settled human groups which make up at least 95 per cent of the population of the planet. Testing the theory involves two steps.

First, a general typology of family structure must be devised. It must be both logically exhaustive, starting from first principles and setting out all the possible family structures; and empirically exhaustive, that is to say taking into account and describing all the family forms which are actually observable on the surface of the planet.

Second, it must be shown that to each family form described there corresponds one and only one ideological system and that this ideological system is not to be found in areas of the world which are dominated by other family forms (in mathematical terms one would speak of a bijective relationship between family types and political types).

A further requirement is that secondary variations in family structure within each anthropological type must correspond to secondary variations in the political or religious forms within the corresponding ideological type.

1

The seven families

Le Play's typology, developed for the analysis of family forms within Europe, is incomplete. It fails to take account of one essential aspect of family structure which for ethnologists has become a routine part of their observations: the extent to which marriage is exogamous or endogamous, in other words the existence of certain prescriptions for choosing a marriage partner within or outside the family group. For an anthropologist, especially a structuralist one, this oversight is unforgivable: prohibitions against incest are for a structuralist anthropologist a kind of fundamental mystery, something which affords access to a culture in the same way that the mystery of the Eucharist or of the Holy Trinity brings the Christian into contact with God.

Incest

The almost universal incest taboo — there are a number of important and sociologically significant exceptions — is not a source of uniform family forms for it is applied in a variety of ways. In different parts of the world the frequency of marriage between first cousins, that is between the children of two brothers, two sisters, or of brother and sister, ranges from 0 to 60 per cent of all marriages. In some places there are unions between half-brother and half-sister; sometimes even between brother and sister; or one step further still, some communities allow marriages between non-identical twins of different sexes. Such cases are statistically rare but can be taken into account in formulating global theoretical models. They are also reflected in a particular type of ideological framework.

Le Play's indifference to this aspect of family structure is comprehensible: despite their diversity in terms of inheritance systems and household forms, European countries are almost unanimous in observing very strict rules about consanguinity. Everywhere, from Scandinavia to Italy, from Portugal to Russia, whether the family is of nuclear, authoritarian or community form, people very rarely marry their first cousins.

If we add two levels of endogamy — which can be present to a high or a low degree — to the corrected form of Le Play's model (containing four rather than three categories), we would expect to end up with a classification containing eight family forms. However, in the anthropological equation four multiplied by two does not equal eight. The combination of the principles underlying Le Play's typology with those that determine the type of endogamy produces some forms in which the principles conflict and one in which they double up. The result in this case is that four multiplied by two equals seven, because preferential marriage presupposes a certain type of relationship between brother and sister that clashes with the principles of equality or of inequality that Le Play identifies.

Not all of Le Play's family types are affected in the same way by a relaxation of the exogamy requirement. The community family can be divided, if the incest taboo is weak, into two new types: the endogamous community family and the asymmetrical community family. The authoritarian family remains essentially unchanged by a relaxation of the taboo and does not produce any new forms which are fundamentally different from the 'exogamous' authoritarian family. The absolute and egalitarian nuclear families change in the same way if restrictions on the marriage of close relatives are reduced: they merge to form a single model, the anomic family, which may be defined as an out-of-order nuclear type.

The community family and the relaxation of the incest taboo: endogamy

A familial rather than an ideological phenomenon, preferential marriage between first cousins results from the overdevelopment of fraternal affection. The tie between brothers, the dominant human relationship within the family system, not only brings brothers and their wives under the same roof: it is reinforced by marriage between the children of these brothers. The ideal of fraternal affection attempts to get round the interdiction on consanguinity, respecting it but limiting its scope as much as possible to simply the taboo on sexual relations between brother and sister.

Resulting from solidarity between brothers, what is called the FBD marriage (ego marries father's brother's daughter) must belong to a dense, community family structure (type 4 in the amended Le Play typology). In this interpretation there is no longer any difference in quality between marriage ties and ties of descent, unlike in the classic anthropological approach. Descent engenders a fraternal relationship which in turn gives rise to a matrimonial relationship. This endogamous community family is typical of the Muslim world. Its emotional substratum is revealed repeatedly throughout the *Arabian Nights*, whose starting-point is the bond between two brothers, and in which a man's love for his wife is inevitably expressed in a leitmotiv which fails to distinguish between marriage and descent: 'I loved my wife greatly because she was my uncle's daughter.'

In practice cross-cousin marriage is also very common in family systems where parallel-cousin marriage is practised. This is only natural. Fraternal solidarity is only one aspect of the global solidarity of siblings. The Muslim family system in fact embodies bilateral endogamy, marriages between the children of a brother and of a sister often being as numerous as those between the children of two brothers.

The community family and asymmetrical marriage

In the Muslim world and in the endogamous community family generally, the link between brothers lies at the heart of a system that emphasizes all sibling relationships. In the case of the Indian community family, a system which is also based on solidarity between siblings, the primary relationship is that between brother and sister. The community household structure places brothers with the same rights within a wider domestic group. But the children of these brothers cannot marry each other. On the other hand cross-cousin marriage is encouraged. Thus cross-cousin marriage is accompanied by a taboo on alliances between parallel cousins. This system also encourages marriage between a man and the daughter of his sister, a further illustration of the brother—sister bond.

This particular family model is half-way between the exogamous and endogamous community models. It encourages one type of endogamy while forbidding another. Like the two preceding models, however, it is a variation on the theme of solidarity between brother and sister. The favoured marriage between the children of a brother and a sister is necessarily linked with a community family household. It is this family type which gives rise, on an ideological level, to the caste system.

Logic, and the desire to be exhaustive, dictate that we should now consider a type which is theoretically impossible, the case of preferential marriage between maternal parallel cousins. In reality there is no settled peasant society whose family ideal is an extended group based on an inverted agnatic relationship, in other words on solidarity between sisters rather than between brothers. Only a domestic group consisting of two sisters and their husbands could produce a preference for marriage between maternal parallel cousins. Such a system would, however, be an infringement of the principle of male dominance, a principle whose forms and strengths admittedly vary but which is in practice much more universal than the incest taboo, even if it has not attracted the attention of anthropologists to the same extent.

Relaxing the obligation of exogamy therefore produces two new types of community family: the endogamous community family and the asymmetrical community family. The community family (the patriarchal family in Le Play's terminology) which exists in Europe becomes the exogamous community family.

The authoritarian family and the relaxation of the incest taboo

Relaxing the obligation of exogamy has only a minor effect on the authoritarian family, which is firmly bolstered by its vertical organization and by the principle of indivisible inheritance. The number of marriages between cousins modifies this system very little. The principle of separating brothers makes any real model of preferred marriage impossible.

In practice, a slight variant of the authoritarian family does exist which, while not endogamous, tolerates more frequent marriages between cousins and which is characterized by a degree of warmth between brothers, their lack of equality still allowing a measure of solidarity. It is a combination which is typical of the traditional Jewish family and which may also be found among the Romany gypsies. In both cases the small size of the community encourages a degree of endogamy which, while never becoming an ideal, is accepted as a realistic compromise. Once the size of the community increases there is a return to the normal exogamous type.

The nuclear family and the relaxation of the incest taboo: the anomic family

Fear of incest has a different kind of effect on the nuclear family: based on the principle of the separation of children from parents (complete in the case of the absolute nuclear family, less so in that of the egalitarian nuclear family), its structure is weakened by any relaxation of the principle of separate lines of descent.

Obligatory exogamy is in fact an invisible and unconscious support of the nuclear family: banning marriage between the children of brothers is a logical corollary of their separation. In communities where the children of siblings do marry, yet where the nuclear family is the ideal form, there is a blatant contradiction between theory and practice: in general, census returns reveal households which are not composed simply of parents and unmarried children. Each domestic group contains other adult individuals and often several couples. Parents and married children frequently live together, the dominant relation in these cases normally being between the women. However, this form is never thought to be an ideal grouping even when it is statistically dominant.

In the anomic family the rules of inheritance become less rigid and there is a compromise between the principle of equality and the reality of family life. The house will very often be left to the youngest daughter who looks after her aged parents. This is not the same thing as the indivisible inheritance of the authoritarian family, but rather reflects the hesitation of a nuclear family

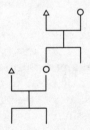

Figure 5   Common household form of the anomic family

system which fails to separate its members when the children reach adulthood.

This family form is dominant in South-East Asian countries which have a tradition of Hinayana Buddhism: Burma, Thailand, Cambodia. It is also found in countries in the same area which were relatively recently converted to Islam such as Malaysia and Java – or even to Christianity – such as the Philippines. It is typical too of certain Indian cultures in Central America and of all the Andean civilizations, especially the Aymaras and the Quechuas.

To define this particular family form John F. Embree developed the concept of the loosely structured society, which he first applied to Thailand although this is not the most extreme example. (In countries such as Burma and above all Cambodia the disintegration of the usual anthropological forms has gone much further.) Well acquainted with Chinese and especially Japanese society, Embree was struck by the contrast between their rigidly structured family systems – a community type in the case of China, an authoritarian type in Japan – and the amorphous character of the Thai model. Absence of structure in itself thus became a particular type of grouping. I will call this faulty nuclear model the anomic family, as a tribute to Emile Durkheim.

The existence of this type is very important for our understanding of Western models of the nuclear family. From an anthropological point of view they are rigidly regulated. The existence of the nuclear family requires the strict observance of particular anthropological norms, especially that of exogamy.

Relaxing the obligation of exogamy increases the number of family models from four to seven. The absolute nuclear, egalitarian nuclear, authoritarian and community families are joined by three new types: two community models, each with a system of preferred marriage, the endogamous community family and the asymmetrical community family; one malfunctioning nuclear family, the anomic family.

This analytical grid has one flaw – it omits to take account of the continent of Africa. Like any typology, it is based on the application of a number of a priori principles; it is one description, among an infinite number of possible descriptions, of the reality of the family. Like Le Play's typology it is based on unstated premises. Implicitly it assumes the existence of constants, of structural characteristics which because they are common to all families have no part in a comparative analysis. Le Play passed over the exogamy/endogamy opposition because all European cultures were exogamous. In the same way the typology of seven families ignores the existence of unstable household forms, because all the systems studied have one characteristic in common: a certain degree of stability in relations between individuals, for which the model is the stability of the married couple.

Africa: the unstable household

In Europe, in South and North America, in Asia and in Islamic countries, mutual relations between individuals — between parents and children, husband and wife, brothers and sisters — are relatively stable. The household, the domestic unit, is a basis for analysis. This is not true of the African systems where the relationships between individuals are in a constant state of flux. The story of a domestic group cannot be summed up here, as it might be elsewhere, in terms of a few major events — births, marriages, deaths. In the innumerable African models, men, women and children are forever on the move, making and remaking, in a single lifetime, domestic forms which cannot logically be called households. A symbol of the mobility in basic human relationships is marriage, which in Africa is an extremely fragile bond.

Although it is found in most non-Christian cultures, polygamy is nevertheless the exception rather than the rule, in Muslim countries as elsewhere. In Black Africa polygamy is the norm, an ideal fully realized in statistical terms. The corollary is divorce, which is more frequent in Africa than anywhere else in the world.

It would be wrong to confuse instability with absence of norms, and to fall into a kind of implicit racism which depicts Africans, once again, as good or bad savages. Polygamy and divorce are the norms. The African models, enormously varied and as yet not fully charted, are in most cases clearly exogamous and obey rules on consanguinity which are much more strict, at least in their rejection of incest, than the family types we have so far classified as anomic.

However, Africa does not represent a single family type but a range of types produced by the new criterion of the stability of mutual relations between individuals. In this context therefore I will speak of unstable systems, reserving the term 'family' for stable domestic groups. In Africa, however, as in other places, one can still identify links between the anthropological base and the ideological forms. But the extreme fragmentation of the data and of the systems permits only a general and incomplete correspondence to be made.

The seven families and liberty

Le Play's typology was deduced from a direct application of the principles of the French Revolution — liberty and equality — to family structure. This is not true of the seven family typology which adds to these concepts the principle of exogamy, achieved to a greater or lesser extent in different societies, but which does not at first sight seem to carry any political significance. Nevertheless, the endogamy/exogamy division is not without consequences for liberty and equality. The choice of a marriage partner expresses an idea about authority and a conception of justice just as much as rules on inheritance and cohabitation. Le Play's conceptualization was based on a double dichotomy: liberty/submission, equality/inequality. Taking the incest taboo into account leads us to distinguish not two degrees of liberty but four, and to place the idea of equality in the wider perspective of symmetry.

Each of Le Play's family types corresponds to one ideal of how matrimonial decisions should be taken. The nuclear family allows the individual freely to choose a marriage partner. The authoritarian and exogamous community families, in which two generations of adults live together, presuppose the active and pre-eminent participation of the parents in the choice of partner: in both practice and theory the marriage is 'arranged'. The two degrees of liberty (liberty/submission) implicitly singled out by Le Play are both to be found in the way matrimony is organized. The form of cohabitation defines an ideal of marriage.

What happens in the case of endogamous marriage? Naturally, the choice of a partner here has nothing to do with the individual who is to be married, since his future wife must be integrated into the community family. However, the choice does not belong to the parents' generation either. An endogamous marriage is decided not by an individual but by custom, and a cousin is from birth a potential marriage partner. The ideal marriage is here beyond individual choices. The mechanism is self-regulating.

The nuclear family allows freedom of choice to the younger generation. The exogamous community family makes the decision that of the oldest generation. The endogamous community family or asymmetrical community family, which also has preferred partners, refers marriage arrangements to an impersonal principle, custom. Thus a third approach to liberty is introduced: the individual submits to a power that no one exercises. This system seems more immovable and powerful than the distribution of authority in exogamous families: because it is impersonal its authority may not be challenged; the system is not embodied in a fallible individual whose judgement can be questioned. The fourth approach to liberty is that of the anomic family, which leaves individuals free to choose a marriage partner but unlike the exogamous nuclear family does not oblige them to avoid close relatives. The anomic approach seems to allow the maximum freedom possible: it has by definition no rules.

Exogamy, on the other hand, is a strict rule, an obligation which seems so normal to Europeans that they are hardly aware of it, but it does exist and it organizes their very existence and their society. It is a negative type of structuring which pushes apart the members of a single family and forces them to choose a marriage partner outside the group they come from. Despite myths about the permissive society, the Western world is very rigidly regulated from a sexual point of view. The anomic family is morally much more tolerant, but with sociological results that are in fact far from happy.

The process of choosing a marriage partner thus allows us to define four types (not two) of liberty (or of absence of liberty) among which the seven families may be divided (see table 1). From the table, it is clear that Le Play's categories occupy an intermediate position in the total range of family types. Types B and C of spouse selection have as their ideological reflection the liberal and authoritarian doctrines of the West. But here we escape from the Eurocentricity of the classical definitions of liberty used by political science and inherited from the English and French traditions, for types A and D also have their ideological reflections, as will be seen later. In this way, going back to anthropology in the analysis of family systems enlarges our conceptual framework and allows us to comprehend Islamic, Hindu and Buddhist conceptions of liberty and authority.

Inequality and asymmetry

The European political concept of equality has wider applications than that of liberty. Six of the seven families can be classified

Table 1   Form of spouse selection in relation to family type

Form of spouse selection	Family type
A Determined by custom ──────────▶	Endogamous community family Asymmetrical community family
B Determined by parents ──────────▶	Exogamous community family Authoritarian family
C Determined by the individual with ──────▶ a strong exogamous obligation	Egalitarian nuclear family Absolute nuclear family
D Determined by the individual with ──────▶ a weak exogamous obligation	Anomic family

according to this principle. In order to classify the seventh we must refer to the wider concept of symmetry which wholly embraces that of equality.

The asymmetrical community family gives its members a sense of heterogeneous social space, partially allocated so that not everyone has an equivalent place: certain relatives are eligible as marriage partners; others are not. An asymmetrical structure and perception of the world also occurs in the authoritarian family which excludes some of the children from the inheritance, and creates two categories of men: the first-born and the younger sons. Although very different in many respects, the authoritarian and asymmetrical community families share a heterogeneous view of human relations and thus of social and ideological life. Unable to develop a homogeneous, undifferentiated view of social space, cultures with asymmetrical family systems cannot accept the idea of universal man or the diverse political or religious doctrines which correspond to it.

The symmetry/asymmetry opposition, however, does not allow us to classify the anomic and absolute nuclear families which do not see equality between the children as an important ideal. The common characteristic is precisely that they are indifferent to the ideal of equality and more generally to that of symmetry.

We end up, then, with three attitudes towards symmetry in family and social relations: symmetry, indifference and asymmetry (see table 2).

A general table (table 3) allows us to see where all seven family types stand with regard to ideas on liberty (four levels) and on equality (three attitudes towards the principle of symmetry).

Planisphere

Charted on a planisphere the seven families produce a map which is eminently political, but which bears no relation to traditional linguistic or ethnic frontiers (see map 1). This is only natural, for social anthropology does not recognize the existence of white, yellow, red, black or blue. It is colour-blind and indifferent to racial classifications. It seeks to grasp mental structures not physical appearance, and effectively shows that the two do not coincide.

It also shows that family structure does not coincide with linguistic groups. It would be difficult to pick out on our planisphere the famous Indo-European branch of humanity, much beloved of those racist theories which sought to align race, language and mental structure. Russia, linguistically close to Poland, is a near neighbour of China or Vietnam in its family system. The only obvious, verifiable coincidence is between family form and ideology, which each time represent the expression, on two different levels, of one and the same system of values, defining and organizing the concepts of liberty and of symmetry in human and social relations respectively.

The exogamous community family, both authoritarian and egalitarian, in demographic terms dominates the other anthropological categories. But it is still not in the majority, for it represents only some 40 per cent of the world population.

Everywhere that it occurs the exogamous community family encourages the appearance of powerful communist movements. All the great revolutions of the twentieth century are present and accounted for: Russia, China, Vietnam, Yugoslavia and Cuba are all countries dominated by this family type. We could also add Hungary to this list, whose communist revolution of 1918 was crushed, although with difficulty, by foreign intervention.

Table 2 Attitudes towards symmetry in family and social relations

Symmetry	Indifference	Asymmetry
Egalitarian nuclear family	Absolute nuclear family	Authoritarian family
Exogamous community family	Anomic family	Asymmetrical community family
Endogamous community family		

Table 3 Attitudes towards liberty and symmetry according to family type

Attitudes to liberty (defined by type of spouse selection)	Attitudes to symmetry (defined by spouse selection and inheritance system)		
	Symmetry	Indifference	Asymmetry
Custom	Endogamous community family		Asymmetrical community family
Parents	Exogamous community family		Authoritarian family
Free, with obligatory exogamy	Egalitarian nuclear family	Absolute nuclear family	
Free, without obligatory exogamy		Anomic family	

Table 4   Distribution of anthropological categories in the world

Family type	% of world population
Absolute nuclear family	8
Egalitarian nuclear family	11
Authoritarian family	8
Exogamous community family	41
Endogamous community family	10
Asymmetrical community family	7
Anomic family	8
African family systems	6

Table 5   Distribution of anthropological categories in Europe
(only four family types, all exogamous)

Family type	% of European population
Absolute nuclear family	12
Egalitarian nuclear family	25
Authoritarian family	26
Exogamous community family	37

The exogamous community family is only hindered from inculcating communist values — authoritarian and egalitarian — in those places where it is part of a composite anthropological structure: in north India, in central Italy, in Finland — three countries where the intellectual and electoral influence of the communist party is nevertheless far from negligible. Where the exogamous community family is present only in isolated pockets, communism retains a stable electoral implantation, regional but strong: for example, in central France, southern Portugal and northern Greece.

Conversely, in countries where the exogamous community family does not exist communism has never gathered any irresistible, extensive and spontaneous support. Initially produced by a particular anthropological structure, its subsequent progress is blocked. The rest of the story is military. Wherever the different red armies try to impose communism from the outside the anthropological base rejects it, always violently and sometimes in a rather bizarre way. Hybrid political forms appear. The army replaces the party in Poland. The general secretary introduces hereditary succession in North Korea. The single party divides along the usual clan lines in Afghanistan, or it collapses in on itself, along with the whole country, as in the case of Cambodia.

When sheltered from the Soviet, Chinese or Vietnamese armies, the rest of the world, divided up among six family types, lives out its own ideological dreams. To each of these types, too, correspond particular religious and political forms.

2

Community

Characteristics of the exogamous community family:

1 equality between brothers defined by rules of inheritance;
2 cohabitation of married sons and their parents;
3 however, no marriage between the children of two brothers.

Principal regions concerned: Russia, Yugoslavia, Slovakia, Bulgaria, Hungary, Finland, Albania, central Italy, China, Vietnam, Cuba, north India.

According to the handbooks of the Third International, communism is the dictatorship of the proletariat. But I would like to suggest another definition which seems to correspond more closely to the sociological and geographic reality of the phenomenon: communism is a transference to the party state of the moral traits and the regulatory mechanisms of the exogamous community family. Sapped by urbanization, industrialization and the spread of literacy, in short by modernization, the exogamous community family passes on its egalitarian and authoritarian values to the new society. Individuals with equal rights are crushed by the political system in the same way they were destroyed in the past by the extended family when it was the dominant institution of traditional Russian, Chinese, Vietnamese or Serbian society.

We must nevertheless explain the disintegration of this anthropological base, and the extraordinary hatred that all communist regimes display towards the exogamous community family even though they adopt its fundamental values. For in China and in Russia, ideologists consider one of the first tasks of the regime to be the abolition of the constraints imposed on society by the patriarchal family (their vocabulary is fairly close to that of Le Play). The anthropological individualism of the different communist regimes is clear, for they proclaim the abolition of paternal power and the autonomy of the couple. Wherever one looks in the world or in history, only the exogamous community family provokes such hatred and such a desire for sociological murder. Nowhere else do reforming movements, be they Islamic, Hindu, Christian or Buddhist, social democratic or liberal, threaten the family unit to such a degree. The contrast is particularly striking between communist and Islamic countries which are dominated by two forms of community family, exogamous and endogamous respectively. The Islamic family does not produce, like Russian or Chinese families, a violent desire for its own destruction. It is a stable structure, and is perceived as a form that nurtures rather than oppresses.

Spontaneous disintegration

The exogamous community family is by contrast an unstable structure, capable of spontaneous disintegration. Its fragility results from the fulfilment of an exogamy requirement within a system which simultaneously stresses solidarity between brothers and paternal authority. Exogamous spouse selection introduces a stranger into the household and this transplant provokes considerable anxiety. It implies a modification of the multiple bilateral relations which make up the affective life of the domestic group. In a nuclear family system exogamy produces only one problem, the creation of a couple, and requires the adjustment of only one relationship, the fundamental relationship between two individuals. Adding a wife who is a stranger to a community household involves establishing and stabilizing seven new functional and emotional ties: the woman must build a new relationship with her husband, of course, but also with her mother-in-law, her father-in-law, her brothers- and sisters-in-law, and with her nephews and nieces. The complexity of this situation makes the exogamous community family in practice an unstable organism.

Traditional Chinese customs recognize this state of affairs. Any violence, either physical or verbal, could lead to capital punishment in the form of strangulation or decapitation, according to the gravity of the crime, for a son who was lacking in respect. A central institution of Confucian China, the exogamous community family was implicitly considered rather fragile by social thinkers of the time. Filial reverence was elevated to the level of ideology, but was the opposite of the family affection of the Islamic countries which by contrast seems natural, spontaneous, uncodified and above all completely free from sadism. The most powerful and most stereotyped form of filial devotion in China was for the son to offer a piece of flesh taken from his arm or calf in order to provide a healing potion for his sick parent. The Chinese ancestor cult ensured the permanence of parental authority, which was believed to continue even after death with the father simply retiring to another world never far from that of the living.

Russian women

The Russian peasant family, which unlike its Chinese counterpart was never elevated to the status of an institution and an ideology by the former regime, nevertheless had an even more trouble-torn and pathogenic history because it insisted so little on male superiority and agnatic solidarity. The most striking characteristic of the Russian family — a quite untypical phenomenon in an exogamous community system — is the marked egalitarianism of relations between the sexes, evidenced by the very slight age difference between husband and wife. In China, on the other hand, in Tuscany, central France, northern Greece and India (all exogamous community family regions), a considerable age difference gives the husband—wife bond some of the features of the father—daughter relationship, so that it is essentially hierarchial even if it does not rule out affection. This distinctive characteristic in the make-up of the Russian family has been confirmed by recent historical and statistical studies of the local censuses of the first half of the nineteenth century. In 1849 in one district of Great Russia close to Riazan, the average age difference between husband and wife was only 0.6 years.[1] In the domain of Mishino which forms part of this district the age difference between marriage partners was 1.7 years in 1814; but most significantly 43 per cent of the women were older than their husbands. At the same date 78 per cent of households (or domestic units) represented the 'ideal' form of community family: that is they brought together under the same roof several married couples, parents and adult children. The average age of men at marriage being around twenty suggests the cohabitation of fathers-in-law aged

---

[1] P. Czap, 'Marriage and the peasant join-family in Russia in the era of serfdom', in D. Ransel et al. (eds) *The Family in Imperial Russia* (Illinois, University of Illinois Press, 1978).

from forty to forty-five with daughters-in-law between twenty and twenty-five married to husbands who were slightly younger. This peculiar demographic equilibrium permits the development of the traditional syndrome of Russian culture, incest between father-in-law and daughter-in-law, which is expressed with feeling in popular stories familiar to nineteenth-century folklorists and mentioned by Friedrich Engels in *The Origin of the Family, Private Property, and the State*. Father—son rivalry appears, transposed and watered down, in Turgenev's *First Love*.

This conflict is exacerbated in the Russian family model by the egalitarianism of relations between men and women; but it is latent in every exogamous community household. The incest taboo, although present, is not in this case based on the powerful mythology of blood. The prohibitions of affinity, forbidding sexual relations between individuals who are related by marriage, do not, despite the efforts of different Christian churches, have the solidity of prohibitions of consanguinuty.

The exogamous community family creates rivalry between males, a rivalry that is all the more acute when the system is less strongly agnatic. On the shores of the Mediterranean, in central Italy and in northern Greece, and to a lesser extent in Yugoslavia and Bulgaria, the exogamous community family is reinforced as in China by an inequality of the sexes which encourages male solidarity.

Russian radicalism and Chinese moderation

A relatively small age difference between marriage partners is a typical feature of all the nuclear family systems, whether absolute, egalitarian or anomic. In England, in the north of France and in Indonesia, the husband is rarely much older than his wife. Based on a single tie, that between the married couple, the nuclear family must insist on their mutual solidarity, and this insistence implies a certain egalitarianism. The traditional Russian family, which is egalitarian with respect to the ages of husband and wife, therefore resembles a collection of nuclear families just as much as it resembles a typical community family model. Structurally it seems destined to explode, to release the conjugal nuclei of which it is composed. This is what modernization, first Tsarist and later Soviet, achieved in the nineteenth and twentieth centuries. It is not simply a matter of urbanization. In the rural village of Viriatino, which has been closely studied by Soviet ethnologists, the community family has virtually disappeared.[2] The Soviet census of 1970 shows that at this date the relative frequency of multiple households (that is those containing several married couples) had gone down to 4.4 per cent in the Ukraine, 2.6 per cent in Belorussia, and to 3.1 per cent in Russia itself, compared with 12.5 per cent in Bulgaria (1965) and 6.2 per cent in Hungary (1970) where a parallel evolution was obvious although less brutal. There are few examples of this kind of disintegration of an anthropological system.

China in particular has not gone so far. It is difficult to know exactly what is happening there given the fact that the present regime has been unable to hold a satisfactory national census, but the publication in September 1980 of a law on marriage affords a reasonably precise idea of current trends.[3] First reaffirming the principles of equality between the sexes, of the autonomy of the couple, and of the free choice of marriage partners in the great communist tradition (articles 2, 3, 4), the law subsequently outlines the rights and duties that are typical of the community family: the obligation for grandparents to look after their grandchildren if the parents die; for grandchildren to see to the needs of their grandparents; for the eldest brothers and sisters to look after the youngest if the parents die (articles 22, 23). The state itself thus refuses to nationalize medical insurance. The rapid growth of the exogamous community family form, complete in Russia, has only been partially successful in the Chinese countryside. But exceptionally great anthropological strain is required to produce communism, which in Russia was born of a family structure that is both banal and extreme. Unlike China, Yugoslavia, Vietnam and Cuba, Russia was not content to apply a communist system of government. Starting from the few vague and negative recommendations of Marx, from an abstract criticism of a form of capitalism that only existed in England, Russia conceived a regime that involved agrarian collectivization, total nationalization of the economy and militant atheism. It put into practice something that no one had ever dreamed of.

Furthermore, the originality of communism lies less in industrial planning, which was anticipated by seventeenth-century mercantilists and implemented in the war economies of the West between 1914 and 1918, than in the destruction

---

[2] S. Benet (ed.), *The Village of Viriatino* (New York, Doubleday, 1970), ch. 4.
[3] *Population and Development Review*, vol. 7, no. 2 (June, 1981), pp. 369–72.

of the social and economic structure of rural areas, the most traditional of all. Today most of the Third World regimes which adopt socialism — whether the Buddhist or the Arabic kind — accept the idea of nationalizing industry; but they refuse to attack religious and peasant customs. They want to construct the future but refuse to destroy the past as the Russians did or, with less success, the Chinese, the Vietnamese, the Serbs and the Cubans. All these Marxist-Leninist regimes, to differing degrees, consider agrarian collectivization and atheism to be fundamental ideological principles. Communism is peculiar in its desire to attack the anthropological base, an attitude which distinguishes it from all other ideologies, which are neutral or tolerant in their relations with religious and peasant traditions.

The desire to kill God

If one accepts the psychoanalytic interpretation of religion which sees God as a father-figure, it is no more difficult to interpret atheism, negative religious belief, than to explain the positive belief, Catholic, Protestant or Jewish, which forms Freud's intellectual raw material in *The Future of an Illusion*. If God is an unconscious representation of the father, then his execution by atheism is simply an intellectual rendering of a perfectly banal parricide. And it is not difficult to find the assassin. There is not one but several; and they are brothers.

The liquidation of God and of the father only occurs on a large scale in certain societies, in Russian or Chinese societies for example, where a particular family form is dominant: the exogamous community family in which patriarchal authority is both strong and intolerable, demanding and fragile, because it weighs on several equal brothers who can conspire against paternal power. A kind of delinquent solidarity gives the brothers the courage to shake free.

Le Play, conservative and even reactionary, desiring the re-establishment of paternal authority in France, had a certain admiration for the Russian family. He appreciated its disciplinary ability and its vigorous oppression of the individual. But he had not noticed its potential for egalitarianism, for rebellion and for revolution and self-destruction.

Freud, had he taken an interest in family forms other than German and Jewish models, would no doubt have been more perspicacious. Focusing mainly on the father—son relationship, he readjusts his archetypal family when he moves on to play out a mythological parricide: in *Totem and Taboo* the father is executed, not by his son, but by a group of brothers. Is Freud unconsciously disturbed by the indestructible solidity of the authoritarian family (Le Play's stem family), which sets father and son face to face in an unequal dialogue in which the adult child is always materially and psychologically dominated, never freed? In many psychoanalytical cases, taken from Germanic countries, the natural death of the father fails to free the son, precipitating instead a neurotic depression, the result of a relationship which was too strong to be mastered. It is what happens to President Schreber, studied by Freud himself. But it is also true for Max Weber: his first psychological disturbances appear soon after the death of his father. Paternal power is, in the authoritarian system, invulnerable; but in the exogamous community type, solidarity between brothers makes it fragile.

The end of the story

It is not sufficient to shatter the exogamous community family in order to free men and to destroy their habits of discipline and egalitarianism. The destruction of the family form does not extend to the value-system which underpins it. Liberty, once achieved, is seen as anarchy, as a source of anxiety rather than of pleasure. The creation of a communist structure allows individuals to be reintegrated into a family setting which is authoritarian and egalitarian. The party replaces the family. Its cells artificially reproduce relationships of fraternity which are dense and intolerable. Even deadly. Its hierarchy replaces paternal authority literally on every level. At the base, the secretary of the cell intervenes in the family life of Soviet couples. At the top, the fathers follow one after the other: a dynamic, talkative and violent father in Lenin; a sadistic father in Stalin; an aged father in Brezhnev, who carried the metaphor of the Russian political family to its limit. The senility of the Soviet leaders is the destiny of all patriarchs. Today the USSR, China and Vietnam are old community families, feeble and sclerotic.

The Cuban mystery

The traditional family systems of Russia, China, Vietnam, Yugoslavia, Albania and Hungary — that is of the six old-world countries which spontaneously produced communist revolutions – are all of the exogamous community type. They are recognized as such by ethnologists and pose no further theoretical problems. Not even the Chinese system presents difficulties any more, although for a time it was believed to practice asymmetrical cross-cousin marriage, a belief proved incorrect by the most recent statistical studies. Nor does the Albanian model, which although Islamic, avoids preferential parallel-cousin marriage.

The case is not so simple with Cuba, which theoretically forms part of the Latin-American world but in practice belongs to the Soviet goulag. The Cuban anthropological base, a local mutation of Hispanic culture which arises from contact between Castilian, Galician and African anthropological systems (the country is perhaps 50 per cent black), has never really been studied. It is regrettable: knowing what makes Cuba peculiar might have saved us the wait, now twenty years long, in anticipation of a generalized, Castro-style revolution on the continent of South America. This hope or this fear, depending on one's point of view, is based on an implicit and erroneous premise: that the Cuban and Latin-American social systems are exactly the same.

The linguistic evidence seems to indicate that Cuba, like the other countries of Spanish origin, such as Argentina, Mexico, Uruguay and Guatemala, should have a nuclear, egalitarian family tradition. This is not so. But the absence of anthropological fieldwork obliges us to illustrate the point indirectly, by means of a detour which involves both statistical and anthropological methods: measuring suicide rates and analysing census information on household structure from around 1970.

The anthropology of suicide

Suicide rates, the classic indicator used by Durkheimian sociology, allow us to assess the untypical nature of Cuban society and to demonstrate that it is an exception within the anthropological corpus of Latin-America. In general, the frequency of suicide increases with the density and verticality of the family system, and with heavier emphasis on the mutual dependence of parents and children. In this respect the statistics confirm Freudian intuition about the potentially pathological nature of the father–son relationship. Authoritarian and exogamous community family systems are markedly more anxiety-producing than nuclear family models: they therefore give rise to a higher suicide rate.

The degree of verticality in family relations is not, however, the only factor in suicide rates: equality and stability in the husband—wife bond is another that is just as important, as Durkheim was well aware. In Europe, the coefficient of correlation between suicide and divorce rates was +0.62 (twenty-one countries) around 1975. The importance of the husband—wife relationship among the causes of suicide explains why throughout the world exogamous systems produce suicide rates which are significantly higher than in endogamous systems. Suicide is statistically insignificant in Islamic countries. The analysis of suicide rates thus confirms the anxiety-producing nature of exogamous systems.

In this way, the highest suicide rates are found in countries whose exogamous family structure includes at the same time strong vertical ties, egalitarian relations between men and women, and a high divorce rate. It is possible to work out average suicide rates around 1975 for each of the main exogamous family types: the highest is that of the community family (20.2 suicides per 100,000 population), second is the authoritarian family (18.0), followed by the absolute nuclear family (12.3), and finally the egalitarian nuclear family (5.9) (see table 6).

The Cuban suicide rate is not, like those for the nuclear, egalitarian, Latin-American countries, in the vicinity of 5 per 100,000 population. At 17.8, in 1974, it is close to the rates for central and northern Europe, an area of authoritarian or community family structure. How can this anomaly, which dates from the 1930s, be explained? By a simple hypothesis: despite linguistic appearances, Cuba is dominated by the community family. This is confirmed by analysing the census of 1970.

Hidden values

It is fairly difficult to grasp the true nature of a family system by studying a census. Describing a household structure, the form of the domestic group, raises few problems when defining the concepts and the analytical framework. The major difficulty arises from the fact that in practice the formation of an ideal family, the physical creation of a household incorporating two or three married couples (or only one in the case of a nuclear household), depends not only on family values but also on material circumstances and constraints. There are always fewer

Table 6   The anthropology of suicide (suicide rates and family type)

Authoritarian family		Egalitarian nuclear family	
Country and date	Suicide rate[a]	Country and date	Suicide rate[a]
East Germany (1976)	34.0	Poland (1977)	12.4
Slovenia (1969)	30.5	Uruguay (1976)	10.8
Austria (1976)	22.7	Argentina (1977)	7.8
Bohemia (1977)	22.7	Chile (1977)	5.7
West Germany (1976)	21.7	Costa-Rica (1977)	4.4
Sweden (1975)	19.4	Spain (1975)	3.9
Japan (1977)	17.8	Guatemala (1972)	3.4
Croatia (1969)	17.5	Greece (1976)	2.8
Belgium (1976)	16.6	Mexico (1975)	1.7
Norway (1977)	11.4		
Scotland (1977)	8.1		
Israel (1977)	6.5		
Ireland (1975)	4.7		
Average	*18.0*	*Average*	*5.9*

Exogamous community family		Absolute nuclear family	
Country and date	Suicide rate[a]	Country and date	Suicide rate[a]
Hungary (1977)	40.3	Denmark (1976)	23.9
Finland (1974)	25.1	Canada (1976)	12.8
Slovakia (1977)	18.2	USA (1976)	12.5
Bulgaria (1976)	14.1	Australia (1977)	11.1
Hong Kong (1977)	12.3	New Zealand (1976)	9.2
Serbia (1969)	11.2	Netherlands (1977)	9.2
		England (1976)	7.8
Average	*20.2*	*Average*	*12.3*

[a]Annual suicide rate per 100,000 population.

dense, complex households in urban areas than in rural districts. This in no way implies a priori a weakening of family values, which in the cities are no longer expressed in shared households and common work but in other ways. It is simply that the family is no longer a visible entity. Values which are incarnate in peasant life are relocated in the towns on the level of immaterial mental structures. Identifying them requires complex research into forms of education, into psychological attitudes within parent—child relations, into the frequency of contact between adults and into the degree of financial help they give to each other. Mechanisms of professional continuity can also be examined — whether sons choose professions similar to those of their fathers — a far more important factor in modern technical and industrial life than is generally admitted, although it varies considerably in different countries. For the moment such research is still lacking, at least on a wide and international scale which would allow comparisons to be made. We must settle for censuses which describe actual family form. But in assessing the significance of statistics which indicate, for example, the frequency of households containing several married couples ('multiple family households' in Peter Laslett's typology, the most accurate to date), it is essential to take into account the level of development of the country, the degree of urbanization, of literacy, of industrialization, and its demographic evolution. Luckily the results are sufficiently clear in the case of Cuba to draw some definite conclusions.

The community family in Cuba

In 1970, the average number of people per household was 3.8 in Argentina and 3.8 in Spain, but 4.5 in Cuba. This is despite the fact that the three countries are very close in terms of cultural and demographic development. Their birth-rates from 1976 to 1977 were almost identical: 23, 18 and 20 respectively. Life expectancy was similar: 66 in Argentina, 70 in Cuba, 73 in Spain. The Third World mythology surrounding Castro's regime tends to make us forget that this large Caribbean island was, on the eve of the revolution, very close to being a developed country.

In this virtually developed country — developed in cultural terms, for let us ignore its socialist poverty — the proportion of multiple family households, those including at least two married couples, was 12.9 per cent in 1970 as opposed to 5.8 per cent in Spain, a country with an egalitarian nuclear family system the north of which (from Galicia to Catalonia) is, however, largely dominated by an authoritarian structure and by rules of primogeniture.

The higher family density of Cuba is not the result of a lower level of urbanization: the family structure is slightly more dense in urban areas than in rural ones. With 13 per cent multiple family households the Havana province is ahead, in terms of community family structure, of Singapore (11.7 per cent) and Hong Kong (5.9 per cent), countries which nevertheless belong to the Chinese family system. (Compare this with France where the proportion of multiple family households in urban areas was 1.1 per cent in 1975.) As a whole Cuba is similar to Bulgaria (12.5 per cent of multiple family households), a country whose family structure is undeniably a community one.

A final check can be made. The Cuban and Mexican censuses of 1970 illustrate the greater complexity of family structures on the Caribbean island despite its more advanced demographic and economic development. These two documents describe the different types of family relations within each household, clearly distinguishing close ties — between husband and wife, parents and children — from more distant ones — grandparents, uncles and aunts, nephews and nieces, cousins. In Mexico, for each head of the household there are 0.23 distant relatives, but in Cuba there are 0.59: in other words there are two and a half times as many in Cuba than in Mexico, an indication of the much greater complexity of Cuban household structure. The existence of households containing at least three married couples (1.5 per cent) in Cuba allows us to conclude that the family model in this country is of a community rather than an authoritarian type, because the latter allows no more than two couples in one household.

Behind the short-lived Cuban carnival we thus find in the long term the same anthropological structure as in Vietnam: the exogamous community family. Social anthropology allows us to go beyond mere exoticism and to reach hidden but powerful mental structures, to identify the basic values of discipline and of equality which characterize family forms throughout the country and against which American or Western intervention is impotent.

The electoral geography of communism

Communism has triumphed and suppressed freedom in only a few countries. Elsewhere it exists in the form of political parties which may be either tiny groups or powerful forces. If a liberal political system allows, communist strength is expressed by a substantial and stable electoral implantation. But these secondary growths are no more randomly determined than the principal developments in Russia, China, Vietnam, Cuba or Yugoslavia. Here too anthropology provides the explanation.

The structural features of the communist vote in Berry or Arauco, Tuscany or Kerala, Finland or Bengal, in themselves suggest that there is an anthropological dimension to the phenomenon. The Marxist-Leninist electorate has two main characteristics, both of an anthropological nature: it is strongly regional and it is extremely stable over time. In technical terms the communist vote displays high regional variability and low temporal variability.

Electoral geography in France over the years has clearly demonstrated the characteristics of the French Communist Party's implantation, support for which, after a period of rapid growth between 1936 and 1946, levelled off and oscillated from 1946 to 1978 between 20 and 25 per cent of the vote, blocking political movement in France to the frustration of the socialist Left. But the consistency of the support for communism in France hides enormous regional variation: in 1973, for example, it obtained 30.3 per cent of the vote in the Allier department but only 6.4 per cent in Mayenne.

This sort of geographic fluctuation is typical of most of the major communist parties. It is exactly the case in Italy where the Italian Communist Party, despite a period of slow but steady growth between 1945 and 1970 which has made it the dominant left-wing group, is not as strong in the north or south of the country as it is in the centre: for example, it receives 47 per cent of the votes cast in Emilia, compared to a mere 20 per cent in Venetia, 120 kilometres away.

The greatest regional variation in the communist vote in Europe occurs in Portugal: over 40 per cent in Alentejo, in the south, but less than 10 per cent in the northern half of the country in the 1976 elections. In Chile it is the same. From 1932 until 1973 the Chilean Communist Party gained between 2 and 5 per cent of the vote in the provinces of Maule and Linares, compared with 30 per cent in those of Arauco and Taracapa. The situation is similar in India where once again regional variation and stability go together: 39 per cent of the vote in Kerala in 1962, 0.2 per cent in Gujarat. The total communist vote was 8.9 per cent in 1957, 9.8 per cent in 1971 (if the scores of the two parties which were produced by the 1964 split are added together). Here too a period of rapid growth, from 3.3 per cent of the vote in 1952 to 8.9 per cent in 1957, was followed by complete stagnation. In each case the initial ease with which the communist party first became established has created illusions about the ultimate power of communist ideology. During the initial phase it seems irresistible; in the next phase it is imprisoned in particular places; finally it prides itself on being ineradicable. Having discovered a niche for itself within an anthropological and familial structure whose values are its own, it can go no further. It has found a home.

Nivernais, Tuscany, Finland

In Tuscany (where the communist vote is approximately 45 per cent of votes cast), in Finland (where it is 20 per cent), and in the Nivernais, Berry and Bourbonnais regions (25 to 30 per cent), the traditional family structure is indisputably of an exogamous community type. Le Play's own research shows this for central France. A number of recent studies on seventeenth- and eighteenth-century village censuses suggest that the community type came from Morvan to the Dordogne, following a north-east/south-west line which marks the frontier between the authoritarian family areas of the south-west and the nuclear, egalitarian region centred on Paris.[4] The implantation of the French Communist Party follows this line faithfully.

The classic studies of Scandinavian ethnology have always insisted on the difference between the authoritarian Germanic system found in Norway and Sweden and the exogamous community family model in Finland. The political significance of this model — which is quite clear, since Finland is the only Scandinavian nation with a powerful communist party — is nevertheless attenuated by the cultural influence of Sweden and by the very understandable anti-Soviet feelings of the population, resulting from the accident of geography. In small countries the normal operation of anthropological parameters is often disrupted by phenomena of attraction or repulsion created by the dominant ideological centres.

In Tuscany numerous religious censuses of the eighteenth century — *stati d'anime* in Italian — describe family composition in detail. In the Pratolino parish near Fiesole, for example, 75 per cent of households in about 1730 included at least two

---

    [4] J.-C. Peyronnet, 'Famille élargie ou famille nucléaire? L'example du Limousin au début du dix-neuvième siècle', *Revue d'histoire moderne et contemporaine*, 22 (1975), pp. 568–82.

married couples, in most cases brothers and their wives. It would be difficult to imagine a more perfect community model. Christiane Klapisch's studies on fourteenth-century Tuscany suggest, furthermore, that between the sixteenth and eighteenth centuries the visible community structure was reinforced, a phenomenon related to the ruralization of the Italian economy during this period. A weakening of urban, commercial and industrial life allows complex domestic forms to reappear, underpinned by a value-system which had in no way been eroded by the cultural and urban progress of the Middle Ages.

Emilia, Alentejo, Provence

The examples of Emilia (where over 45 per cent of the vote is communist), of Alentejo in Portugal (where it is over 40 per cent), and of Provence and coastal Languedoc (25 to 30 per cent), are more difficult to analyse. A look at the national census shows that community-type households are more numerous there than in nuclear family regions; but the evidence is not as clear as in the examples of Tuscany, Nivernais or Finland, regions for which there is good historical and ethnological material.

The disappearance of the traditional peasantry is not a recent phenomenon in Provence, Emilia or Alentejo. The Mediterranean seaboard of France was an area of early, indeed pre-industrial urbanization: rural life has long been of secondary importance. Alentejo and Emilia, unlike Tuscany and central France, are not areas of medium-sized properties but regions where agricultural capital is heavily concentrated, with a large wage-earning work-force. The traditional peasant family, providing labour and sharing the work, is economically impossible.

In this economic context the community family cannot normally appear. What indicates its existence above all — in terms of its value-system — is the presence in these regions of fiercely egalitarian inheritance rules which take the principle of equality between brothers to incredible lengths. In the department of the Var in Provence, urban and village houses are divided up vertically or horizontally. In Alentejo the tiniest savings left by agricultural labourers give rise to interminable discussion: the *partilhas* (dividing-up) is a ritual institution of family life. Similar conflicts are to be found in all areas of community families, in Russia or in China, where the death of the father always leads sooner or later to the brothers separating, and the division of the inheritance almost inevitably becomes a real drama. The death of the patriarch is a high point which reveals the extreme egalitarianism of family values.

The Indian problem

North India is probably the only area of the world where the exogamous community family has not given rise to a very powerful communist movement, the percentage of votes gained by the Marxist-Leninist party or parties having always been less than 10 per cent in this part of the country (in 1962 for example), reaching 25 per cent only in West Bengal. The ideological impotence of the exogamous community family in north India, however, is not really surprising: the subcontinent has a complicated structure, combining the exogamous community family of the north and the asymmetrical community family of the south. The latter, which produces the caste system, dominates the country culturally. Only an overall study of the caste system would allow us to explain the relative failure of communism in north and south alike.

It will suffice here to emphasize the peculiar solidity of the exogamous community family in north India which makes it, within this category of family form, the theoretical opposite of the Russian community family. Actively agnatic and anti-feminist, the Indian family is extremely resistant to disintegration. Less anxiety-producing, it is also less inclined spontaneously to produce communism. But where it is weakened by particularly strong tension between men, notably between father and son, it disintegrates in the usual way and easily produces, despite the influence of the caste system, a 25 per cent communist vote – for example in West Bengal.

Female infanticide

Undoubtedly the best indication of the fiercely agnatic character of the Indian family is the existence of a virulent tradition of female infanticide, more marked in north India even than in China. Recent Indian censuses consistently reveal a striking imbalance between the sexes: an excess of males denotes a massacre of female babies. A special supplement to the 1971 census was devoted to the sex ratio which, while normal in south

India, frequently falls below 9 women to 10 men in north India (8.8 in Uttar Pradesh, near Delhi). In one group of villages in the Kangra district (Punjab) where a census was held in 1855, there were among children aged 4 to 14 only 393 girls for 1,000 boys.[5]

The idea of property which corresponds to this particular structure is unusually collective in nature. According to the inheritance rules of the Mitakshara judicial school the children have a share in the ancestral property from the moment of conception. The father has no more than usufruct and has no right to sell land or collective property without the agreement of his co-owners, usually his sons. This kind of paternal authority is somewhat removed from the Russian or even the Chinese models. It comes close, although there is no endogamy, to the Islamic model, and it is derived in a similar way from an extreme application of the agnatic ideal. It gives the Indian exogamous community family a particular solidity, in so far as it reduces the sources of tension between father and sons.

Where the Mitakshara school does not hold sway the exogamous community family resolves its problems with its usual tension and internal rivalry. It retains its propensity to disintegrate. In West Bengal where a different set of inheritance rules applies — Dayabhaga — property is not shared by all the men in the family. The sons inherit their father's wealth only after his death. Here, as in China or Russia, ethnologists have been struck by the strained interpersonal relations within the family. Bengali brothers often refuse to live together once their father has died. In the village of Tarkotala, where ties between brothers could have comprised 20 per cent of the household's community bonds, the actual proportion was only 5 per cent.[6] A substantial communist vote corresponds to the broken family structure of West Bengal; although they fall behind the Tuscans (45 per cent), the Bengalis (25 per cent) nevertheless reach the same figure as in the French province of Berry.

Communism away from home

In countries where the exogamous community family is not the dominant family form, is not in the majority, or even a substantial

---

[5] J. Parry, *Caste and Kinship in Kangra* (London, Routledge and Kegan Paul, 1979), p. 218.

[6] M. Davis, 'The Politics of Family Life in Rural West Bengal', *Ethnology*, 15 (1976), pp. 189—200.

element in society, the communist vote falls below 20 per cent. This does not mean that it escapes the silent influence of anthropology. The different family models — anomic, authoritarian, egalitarian nuclear and absolute nuclear, endogamous community and asymmetrical community — do not react in the same way to the electoral efforts of the communist party. Unfortunately, the classic methods of electoral sociology do not allow us to cover places where free elections are not the dominant political form. But Western Europe and Japan provide reasonably accurate information owing to their stable electoral systems. For the moment I will leave India out of this account, despite the good political information available there: with India — as with the Islamic world and with areas which have anomic family systems — political analysis requires more refined concepts which recognize the existence of four degrees of liberty and which make use of the idea of symmetry as well as that of equality. I will examine more closely in the chapters specially devoted to the endogamous community, asymmetrical community and anomic family types, the relationships of affinity or repulsion between communism and those family structures which relax the requirement of exogamy. Here I will look only at the reactions of the three forms which are exogamous but not of the community family type. To study them we need only consider the classic dichotomies: liberty/authority and equality/inequality. Anthropology provides the means of understanding and bringing order to the disconcerting electoral geography of Europe and Japan.

Ranking the three families

The evidence reveals that in the mid-1960s the electoral implantation of Marxism-Leninism was slight in countries where the family type is nuclear and egalitarian (10 per cent of the vote on average); very slight in countries with an authoritarian form (4 per cent on average with greater variability: between 1.5 and 7.9 per cent of the vote); and insignificant in areas of absolute nuclear family (less than 1 per cent). The scores of the different communist parties are almost perfectly ranked according to family type. This classification allows us to pick out the specific influence of each of the two fundamental principles — equality and authority — which combine to form the essence of communist ideology. Family egalitarianism on its own can produce a degree of communism, as can authoritarianism. Where both of these

Table 7 Support for communism in relation to family type

Country and date	Communist vote (%)	Dominant family types (secondary types in brackets)
Kerala (1962)	39.1	Disintegrated matrilineal (see chapter 6)
Italy (1968)	26.9	Egalitarian nuclear in north and south Exogamous community in central regions
Bengal (1962)	25.0	Exogamous community — Dayabhaga inheritance rules
Finland (1966)	23.0	Exogamous community
France (1968)	20.0	Four exogamous types
Portugal (1975)	12.5	Egalitarian nuclear (but authoritarian in north and partially exogamous community in south)
Chile (1964)	12.2	Egalitarian nuclear (exogamous community in south)
Greece (1977)	9.4	Egalitarian nuclear (exogamous community in north)
Spain (1977)	9.2	Egalitarian nuclear (authoritarian in north)
Japan (1971)	7.9	Authoritarian
Sweden (1973)	5.3	Authoritarian
Austria (1953)	5.3	Authoritarian
Denmark (1975)	4.2	Absolute nuclear (but authoritarian Hanseatic influence)
Belgium (1968)	3.3	Authoritarian
Netherlands (1967)	3.1	Absolute nuclear (authoritarian in east)
Norway (1965)	1.5	Authoritarian
Australia (1967)	0.4	Absolute nuclear
Great Britain (1964)	0.2	Absolute nuclear (authoritarian in Scotland)

principles are absent, in areas of absolute nuclear family structure, Marxism-Leninism is almost insignificant. It drops below 1 per cent of the vote, notably in the Anglo-Saxon world. The fall is attenuated in the Netherlands (3.1 per cent) and in Denmark (4.2 per cent) by the presence or the influence of authoritarian anthropological structures. The situation is the same in Scotland where communism, while extremely weak, is nevertheless slightly stronger than in England because of its influence on a number of important unions, notably the miners' union. The vertical authoritarian ideal is not absent from Scottish family culture; and even an ideal of discipline will create a slight predisposition to communism.

The especially strong resistance of the absolute nuclear family to Marxism-Leninism can be seen in one region of France, the centre-west (which has a nuclear household structure like the Paris region but an inheritance system that is not dominated by the idea of the division of goods as well as the total value of the estate). While in practice it is often egalitarian, as in England, the inheritance system in Anjou, Maine and French-speaking Brittany works in a subtle way; one of the brothers takes the property, the others the money. It is in this area that the French Communist Party receives the lowest proportion of the vote: 6.5 per cent in the Mayenne department in 1973. The national importance of communism prevents the party vote from falling to an insignificant level, as in England or Australia. It is nevertheless remarkable that in France, where the implantation of Marxism-Leninism is very uneven, it is weakest in those areas where in 1975 the structure of rural households was the simplest. In fact it is in the centre-west that the percentage of households containing two married couples is lowest: less than 1 per cent of the total in Sarthe, Mayenne, Ille-et-Vilaine, Manche. In the Paris region, nuclear and egalitarian, the proportion of households of this type, while low, is still slightly and significantly higher: it varies from 1 to 2 per cent. The absolute nuclear family, neither egalitarian nor authoritarian, is, of all the exogamous family systems, the anthropological negative of the community family: thus communism is almost non-existent in the areas where it is dominant.

Electoral geography thus allows us to test empirically the logical independence of egalitarian and authoritarian ideals. A family type which is egalitarian without being authoritarian produces a measure of communism. Similarly, a family type which is authoritarian without being egalitarian also produces a measure of communism. In the mid-1960s the ideal of equality seemed slightly more influential than that of authority: the first produced an average of 10 per cent of the vote for Marxism-Leninism, the second only 4 per cent. This has not always been the relationship between the two ideals, however. Before the Second World War, areas with authoritarian family systems although recording communist votes below 20 per cent were nevertheless more open to the development of Stalinism than egalitarian nuclear family regions. The rising star of the Third International at the beginning of the 1930s was the German Communist Party, which reached 16.9 per cent of the vote in November 1932. Its Czech counterpart, likewise in an authoritarian family area, was at the same period fluctuating at about 12.5 per cent. The French party did not reach this figure until 1936 and its implantation was greater, if we exclude the capital, in community family areas than in the egalitarian nuclear zone of the Paris basin.

There were no doubt ideological nuances corresponding to each of these types of incomplete communist implantation in countries with authoritarian and egalitarian nuclear family types. German communism was no doubt more authoritarian and less egalitarian than the Spanish variety. These nuances have not been studied in much detail, for empirical research here reflects its conceptual inadequacy.

The critical threshold

Anthropology serves to explain communism but does not legitimize it. Nowhere in the electoral history of the world has a communist party succeeded in winning 50 per cent of the vote, neither in Russia nor in China, nor in Vietnam, Cuba or Yugoslavia. Marxism-Leninism always comes to power through an act of violence and immediately suppresses — as a matter of principle — the very concepts of political liberty and free expression of opinion.

Even in Emilia the Italian Communist Party cannot exceed a maximum of 47 per cent of the vote. In the exogamous community family areas of central France, Finland, and southern Portugal, there is always a majority of 60 to 75 per cent of the electorate who refuse the collectivist option and who do not conform to anthropological determinism. This is a reassuring observation, but it is not enough. Three communists acting in unison will always be stronger than three liberals who are free to express their differences. The very idea of communism involves a superior organizational ability which arises from the abolition of individual will and from the imposition of discipline. There is a threshold beyond which a substantial communist minority takes control, if there is no outside intervention, and suppresses the electoral process. A system where the communist party wins over 40 per cent of the vote is soon lost; a communist state will be formed there and will oppress 60 per cent of the population. The Tuscans and the Emilians are spared this disaster only by the overall balance of forces in Italy which neutralize the locally irresistible power of the Italian Communist Party.

This critical threshold is never reached in countries where the exogamous community family is not clearly dominant. It now remains for us to turn to the countries and regions where political dreams cannot be of a communist kind because their family structures produce other value-systems. They form a huge but fragmented mass, more difficult to grasp conceptually. But they are just as important in distant and recent history, and in the future of the world.

3

Authority

Characteristics of the authoritarian family:

1 inequality of brothers laid down by inheritance rules, transfer
   of an unbroken patrimony to one of the sons;
2 cohabitation of the married heir with his parents;
3 little or no marriage between the children of two brothers.

Principal regions and peoples concerned: Germany, Austria, Sweden,
Norway, Belgium, Bohemia, Scotland, Ireland, peripheral regions of
France, northern Spain, northern Portugal, Japan, Korea, Jews,
Romany gypsies.

In the Bible the most famous family crime is not the murder of
a father or even of a son — Abraham was stopped before he
struck down Isaac — but the murder of a brother: Cain killed
his brother Abel. This strained fraternal relationship can be seen as
a dramatization of the normal relations between brothers born of
the same father within the authoritarian family. One is chosen,
the other rejected. The procedure of primogeniture, of ultimogeniture, or any other form of block transmission of the
patrimony, is as much a rejection as an inheritance. It implies
that the brothers are not equal and conveys an asymmetrical
view of social space. Not all the individuals in a given family
have the same position or value. All men are not considered
equal. One could go further: not all peoples are considered equal.
The list of those groups who adopt an authoritarian ideal of the
family is eloquent. It epitomizes all the forms of parochialism,
all types of ethnocentricity, and all the diverse refusals of human
universality.

The refusal of universality

The principal authoritarian family systems are found among
the following peoples: Jews, Germans, Japanese, Basques, Irish,

Catalans, Flemish, Walloons, Galicians, Occitans, Bretons, Norwegians, Gypsies, Czechs, Swedes, French Canadians, Scots, Koreans. The list is surprising in its consistency, for it seems to contain not family systems but ethnic conflicts. Over three-quarters of the names given evoke claims to autonomy or superiority, or declarations of neutrality – in other words indifference to others.

Most of the universalist ideologies agree in their portrayal of the idea of fraternity: from Christianity, which holds that all men are brothers, to the Third International which co-ordinates fraternal relations between parties. Displaying greater gallantry, the French Revolution supported sister republics. Human inability to conceive of international relations other than in family terms is striking. But what sense can such metaphors have for a Japanese male who has learnt from one of his nation's classical proverbs that 'a brother is the first foreigner'?

The ancient world provides a final test of the historical and anthropological law which allows us to pair universalism with fraternal equality and ethnocentricity with fraternal inequality. Athens, where primogeniture was the rule, had a restrictive definition of citizenship, which was refused to *metics* – that is to foreigners living in the city – and to its allies. Rome, which was egalitarian in its inheritance system, extended citizenship throughout the empire.

Max Weber perceived, although he was unable to explain it, the existence of a relationship between community family structure and the building of world empires. The similarity between the Roman, Chinese and Russian kin systems is particularly marked. The exogamous community family which is present in all three is based on an especially strong feeling of brotherhood. It engenders a great ability to assimilate, and a special capacity to refuse to admit that men or races are different. China, Rome and the Russia of Ivan the Terrible all carried out vigorous assimilation policies and expanded by proclaiming conquered peoples Chinese, Roman or Russian. The process was often brutal: it required an acceptance of the values dominant in the victor's society, universal in aspiration but in practice no more universal than others. The French Revolution and Islam, other universalist historical phenomena, are likewise based on egalitarian anthropological premises: the egalitarian nuclear family and the endogamous community family respectively.

The relationship between family egalitarianism and ideological universalism, on the one hand, and between a refusal to accept the equality of brothers and particularism, on the other, can be seen on a regional level just as much as on a national one. The different regions of France which vary considerably in their family structure are typical in this respect. In those where the inheritance system is egalitarian, where each brother is as good as the others, there is no particularism and integration into the nation is accepted naturally. Provence, Burgundy, Poitou, Lorraine, Limousin and Berry all have their customs and traditions, but do not exaggerate their 'uniqueness': their inheritance systems are egalitarian. The south-west of the Occitan-speaking areas, the Basque country, Brittany and Alsace are provinces which are conscious of their individuality: their inheritance rules are inegalitarian.

Another European example is the Spanish provinces. Castille is the only one of the medieval Hispanic kingdoms whose family structure was egalitarian. It was far ahead of the other areas of the north — Aragon, Leon, Galicia, Catalonia — in the process of reconquest and unification. Was it more open to universalist ideals and to the principle of assimilation? The suggestion that this may be so is confirmed by the present-day persistence of Basque, Galician and Catalan particularism, based on asymmetrical family structures.

The failure of Germany in Western Europe illustrates the reverse process of military and cultural expansion which refused to accept the equality of the conquered peoples. Although Germany, since the Middle Ages, has been represented everywhere beyond the Oder River by its merchants, its artisans, its language and its extraordinarily dynamic culture, it has never succeeded in assimilating the Slavic and Magyar peoples whose civilization owed so much to its influence, and this part of the continent remained a cultural mosaic. After contact with these races for over a thousand years Nazism declared the peoples of the East inferior. In 1945 the tragedy ended. A thousand-year Reich cannot be built on the principle of human inequality, which in Germany as elsewhere arose from an authoritarian family structure proclaiming the inequality of brothers.

Most cultures dominated by the authoritarian family are represented by small nations. This is no coincidence; it is not their vocation to expand by assimilation. Germany and Japan are two notable exceptions. But today the school textbooks of the German Federal Republic often show, in a series of maps, the various stages of Germany's contraction from the Germanic

Holy Roman Empire to its present state. It is a strange example of a civilization that sees itself as a diminishing force.

Fragmentation

If the egalitarian systems excel in denying the existence of real difference, the inegalitarian models, on the other hand, are expert in spotting differences that do not exist. Regions with an authoritarian family structure tend to invent ethnic traits. Their culture breaks down nations which are objectively uniform. The assimilation ability of the egalitarian systems is reversed and turns into a propensity for disintegration. It is a characteristic of authoritarian family areas that they are strikingly incapable of forming unitary states.

Germany, which was only unified with difficulty, is the best example. A hundred or a thousand dialects are still spoken, giving to each city, province or *Land* a specificity which has no real basis on an anthropological level. Germany as a whole has an authoritarian family structure. The only exception is the Rhineland where egalitarian inheritance systems seem fairly common. Apart from these, only secondary nuances separate the various provinces.

The example of Japan is still more remarkable. Anthropologically it is absolutely homogeneous, being entirely of the authoritarian family type except for the unassimilated Ainus of Hokkaido. And yet feudalism with its fragmentation of political power ravaged the country for centuries. Regional factionalism is just as strong in Korea which is perfectly homogeneous and authoritarian in terms of family structure.

The Basques speak Spanish but detest Spain. The Irish speak English but hate England. The Flemish and the Walloons, near to one another in anthropological terms, are incapable of co-operating. Everywhere the authoritarian family produces a belief in ethnic differences.

Anti-Semitism: looking for an invisible difference

It is ironic to note that the German and Jewish family systems are essentially very similar. The two peoples are peculiar in their ideological particularism, be it political or religious. Israel invented the one God and the idea of the chosen people, but it was Germany which, politically, murdered its brother in a massacre which has no equivalent in all human history. German anti-Semitism was not just any anti-Semitism; it was not that of the Russian communists or of Christians who hated Jewish separatism. Nazism refused to accept precisely that integration which European Jews in the 1930s were seeking. Medieval and Tsarist pogroms were directed against a minority which proclaimed that it was different. The gas chambers of the twentieth century were designed to eliminate the Jewish community at the very moment when it accepted its integration into European culture, when it tried to become German in Germany, French in France, British in Britain. To justify their actions the Nazis invented differences. The most scurrilous and the least intelligent ideologues sought out secondary morphological characteristics, the shape of the nose or the ears, for example. The more open or the more subtle theorists, like Spengler — who was not strictly speaking a Nazi — frankly admitted that they were looking for something invisible and ineffable, some racial essence that had nothing to do with cranial morphology or bone structure.

The Germans, in order to invent a difference, made use of a genuine Jewish tradition; and indeed it is possible to create something from nothing. The Japanese, who consider themselves ethnically pure and who have an extreme horror of mixed blood, created a group of untouchables, the Burakumin, two and a-half million of them, whose sociological situation cannot be explained in terms of any genuine historical peculiarity.

Asymmetry and anarchy

The tendency towards fragmentation which arises from an authoritarian anthropological system is all the more surprising because it is combined with an extremely strong sense of discipline, a political result of vertical family organization. The coexistence of discipline and anarchy is particularly obvious in Germany and in Japan in the years before the Second World War. Hitler's regime, despite the existence of the Nazi party, and the Japanese imperial regime, despite the effective seizure of power by the army, had no stable, ordered structure.

Franz Neumann described in *Behemoth* the bureaucratic anarchy which reigned under Hitler, the rivalry between organizations, between the party, the army, the SS, the SA, the Gestapo, a cancerous proliferation of organs. The specialists on Japanese political history are incapable of explaining the typical decision-making process, and in particular that which led to the attack on Pearl Harbour.

There is nothing comparable in the Russian and Chinese forms of totalitarianism, which are based on the principle of symmetry as much as on obedience. In China and in the USSR the Party and the state are perfectly synchronized and are based, like the community family, on a symmetry which implies that the system has a centre. The Russian household in fact was no less democratically centralized than the Soviet Communist Party. In Germany and Japan, on the other hand, an asymmetrical family structure produced an asymmetrical political system which was disordered and confused.

The temporal dimension

The principal foundation of those societies which are based on an authoritarian family model is a temporal one. The peoples concerned all have a strong historical awareness and a sharp sense of linear time, a natural reflection of the importance of lineage in this anthropological form. The aim and function of the authoritarian family is to ensure succession from one generation to the next, a theoretically eternal continuity of the domestic group. The son succeeds his father, the grandson replaces the son, and so on. The Japanese imperial family emphasized its genealogical continuity, theoretically tracing its origin to the union of the gods. The best-known example of this historical awareness is that of the Jews, who have a history going back five thousand years.

The very survival of tiny ethnic groups which have an authoritarian family model is the best illustration of their historical awareness. In most cases belief in a special mission, shared by the Jews and from time to time by the Germans, is not a prerequisite for ethnic continuity. The gipsies, whose family system is identical to that of the Jews down to the tiniest detail, have no special religious beliefs and are content to pass down through the centuries no more than their nomadic way of life and a marked sense of superiority.

Unlike ethnocentric ideologies, communism is not in love with history or with historical continuity. It includes time in its interpretative dogmas, but seeks to destroy the past. Since this is impossible it excels in falsifying history by a process of repeated amnesia, of which the Russian Revolution from Stalin to Brezhnev provides the best example. Here too, Marxism-Leninism is only reflecting in its relationship to time the anthropological substrate which produced it, the exogamous community family. Unlike the authoritarian family it does not aim for continuity. Its cycle is repetitive. The death of the father always leads sooner or later to the brothers separating and to the dissolution of the original domestic group. New households are created and the cycle continues in an endlessly repeated family history. With each new generation the community family starts afresh. Modelled on this cycle, Marxism-Leninism tries to destroy time. It abolishes the past and announces the end of history.

At the other end of the scale, the authoritarian family's obsession with time and its constant exposition of household continuity often leads to racism, in other words to a biological definition of social status. The genetic capacity to conserve and to transmit specific attributes of a race is often attributed to blood: be it the blue blood of *ancien régime* European nobles, the energetic blood of Spengler, or the *limpieza di sangre* of the northern Spaniards in the fourteenth century. Ethnocentric ideologies aim to divide up the world, yet they all resemble each other. The world of racism is as little varied as that of communism. Like the latter, racism sets up in ideological form a latent family structure, perfectly formed. Wherever this anthropological base does not exist, and whatever the local conditions, true racism cannot take root. Fascist Italy, based on nuclear or community family models (both of which are egalitarian), never really managed to follow in the anti-Semitic footsteps of its northern ally, Nazi Germany.

The dream of inequality

The authoritarian family is based on an aristocratic exclusion from inheritance of all but one of the brothers. Accepting the principle of inequality in interpersonal relations, it transposes this ideal onto the ideological plane, creating the inequality of men, of peoples and of races. But economic logic undermines this ideological dream. Ironically, the economic structure of countries with an authoritarian family system is almost always relatively egalitarian.

Thus the authoritarian family combats the fragmentation of peasant holdings and prevents capitalist concentration in the countryside. It sets up a peasant ideal of stability: each family, in order to perpetuate itself, must cling to its house and land; its ultimate political aim is to win recognition of its property rights. In this way, the Japanese, German, Swedish, Norwegian, Occitan, Basque, Catalan, Savoyard, Korean and Irish (since the English withdrawal) societies are egalitarian in their internal structure, and are dominated by a middling peasantry in which every family behaves as if it had an aristocratic lineage.

German and Japanese societies are particularly good examples here: they have never disputed the noble ideal, yet have no difficulty in accepting educational equality, and their middle classes are notable for their attempts at upward social mobility. In the nineteenth century the German *petite bourgeoisie*, rejecting the principles of the French Revolution, displayed unlimited affection for their emperor and for their extremely aristocratic army. Today, however, the destruction of the German *ancien régime* is at last complete: the Federal Republic, which did not live through 1789 or 1793, has nothing to learn from France about egalitarian social measures — quite the contrary. The range of incomes is much more restricted and objective class distinctions are much less noticeable in West Germany than in countries like Italy, Spain and France which, while generally egalitarian in their moral principles, are extremely inegalitarian in the social distribution of wealth and income.

Rural societies whose family and political ideals are egalitarian in practice turn out to be inegalitarian. The division of inheritance — by the egalitarian nuclear family or by the exogamous community family — leads to a fragmentation of peasant holdings which only serves to help those rural capitalists who collect plots of land. Since pre-industrial times the major part of the population of the Paris basin, Poland, northern and southern Italy, Spain and Portugal (except in the north) and the whole of Latin America has been made up of a rural proletariat. All these countries have predominantly egalitarian inheritance systems.

The absolute nuclear family — which in practice divides up inheritances, although without making equality an article of faith — often produces a similar situation because it has no interest in household continuity and in retaining the family holding. The unification of estates and the concentration of agriculture were achieved very early on in countries where it is now dominant. England has had an extensive rural proletariat since the seventeenth century.

The mechanism of division which is typical of the exogamous

community family does not lead automatically to the fragmentation of holdings. The ideal of fraternal co-operation works towards unification. It does not check the division of property, but does allow a joint labour force. This is why we often find in regions of exogamous community family intermediate structures where the ownership of the land tends to be concentrated among only a few hands but the actual working of the soil is done by an extended family. The sharecropping system (*mètayage*) typifies this, placing a complex family group at the disposal of a landowner. It is found in Tuscany, in central France, and in large parts of India and China. Everywhere, the community family (exogamous, endogamous or asymmetrical) seems to favour its appearance.

The Russian agrarian system, although not based on share-cropping, combines unequal distribution of land with work done by an extended family — without the formation of a very large rural proletariat. It is complicated by village practices of land redistribution according to family size. Here the inability to conquer time and to conceive of a family line retaining a particular plot of land is pushed to its extreme. There was, incidentally, no difference in this respect between Russian nobles and peasants. The noble inheritance system was egalitarian and divided up property: in 1714 the Russian aristocracy opposed the switch to primogeniture which Peter the Great tried to impose. It was, in its egalitarianism, similar to the Italian nobility and to the Chinese Mandarin elite, which also refused to see brothers as unequal.

But can these social classes be considered 'noble'? Is not the aristocratic ideal *par excellence* one of inequality? The Russian, Chinese and Italian elites, defined as egalitarian by their family values, were to provide the twentieth-century revolutionary movements with innumerable leaders.

There is some continuity between traditional rural society and industrial urban society. But this continuity is a dual one, working both on a practical level and on the theoretical level of values held. The authoritarian family transmits inegalitarian values but encourages a social practice which is egalitarian. The nuclear and community families transmit egalitarian values but encourage inegalitarian social practice.

Thus the anthropological base does not simply determine the ideological system; it also shapes the economic form of rural society, whose general structure — egalitarian or inegalitarian in terms of revenue and education — remains at the very heart of modern society.

Female authority

Authority does not imply physical violence. The authoritarian family is not marked, any more than other anthropological variants, by the dispensing of blows and injuries to its youngest members. Well-founded quantitative surveys have shown that the German family, despite its poor reputation in Europe, practises corporal punishment less than its absolute nuclear English counterpart. The ban on physical punishment in Swedish law, in an authoritarian family country, also reminds us that violence and authority are separate concepts.

What defines the German, Swedish, Japanese and Jewish family types as authoritarian is their ability to transmit, thanks to their absolutely vertical structure, extremely strong behavioural norms. They shape individuals, but this moulding is achieved through education rather than by blows. The important role of women in this anthropological model adequately illustrates that the transmission of authority is not a matter of brute force. For strangely enough, the emphasis placed on the father–son tie does not prevent the authoritarian family from giving women, in practice, an important position. Certain types, such as the Basque and Jewish forms, recognize this female role officially. Basque custom allows an inheritance to be transmitted in the female line by primogeniture if the eldest child is a girl. As for traditional Judaism, it excludes women from inheritance but uses them to determine the child's religion, which depends entirely on the mother. The overwhelming authority of the Jewish mother is, furthermore, a cultural cliché throughout the Western world.

The Irish, Germanic and Japanese systems are fundamentally the same. The authoritarian family practises wherever necessary the transmission of goods and culture through the female line. This is even true of Japan, where the principle of male dominance was once the strongest. A recent statistical study of a village in the north-east of Japan reveals that in 20 per cent of cases the transmission of the main house and land was through women.[1] The principle of genealogical continuity necessitates this compromise with reality, for not all families have sons. The permanence of the household requires them to use their daughters.

Above all, the 'male' cannot become a sacred figure in a system of primogeniture, simply because he does not exist. There are those who are heirs and those who are rejected, older and younger

[1] M. Suenar, 'First Child Inheritance in Japan', *Ethnology*, 11 (1972), pp. 122–6.

sons. The latter are from the point of view of inheritance in the same theoretical position as women. The younger son's only hope is precisely that of marrying an heiress. Otherwise he will become a soldier, a monk, a priest or a landless labourer in a period of demographic growth and industrialization. Indeed, the authoritarian family in traditional societies incessantly produces priests and warriors, or both together in the case of the Teutonic knights and the Japanese soldier-monks.

Contradictions

The authoritarian family structure is a mass of contradictions. It seeks to apply the principle of authority and produces anarchy as much as discipline. It simultaneously creates a rigid family core, shaping and stifling the individual in its vertical structure, and free men who are rejected by the domestic group and have no previously defined place in society. It preaches inequality but favours the development of rural societies which are in practice egalitarian. Finally, it emphasizes continuity in the male line yet gives women a major role. This combination of characteristics gives the authoritarian family a particularly strong cultural dynamism, combining the vertical integration of society with individualism. The list of peoples who espouse this ideal is extremely informative; it includes cultures which while not universalist have played a particularly important creative role in the history of mankind: Athens, Israel, Germany. Today Japan is upsetting the balance of economic power in the world by the strength of its expansion and Korea is following suit.

The principal problem posed by these social systems — setting aside their reluctance to join with the others in worshipping universal man — is their psychologically pathogenic character. It was on examples of Jewish and German authoritarian families that Freud based many of his theories. Consciously exalting the power of the father and unconsciously elevating respect for the mother, combining discipline and individualism, rejecting all but one of the children, incapable of defining clearly the status of women, the authoritarian family is a neurotic machine. Its activity lies at the root of the Nazi phenomenon, of Basque and Irish terrorism, of the suicidal xenophobia of the Japanese during the Second World War. It equally underlies many of the severe religious creeds which combine discipline and intolerance, respect for the father and rejection of the brother: Lutheran and Presbyterian Protestantism, Judaism and Counter-Reformation

Catholicism. The role of certain forms of the authoritarian family
can also be pointed out in the great witch-hunts of the sixteenth
and seventeenth centuries. Nevertheless, such ideological violence
is not inescapable.

Authority and legitimization

The authoritarian family which includes roughly 40 per cent of
the population of Western Europe also produces, on an ideological
level, bureaucratic socialism and the Catholic Right, rival but at the
same time colluding forces which worked together to bring
stability to Europe immediately after the Second World War.
Political science — polarized between the Anglo-Saxon and the
Marxist approaches — has never resigned itself to treating these
as specific ideologies, as genres with particular laws governing
their appearance and development. Yet social democracy is not
simply a limp or degenerate form of communism; political
Catholicism is not an imperfect version of liberalism, nor merely
a bourgeois alibi. The mass of people who, in authoritarian
family regions, are attached to social democracy or to Catholicism,
are just as certain of their beliefs as are communist activists in
areas of exogamous community family structure.

Social democracy and Catholicism, which are in appearance
more fluid than Marxism-Leninism, are just as strongly determined
by anthropology. Social democracy coincides everywhere with
authoritarian family systems; in each case, political Catholicism
flourished in the same anthropological terrain well before the
Second World War. There are two exceptions to this, however,
both of them recent developments: rebellious Polish Catholicism
and Italian Christian democracy which have appeared in egalitarian
nuclear family areas. But in these two countries Catholicism
acts as an ideological prop in the struggle against communism and
therefore responds to different laws and necessities. Furthermore,
in Poland and Italy Catholicism is accompanied by libertarian and
pro-anarchist tendencies which would be inconceivable in its more
typical authoritarian bastions like Bavaria, Austria, Brittany,
the Basque country, northern Spain and Portugal, Rouergue,
Alsace, Savoy and Ireland. Yet even in the Italian and Polish
examples political Catholicism originally had an authoritarian
family stronghold: in Silesia, in the case of Poland, and in
Venetia in Italy, both regions situated on the fringe of the great
Germanic authoritarian family zone. In 1945 Italian Christian

Table 8   The authoritarian family, socialism and Catholicism in Europe

Authoritarian family regions	Major political forces
Northern Portugal	Catholicism
Northern Spain	Catholicism
Galicia	Catholicism
Catalonia	Socialism
Spanish Basque country	Socialism + nationalism
French Basque country	Catholicism
Aquitaine	Socialism
Rouergue	Catholicism
Savoy	Catholicism
Alsace	Catholicism
Nord-Pas-de-Calais	Socialism + Catholicism
Belgium	Catholicism + socialism
Southern Germany	Catholicism
Northern Germany	Socialism
Austria	Socialism + Catholicism
Sweden	Socialism
Norway	Socialism
Scotland	Socialism (labour movement slightly less pragmatic than in England)
Ireland	Nationalism

The political dominance of Catholicism can take different forms: sometimes it appears as a traditional conservative right-wing force, more often as a Christian democratic movement. The type of socialism referred to here is bureaucratic, but usually respects individual liberty. It is generally called social democracy.

democracy achieved its best results in the north-eastern corner of the country. Before the First World War the German Zentrum, a Catholic party, dominated Silesia (which was then part of the Reich) just as it did southern Germany.

Political Catholicism and social democracy are firm but moderate doctrines. The authoritarian family thus functions, historically, in two modes. The first is pathological – Nazism, witch-hunts – and corresponds to phases of historical transition. The second, which is institutional, coincides temporally with the stabilization of industrial society. At such times the authoritarian family calls forth a political system which is at once bureaucratic and parliamentary, authoritarian and pluralist: in Sweden, in the German Federal Republic, in Norway, in Austria, in Ireland, all countries dominated by social-democratic or Catholic ideologies.

Variants of the same authoritarian and pluralist system, independent of European politico-religious traditions, exist in Japan and
Israel.

The natural and precocious implantation of this constitutional
structure in countries like Sweden, Norway, Belgium, Bohemia
(between the two world wars); its harmonious operation in
Ireland and Israel since these nations achieved independence; its
satisfactory performance in Japan and Germany since 1945, all
seem to indicate that this is the normal result of the authoritarian
family form and that the hysterical reflections of the system −
witch-hunts, Nazism − are the exception rather than the rule.

The following sections therefore analyse successively: the
general features of authoritarian and constitutional political
systems; the breaking-down into parties which characterizes
them, linked to secondary anthropological variations; and the
hysterical developments, small in number but significant from
an anthropological point of view.

Electoral rigidity

Not all free electoral systems are the same. Some are mobile and
conflict-ridden, frequently regrouping the majority and changing
the government. This is the case in Anglo-Saxon countries where
two parties contest power in an uncertain and never-ending
struggle: Democrats and Republicans in the United States, the
Labour Party and the Conservatives in Britain. In these two-
party systems the voters think it quite normal to change their
minds and to vote according to the mood of the moment.
Elsewhere, formal respect for liberal practices − universal suffrage,
secret ballots − gives very different results, producing continual
victories for the government and its majority. Never changing his
mind, the voter makes an identical choice year after year. This
stationary mental and political structure is typical of authoritarian
family countries where free elections in no way prevent permanent
majorities, a phenomenon generally and wrongly interpreted as
evidence of successful policies. The most well-known case is that
of Sweden, where the Social Democrats came to power in 1932
and were not defeated in an election until 1976. But this electoral
continuity − comparable with that among communist voters − is
found in all countries with an authoritarian structure, where
changes of government are rare and normally happen only once
in each generation. In absolute nuclear family countries like the

Table 9   Changes of government between 1945 and 1982

Country	Number of changes	Family type
Great Britain	6 ⎫	Absolute nuclear
United States	5 ⎭	
Germany	1 ⎫	
Sweden	1	
Israel	1	Authoritarian family
Japan	0	
Ireland	2	
Norway	1 ⎭	

United States and England, the government changes on average once every six or seven years.

There are fewer changes of government in countries with an authoritarian family structure which have free elections than there are *coups d'état* in the Latin-American military regimes. The sense of discipline produced by a vertical family system is a stronger guarantee of the continuity of government than is the artificial principle of military discipline.

Asymmetrical pluralism

In an authoritarian system the distribution of votes is unequal, unlike in liberal political regimes of the Anglo-Saxon type where two parties each win more or less 50 per cent of the vote. There is usually a dominant party which has no absolute majority but which is well ahead of the party with the second-largest vote. Most commonly, opposition to the dominant party comes from a clutch of small parties which can only ever hope to win power by forming a stable coalition. Two forces interact: one of domination, the other of fragmentation. In all these respects the political system neatly reflects the organizational principles of the authoritarian family, and in particular its asymmetry: the dominant party plays the role of an older brother, the small parties that of younger brothers who are excluded from the succession, in this case from power. These rules apply perfectly to countries which are more or less homogeneous on a cultural level, like Sweden, Norway, Japan and Ireland.

Where there remain linguistic or religious divisions, in Belgium (between the Flemish and the Walloons), or in West Germany (between Catholics and Protestants), conflict between these blocs introduces into the political confrontation a supplementary dualism which acts as a balancing factor. In Germany in the 1976 elections the national results were more or less even, the Christian Democrats (CDU-CSU) taking 48.6 per cent of the vote, the Social Democrats 42.6 per cent. The Social Democrats then governed with the support of the Liberals, who themselves had only 7.9 per cent. However, if we go down to the level of the *Länder* the impression of a balance between contending parties is somewhat attenuated, for in the south the Christian Democrats occupy the dominant position typical of authoritarian political systems: 60.0 per cent of the vote in Bavaria against 32.8 per cent for the SPD; 53.3 per cent in Baden-Württemberg against 36.6 per cent for the SPD. This regional imbalance is in no way being ironed out. Bavaria has steadily become more strongly Christian Democrat between 1961 and 1975, the CDU increasing their share of the vote from 54.9 to 60 per cent. The asymmetrical pluralism of this province is growing, despite the fact that it stands within the framework of a national state. Furthermore, the Federal Republic as a whole is remarkable for the rigidity of its electoral structure. The few changes which have taken place since the war have simply stabilized it by absorbing remaining small electoral groups, notably communist ones. The overall result of these changes has been a general hardening of regional allegiances. The political U-turn which brought the Social Democrats to power in 1969 was the result of a new coalition rather than of a changed majority. In all these respects the German Federal Republic is most definitely an authoritarian family country.

The situation is comparable in Belgium where confrontation between the Socialists and the Christian Democrats (the same two parties as in Germany) is asymmetrical, although there is no clear indication of dominance on a national scale: 36 per cent of the vote for the Catholics, 25 per cent for the Socialists. The situation is more normal, so to speak, in Flanders where the Catholics gain 43 per cent of the vote and the Socialists only 21 per cent, a typical case of authoritarian asymmetry.

In Israel too the asymmetrical pluralism of the system is partly hidden by the existence of two blocs, people from

Table 10 Major and minor political parties in authoritarian family systems

Country and date	First party (% of vote gained)	Second party (% of vote gained)
Culturally homogeneous systems		
Norway 1967	46.5 (Labour)	10.6 (Conservative)
Sweden 1973	43.6 (Social Democrats)	21.5 (Centre)
Ireland 1927–73	44.2 (Fianna Fail)	30.2 (Fine Gael)
Japan 1974	48.5 (Liberal Democrats)	15.9 (Socialists)
Austria 1979	51.0 (Socialists)	41.9 (People's Party)
Systems with a degree of cultural duality		
West Germany 1976 including:	48.6 (Christian Democrats)	42.6 (Social Democrats)
Bavaria	60.0 (Christian Democrats)	32.8 (Social Democrats)
Baden Württemberg	53.3 (Christian Democrats)	36.6 (Social Democrats)
Belgium 1978 including:	36.0 (Social Christians)	25.0 (Socialists)
Flanders	42.7 (Social Christians)	20.7 (Socialists)
Israel 1973	39.6 (Labour)	30.2 (Likud)

Europe and the East on the one hand, and those from the Arab world on the other. From independence until the 1973 elections the imbalance associated with the authoritarian family was clearly visible: the Labour Party dominated the political scene. Subsequently the increased numbers of the Sephardic community redressed the situation in favour of Menachem Begin. But here again, as in Belgium and Germany, the statistical balance is due more to the existence of two cultural blocs than to an unstable free-choice phenomenon typical of Anglo-Saxon countries.

Austria, culturally homogeneous, provides a final example: that of a formerly balanced system which evolves towards imbalance, towards complete domination by social democracy, a phenomenon which is especially interesting in that it indicates an electoral shift away from populist Catholicism and towards social democracy. The Austrian socialists had 42.5 per cent of the vote in 1966, 48.4 per cent in 1970, 50.4 per cent in 1975, 51.0 per cent in 1979: the Catholics were by then far behind with only 41.0 per cent of the vote. Austrian social democracy thus reached in the 1970s a stable and dominant position considerably more pronounced than that held by any other social democratic party in Europe. Its Catholic opposition is not fragmented, but the socialists regularly win over 50 per cent of the votes cast which gives them greater electoral strength than Swedish or Norwegian social democracy.

It may be, however, that the real social strength of Austrian social democracy, which has a clear majority but is countered by an ideologically united opposition, is no greater than that of its Scandinavian equivalents. The Swedish and Norwegian socialist parties do not win 50 per cent of the vote and did in fact lose elections during the 1970s, but they always dominate the 'bourgeois' coalitions in a socio-cultural sense, particularly through their trade union and consumer organizations.

It is quite remarkable that in three of the authoritarian family countries which do not strictly observe the 'rule' of asymmetrical pluralism and where the majority and the opposition are more or less balanced — Germany, Belgium, Austria — the hub of the Right should be Catholicism. The latter is in each case confronted by the same enemy: social democracy, always strong, sometimes victorious, but never as dominant as in Protestant countries. The interaction of these three ideological forces — social democracy, Protestantism, Catholicism — should therefore be one of the central questions of European political science. Why do some authoritarian family regions tend towards social democracy and others prefer Catholicism? Looking back to the past we could ask: why did some countries choose Protestantism and others Counter-Reformation Catholicism?

At this point one connection is clear: that between political Catholicism, social democracy and the authoritarian family. When the absolute nuclear family dominates, as in the Netherlands and Denmark, the phenomena of dominance and of electoral asymmetry diminish, or even disappear.

Counter-examples: Denmark and Holland

A study of the Danish and Dutch political systems, also situated in the Germanic linguistic and geographic zones, supports the theory of a link between political Catholicism, social democracy and the authoritarian family: in these countries with (for the most part) absolute nuclear family systems rather than authoritarian ones, the party system is at the same time less rigid and less asymmetrical than in Germany, Belgium and northern Scandinavia. The social democrats do not dominate Denmark as they do Sweden and Norway. The Catholics and the socialists do not have the hold on the Netherlands that they have in Germany or Belgium. The Social Democratic Party wins only 30 per cent of the vote in Denmark (1975), the Labour Party only 27 per cent in the Netherlands (1972). There are signs of fluidity: the collapse of the Dutch Catholic party between 1963 and 1972; the strength of the Liberals in Denmark. Liberalism represents 23 per cent of the vote in Denmark (1975), compared with only 9.4 per cent in Norway (1969), 9.4 per cent in Sweden (1973) and 7.9 per cent in Germany (1976).

The mobility and complete fragmentation of the Dutch and Danish political systems, which do not permit particular political parties to dominate, and the strength of the Liberals, are typical features of individualist political cultures, reflecting a nuclear family ideal. But individualism is in this case not the prevailing culture since the east and south of the Netherlands belong to an authoritarian model, and the urban part of Denmark was strongly influenced by German Hanseatic culture, which is also authoritarian.

The political discipline of the northern European countries, therefore, is no mysterious cultural phenomenon but the ideological reflection of a particular anthropological culture. Where the authoritarian family is not dominant — in Holland and Denmark — political discipline weakens.

Political themes

When relations are not embittered by internal regional conflicts — as in Belgium — authoritarian societies work essentially by consensus. They avoid confrontations based, for example, on the idea of class struggle. The parties which dominate their political systems try to achieve a vertical integration of society, drawing in the representatives of different socio-economic groups. This is true of the Catholics, who have their workers' and peasants' associations, their women's and youth movements. But the same can be said of the social democrats: theoretically working men, since the beginnings of German social democracy between 1880 and 1914, they have tried to seduce and integrate the bourgeois and bureaucratic elites, rejecting the notion that there is a fundamental animosity between employers and workers. It is equally true of the dominant Japanese party, on an ideological rather than an organizational level. The Liberal Democratic Party, unlike its Catholic and social democratic counterparts, does not have a strong structure and does not control powerful, vertical, mass organizations. It is a collection of cliques, attached in various ways to the big *zaibatsus*, the industrial groups which as much as, or more than, the state lie at the heart of Japanese life. Impregnated with an ideology of growth and reassertion, Japan has made the economy its central preoccupation. Its most crucial structures of authority thus escape the political domain and are to be found in the economic sphere. Human loyalty, directed towards the party in a social-democratic system, towards the church under Christian democracy, is concentrated on the company in Japan. But it is still the same discipline that rules here, produced by the same authoritarian family structure. Moreover, the main Japanese opposition party takes the organizational form which is usual in Europe: social democratic.

A displacement of the same sort is observable in Ireland, where the political mechanism is also incapable of providing a focus for ideological commitment: the *zaibatsus* are replaced by the church, whose strength reaches levels unequalled anywhere else in the world. The number of priests per inhabitant in Ireland is two or three times what it is in the most Catholic areas of Europe. In this context the existence of a Catholic 'party' is entirely superfluous.

In authoritarian family countries the internal consensus makes the favourite battleground of the parties — unequal in strength —

foreign rather than domestic policy. This is true of Ireland, Japan, Germany and particularly of Israel. In Ireland, the nationalism of Fianna Fail (the dominant party), which wants to revitalize the Irish language, is stronger than that of Fine Gael, which is less hostile to the British and to the 1921 treaty which established the independence of Eire. In Japan social democracy, unoriginal in its domestic policy statements, differs from the political Right mainly in its opposition to rearmament. It plays an important role, for the Socialist Party minority is constitutionally able to block legislation, thus compensating for a relatively mediocre electoral score. The story is the same in Germany, where social democracy is traditionally more pacifist and in favour of encouraging links with the East, than the 'Christian' Right, which is more inclined to seek revenge and which is less ready to accept the partition of the country or the contracted frontiers of 1945. In Israel the primordial importance of foreign policy is quite obvious and is naturally the subject of the most serious disputes between Right and Left.

In the examples of Japan, Ireland, Germany and Israel, one could reasonably maintain that the objective circumstances of their international position make the primacy of foreign policy inevitable. But it can also be pointed out that it is in the nature of peoples with authoritarian family systems, who are strongly ethnocentric, to become engaged in complex international situations.

The particularism of countries with authoritarian family traditions has in general succeeded in preventing the emergence of a political culture common to all of them. Regions of exogamous community family structure, on the other hand, have ended up being united 'fraternally' in a Communist International, often split but always recognizable, and which several times in the history of the twentieth century has acted as a single centralized force. There is nothing similar among the authoritarian cultures, as much like each other as the community cultures, but each striving to magnify their differences and to glorify their distinctiveness. Japan wants to be Japanese rather than authoritarian, Germany to be German, Ireland Irish. The same family structure seems to produce distinct political cultures. The differences are superficial: all these ideologies are bureaucratic, pluralistic and asymmetrical, just as unoriginal, fundamentally, as the communist ideology.

Nevertheless, the authoritarian family systems have, almost despite themselves, produced two transnational ideologies —

political Catholicism and social democracy. In 1914 and 1939 the world witnessed the inability of the church and of the socialists to prevent conflict between states. In 1914 Catholic priests on both sides blessed the soldiers on their way to the front; and the social democrats, without batting an eyelid, voted the war budgets sought by the rulers. The existence of these two international forces is not the result of profound universalist aspirations but of two factors which lead in the same direction. First, the existence of a universalist tradition, Christian or socialist, which predates both the implantation of these ideologies in authoritarian family regions and their deformation by such vertical and anti-universalist cultures. Second, the basic anthropological similarity between different Catholic areas and between different socialist areas.

Whether they like it or not, the Irish, Flemish and Austrians, the people of Rouergue, Alsace and Bavaria, the Bretons and the Basques, whose family structures are similar, conceive authority in the same way, in terms of an unavoidable relationship between man and God. Whether they like it or not, the north Germans, the Swedes, the people of Aquitaine, the Norwegians and the Walloons, all conceive authority in the same way, as a necessary relationship between the individual and the state. The combination of these two factors has led to the formulation of two doctrines of international application, political Catholicism and social democracy. It only remains to describe the structural analogies between Catholicism and socialism, and to explain the laws which allow the passage from one to the other — anthropological laws, naturally.

Heavenly and earthly bureaucracies

The operation of authoritarian family values is equally visible in the social democratic and Catholic ideologies. Both have a vertical vision of social relations, the natural respect for authority which is embodied in a well-developed bureaucratic system: that of the church in the case of Catholicism, that of the state in the case of social democracy. The opposition between heavenly and earthly bureaucracies in fact disappears in the Protestant states established in northern Europe since the seventeenth century in Sweden, Scotland and Prussia. Resting on national churches — which are ethnocentric — these states integrate the Calvinist or Lutheran pastors into their bureaucracies. This synthesis, incidentally, has produced in these three countries the most efficient education systems in Europe, with literacy increasing rapidly since the eighteenth century.

Social democracy, heir to this powerful religious and administrative tradition in Prussia, Scandinavia and Scotland, has re-established the principle of a secular central bureaucracy. But social democracy, unlike communism, is never anti-religious. In northern Europe the work of the Protestant pastors was extremely important in the history of the social-democratic movement. Even in Catholic countries there is no visceral antagonism between the church and social democracy. In France, for example, the Communist party is the only party ideologically committed to atheism. The old SFIO (Section française de l'internationale ouvrière), although heir to the anticlerical tradition of French Radicalism, characteristically retreated during its period of greatest weakness between 1950 and 1965 into areas of France which were not completely dechristianized: the north and the south-west. The excellent surveys of religious sociology carried out in France since the Second World War enable a comparison between the electoral implantation of the different parties and the frequency of attendance at Sunday mass in the early 1960s. Analysis reveals a violent repulsion between Catholicism and communism (a negative correlation of -0.75 in 1967), but a much weaker phenomenon of aversion between Catholicism and socialism (a coefficient of correlation close to -0.39 in 1967 and to $+0.03$ in 1978). Social democracy is never anti-religious even if it is sometimes moderately anticlerical. Catholicism and social democracy are not opposed to each other and seem antagonistic to one another only when their common enemy, communism, poses no significant threat. As soon as communism appears with any force, the complicity between these two ideologies born of the authoritarian family is re-established.

For Catholicism as for social democracy, respect for bureaucratic authority does not entail a rejection of the right to property. This is only to be expected, for the authoritarian family has as its organizing principle and as the aim of its existence, the direct transmission of family property. In this case, therefore, bureaucratic pressure takes the form of high taxation rather than of expropriation or nationalization. The church greatly appreciated its tithes. Social democracy has taken direct taxation to its theoretical limit in Scandinavia: it absorbs more than half of the gross national product in Sweden. But the fiscal situation in countries like Germany, Belgium and Austria, dominated until the mid-1960s by Christian democracy, is not dissimilar.

The authoritarian family particularly favours a dualistic vision of property. Even more than other anthropological systems, it clearly separates real estate, which is indivisible and goes to the eldest son, from money, a secondary asset, which is passed on to the younger son. A glance at post-war Catholic catechisms adequately shows that this conceptual distinction is dear to the church, which despises money but respects property. Social-democratic governments, which tax but do not nationalize, which leave industrialists their factories but tap all monetary revenue, are not greatly different. The socialist and Catholic conceptions of social and economic organization are similar because both derive from the values that are typical of the authoritarian family.

Conceptual clarification

Corresponding to the authoritarian family form there are, therefore, recognizable political forces, but forces which do not quite fit into the categories customarily used to explain ideological struggle. Of all the non-totalitarian socialist parties in Europe, only half have been accounted for: social-democratic parties. The more libertarian, revolutionary and impotent socialist organizations of southern Europe — central and southern Spain, northern Italy, central and southern Greece — are quite distinct from their more bureaucratic and efficient social-democratic brothers and enemies. The anthropological key to understanding these political differences can pin down and explain this division which since the beginning has rent the Second International, setting sullen Germanic bureaucrats against libertarian Latins in a pathetic dialogue. Until now interpretations of this dichotomy, inexplicable in terms of Marxist economic categories, have been based on impalpable cultural characteristics — Germanic or Latin — the division itself being treated as a subsidiary concern, a regrettable theoretical imperfection.

Once bureaucratic socialism and the authoritarian family are brought together the problem is easily resolved. Libertarian socialism corresponds to egalitarian nuclear family areas which seek equality between brothers, but not paternal authority. The anthropological distinction coincides only imperfectly with

linguistic categories: in northern Spain — Galicia, Catalonia, — and
in the south-west of France — Aquitaine — there lies a vast zone
which is Latin in its language but authoritarian in its family
structure, and is dominated by a bureaucratic socialism. The
south-west of France supports the state and furnishes a good
number of its employees.

However, because Western Europe contains three family types
and not two, the Second International embraces three forms of
socialism. The English Labour Party cannot be classified either as
bureaucratic or as libertarian socialism. Unlike social democracy
it does not control its trade unions and has a strong anarchistic
streak. Unlike revolutionary socialism it is calm, strong and has
a vocation to govern. The source of these characteristics is of
course the absolute nuclear family. I will look at these Labour
Party and libertarian variants in chapter 4 which is devoted to
the two forms of individualism: that, is, to the two nuclear
families, the egalitarian and the absolute.

This spectrographic method of dissecting socialism by an
anthropological analysis can be applied to most of the major
political doctrines of Western Europe. There is a tendency for
different ideologies to be disguised by identical terminology,
the interconnected history of the European nations having
given rise to exchanges of words and concepts, without repairing
the anthropological fragmentation of the continent. Each
doctrine — socialism, Catholicism, Protestantism — is deformed
by the family system, nuclear or authoritarian according to the
area.

An ideology corresponds to a basic set of attitudes: it is related
to the unconscious and to family structure. A doctrine, on the
other hand, is intellectually articulated but exists purely on a
verbal level: it is a conscious phenomenon. Protestantism, which
in the sixteenth century was an intellectual revolution, is just
as good an example as socialism. Political scientists have trouble
understanding the different socialist temperaments within the
Second International; historians try unsuccessfully to comprehend
the simultaneous presence, within Protestantism, of liberal and
authoritarian streams. On the one hand there is the disciplined,
state-orientated Lutheranism of Prussia and Sweden; on the other
the more liberal, even anarchistic Calvinism of Holland and of the
English sects. However, even the distinction between Calvinism
and Lutheranism does not sufficiently explain the opposition
between liberal and authoritarian tendencies. For there exists in
Scotland a church which is both Calvinist and bureaucratic, the

famous Kirk. If the hard- and soft-line forms of Protestantism are plotted on the anthropological map the mystery is resolved. Lutheranism and the bureaucratic variants of Calvinism correspond to authoritarian family regions: Prussia, Sweden, Scotland. Behind the less stern variants in England and Holland, in part of Switzerland and in the Jura, lie the different types of nuclear family.

This technique of breaking down doctrines is equally applicable to Catholicism, hierarchical and bureaucratic in authoritarian family areas — by far the most numerous in this case — and more liberal in the nuclear family areas of Poland and of northern Italy. The analysis of religious doctrines according to their basic anthropological components is valid especially for the earlier period of European history. From the eighteenth century onwards, official religion retreated, slowly or suddenly depending on the location, into zones of authoritarian family where the father-image sustained that of God. The nuclear family areas abandoned Protestantism or Catholicism and turned towards English liberalism or French egalitarian individualism.

It was a late version of piety that Freud analysed in *The Future of an Illusion* (1928). His interpretative methodology provides an explanation for authoritarian religions — later Catholicism, Lutheranism and Judaism — but not for the whole metaphysical history of Europe. In the case of Catholicism the general retreat towards the authoritarian family systems, a process which has continued since the Reformation, was accompanied by major doctrinal changes. Medieval Christianity, whose intellectual and demographic centre in the thirteenth century was the Paris basin — today covered with cathedrals but brutally dechristianized — was pluralist, mobile and alive with scholastic debate. Later Catholicism, from the Council of Trent until the second Vatican Council, was authoritarian, even absolutist. In 1870 the first Vatican Council marked the apogee and the consecration of an ideological false turn by proclaiming the principle of 'Papal infallibility'. The church was very much in advance of other European political forces in its invention, *avant la lettre*, of the *Führerprinzip*.

Since the thirteenth century, however, the authoritarian family has been the most widespread family form in the Catholic sphere: 45 per cent of the total population, against 40 per cent for the egalitarian nuclear family, 10 per cent for the absolute nuclear family, and 5 per cent for the exogamous community family. The passing of time has only emphasized a tendency present from the start, as Catholicism has abandoned its individualist and community branches.

Anthropology separates out different types of socialism, Protestantism and Catholicism. But it also allows us to group into a single category all the authoritarian ideologies that are hidden beneath the confusing veil of doctrine. Side by side lie Lutheranism, Scottish Calvinism, Counter-Reformation Catholicism, and why not Judaism? A heterogeneous mixture for anyone interested in the nuances of theology, but one which explains the transformations and reflexes common to the various creeds. Destroying the categorization which separates hard-line Protestantism from authoritarian Catholicism and tracing in both the same underlying family structure affords an understanding of witch-hunts, one of the major ideological phenomena of the sixteenth and seventeenth century. As specialists in this area, like Trevor-Roper, have observed, witch-burning, while not uniformly distributed across Europe, seems to have been practised by Catholics and Protestants alike. Luther's disciples, those of Calvin and of the Pope, all pursued Satan with equal vigour.

More immediately, grouping the authoritarian religious systems into a single category explains why in the twentieth century the Catholic, Lutheran and Jewish religions have managed to produce the same social-democratic, bureaucratic and pluralist systems, respecting both private property and the state. Purely religious oppositions, being more superficial, do not explain why the Swedish political system (Protestant), the Austrian (Catholic), and the Israeli one (Jewish) are so similar. In the same way, the religious history of Japan, Shinto and Buddhist, is completely independent from that of the Judaeo—Christian peoples: yet that country has produced in the twentieth century a major social-democratic party. An anthropological analysis, therefore, does not accord with Weber's conception of fixed religious categories in which the concepts of Catholicism and Protestantism are unified and self-contained.

Conversion: the transition from Catholicism to socialism,
and average age at marriage

Bringing together into a single category both popular Catholicism and social democracy, strongly linked by a shared anthropological origin and by parallel ideological positions, is not to deny one secondary but important difference which divides them. After all, the two ideologies are electorally distinct and in competition. In order to understand this division we must look for a secondary anthropological parameter whose fluctuations might explain the oscillations of authoritarian ideology between the two poles of Christianity and socialism.

The very great variations in matrimonial behaviour within the authoritarian family category supply the key to this political duality. In the authoritarian model age at marriage varies more than in any other family system. The nuclear family, as a simple association between two individuals, does not prompt marriages between children or adolescents because the independence of the married couple in this system requires a degree of maturity and an ability on the part of a husband and wife to provide for themselves. By contrast, the exogamous or endogamous community family positively encourages marriages with children: adding a young wife, incapable of autonomy, to a complex household does not pose any serious organizational problems. In fact the community family cannot tolerate a high marriage-age. The formation of extensive, complex domestic units supposes small or moderate gaps between generations, which marriage at a late age makes impossible. In its ideal form the community family presupposes the marriage of at least two brothers before the death of the parents, which in turn requires a relatively rapid succession of generations.

In order to assume its ideal vertical form the authoritarian family requires no more than the marriage of one son or daughter and in this way it can tolerate considerable age differences between generations. But its form of organization, unlike that of the nuclear family, is also perfectly compatible with a very low marriage-age: the young couple remain after marriage under the protection and control of the adult parents. In practice, then, the authoritarian family can accommodate marriages at any age. An examination of the available evidence shows a wider range of variation for the authoritarian family than for other anthropological models.

Marriage-age can also be logically and empirically linked to the intensity of religious feeling in different societies. Of all the universalist religions, Christianity is the one which has most insisted on the virtue of chastity, either in the form of sexual abstinence within marriage or of permanent celibacy. The most edifying models provided by Catholicism are the Virgin Mary, mother of Christ, married but chaste; and the priest, celibate

Table 11   Theoretical age at marriage of women according to family type

	Low (before age 19)	Middling (19–24)	High (over 24)
Nuclear family	no	yes	yes
Community family	yes	yes	no
Authoritarian family	yes	yes	yes

and chaste. Max Weber, who was fascinated by the effects of religious asceticism on different areas of social life, would no doubt have considered the attitude of the church to be primordial, the cause of other human actions, particularly economic behaviour. But it could also be asked whether in fact the affection in which Catholicism is held in certain regions of Europe is not a result of pre-existing local models of late marriage. The present-day correlation between Catholicism and a matrimonial model which encourages celibacy is striking, even if the direction of causality is not immediately obvious. Is it Catholicism which creates widespread celibacy or popular abstinence which engenders Catholicism? A few coefficients of correlation in several European countries, each of which includes at least a large minority of regions where the authoritarian family prevails, leave no room for doubt about the strong link between the Catholic Right and marriage late on in life. In France, in Spain, in Belgium, the administrative divisions of the country allow a convincing statistical demonstration (coefficients of correlation between +0.40 and +0.55). But this coincidence of marriage-age and political religiosity is valid for most other European countries, even if the quality of the regional evidence does not allow significant statistical tests. In Germany the Catholic southern *Länder* traditionally have a later marriage-age and higher levels of celibacy than the northern and eastern provinces of the former kingdom of Prussia, largely socialist since 1914.

Sweden, Norway, Austria: the advent of socialism

In the case of Scandinavia, and therefore of Lutheranism rather than Catholicism, the relationship between late marriage and

Table 12 Some correlations between late marriage and political religiosity

	Political/religious character	Marriage characteristics	Coefficient of correlation
Catholicism			
France (90 *départements*)	Right wing with strongly Catholic core (Giscard vote 1974)	Average marriage-age of women, 1955	+0.45
Belgium (30 regions)	Chrétiens-sociaux (1978)	Percentage of women married after age 20	+0.53
Spain (50 districts)	Catholic extreme Right (voted no in 1978 referendum)	Percentage of women married after age 20	+0.47
Buddhism			
Japan (47 prefectures)	Komeito, political wing of the nationalist Buddhist sect Sokagakka (1974)	Percentage of unmarried males 1975	+0.63
Communism			
Japan (47 prefectures)	Japanese Communist Party (1974)	Percentage of unmarried males 1975	+0.49

In each of the five cases above, a coefficient of correlation is calculated between the percentage of votes held by a given political/religious group in a given election and a statistical indicator representing age at marriage. The regional units used for the calculation of these ecological coefficients are given in column 1.

political religiosity holds good: higher age at marriage goes with a general propensity for mysticism rather than specifically this or that religious form.

Throughout Europe in the twentieth century, the trend has been towards a decline in marriage-age, once very high throughout the continent. In authoritarian family regions each stage of this decline is accompanied, locally, by a phenomenon of conversion to bureaucratic socialism and a drift away from traditional religiosity. In Scandinavia a massive drop in age at marriage first appeared in the years between the wars: the age of women on their first marriage in Norway then fell from 26 to 22, in Sweden from 27 to 23. At the same time passionate debates took place in both these countries about the decline of mysticism; simultaneously, from the 1930s onwards, the ideological supremacy of social democracy became established.

The authoritarian family areas of continental Europe — Germany, Austria, the fringes of France — did not witness any significant drop in age at marriage before the Second World War. But after 1945, in the space of a generation, the matrimonial model changed completely. Between 1937 and 1971 the average age of Austrian women on their first marriage fell from 26.5 to 21.7 years. Progressively but irresistibly, Kreisky's social democracy came to the fore, forty years later than its Swedish counterpart. The demographic evolution is less clear in Germany, which probably explains the greater resistance of Christian democracy there, notably in Bavaria: the fall in the female marriage-age between 1950 and 1971 was only 2.5 years in Germany (from 25.4 to 22.9), which suggests an average in the south today higher than 23. (Unfortunately there are no reliable statistics available on marriage-age by *Land*.)

France

France's evolution from 1967 to 1981 is not unique. Its socialism is more complex and more composite than that in Austria, because it covers regions both of authoritarian and egalitarian nuclear family structure. But the electoral resurgence of the Socialist Party took place largely, if one looks at votes rather than seats, in the Catholic provinces on the fringes of the national territory, authoritarian family areas where the age at marriage was still high in 1945, as in Austria. The development of earlier marriage led to the classic transition, the population moving on the political plane from Catholic Right to social democracy. The coefficient of correlation between attendance at Sunday mass around 1960 and the growth in the socialist vote between 1967 and 1978 is high, +0.49 (90 departments). In the Paris region, an egalitarian nuclear family area, the Socialist Party won many more seats but far fewer votes, the heart of France being equally supportive of both Left and Right, as in Anglo-Saxon countries. Unlike Brittany, Rouergue, Alsace, or the Basque country, Paris does not practise asymmetrical pluralism.

Socialism therefore follows on quite naturally from Catholicism. An analogous phenomenon can be observed in many small countries and provinces where an authoritarian family ideal is dominant: in Quebec, in the Spanish Basque country, the separatist movement produces mixed forms, at once socialist and nationalist. The xenophobic component of the authoritarian family (murder of the brother) is accentuated by the minority position of the group concerned. In all these regions the collapse of matrimonial discipline and of sexual asceticism opens the way to social democracy.

There is, however, a counter-example. Ireland is the only authoritarian family country in Europe where age at marriage has not fallen to a very low level since the war. Socialism, represented by the Labour Party, continues to languish in insignificance.

Japan: from socialism to Buddhism — history in reverse

In twentieth-century Europe the general tendency has been for age at marriage to fall, while in Japan it has risen, as in most of East Asia. And logically Japanese political life, whose overall structure is determined by the authoritarian family, has witnessed an inverse temporal and geographic distribution of its secular and religious components. Modernization, as in Europe an urban phenomenon, has produced different effects in Japan — a rise rather than a fall in marriage-age. Ideology has followed. Religious feeling has grown stronger in the cities where unmarried men and women are more numerous. The Komeito, the political wing of the nationalist Buddhist sect Sokagakkai, has achieved its maximum power in urban areas; its electoral strength in 1974 correlates closely with the level of celibacy (+0.63) and with the percentage of the work-force in the tertiary sector (+0.49)

(1975 census). In Austria or Belgium, by contrast, political religiosity has retreated into the countryside where the marriage-age is higher. By the same token the strength of the Japanese Socialist Party is, unlike in Europe, in positive correlation with the proportion of the population engaged in agriculture (+0.50). However, as in Europe it is also in positive correlation with a low marriage-age (+0.43). The Japanese example is crucial. It projects political anthropology into truly universal relationships, breaking away from Western and Judeo-Christian religious symbolism. In both Japan and Europe the same correlations between authoritarian family and bureaucratic system, and between high marriage-age and metaphysical orientation of political behaviour, can be observed.

Buddhism − particularly that of the Greater Vehicle − does not make chastity a primordial virtue to the same extent as Christianity. But in Japan as elsewhere the rise in celibacy precedes and shapes a mystical mutation of political life. In this way, it is anthropology that engenders the religious system and not the reverse. Theology does not determine age at marriage. Each family system selects its own doctrine, crystallizes it and transforms it into ideology. Unconscious family values give the doctrines formulated by intellectuals (lay or religious) the mental rigidity and the mass support vital for their ideological solidification.

Sexuality and politics

In the 1960s and 1970s Europe was the scene of a sexual revolution, of a rejection of traditional values in the area of morality: with the spread of modern methods of contraception, the generalization of premarital sex, the greater value placed on sensuality within marriage. Demographically this behavioural evolution appears principally in two ways: a fall in marriage-age and a collapse in the birth-rate. These statistical transformations confirm that the sexual revolution was not simply a fashion but a mass phenomenon.

Interpretations of the ideological consequences of these changes, strongly influenced by psychoanalysis, have taken uncertain and mythicizing directions. Some political scientists have tried to show a link between sexual liberty and political liberty, arguing that the emancipation of the body leads to the emancipation of the mind. This is to accord, in the great tradition of Christianity, considerable importance to sexuality, making it the motive of all human behaviour. Above all it involves a factual error: an affirmation of the state's authority is frequently the obvious result of sexual liberation. The fall in age at marriage leads not to a libertarian system but to social democracy in countries where the family structure is authoritarian.

The anthropological value-systems — liberty, equality and their negations — are more stable, strong and profound than sexual behaviour, which varies with the passing of time and which is only a secondary cultural factor. The transition from political religiosity to social democracy is a secondary transformation from the point of view of liberty. From being heavenly, the bureaucracy becomes terrestrial: it ceases to control sexuality but takes hold of the economy. Fiscal pressures replace sexual abstinence. Sexual freedom, in authoritarian family countries, leads not to anarchy but to Aldous Huxley's *Brave New World*, which crushes the individual in every way while allowing sexual pleasure free reign.

Although particularly pronounced in authoritarian family regions, fluctuations in age at marriage occur in all anthropological systems. The values which underlie these other structures, however, lead to the elaboration of other ideologies. Yet in every case a rise in marriage-age is followed by an increase in the general level of mysticism in the society concerned. A mysticism which it would be wrong to consider, as do the least respectable psychoanalytical interpretations, as an ideological consequence of sexual frustration. Celibacy is much more than abstinence: it undoubtedly involves sexual privation but it also entails individual isolation, creating a consciousness independent of family life with a potential for introspection, reflection, creation and neurosis which has nothing to do with sexuality.

A rise in the marriage-age can thus intensify religious anxiety although this does not necessarily fit in with the conception of society produced by the authoritarian family. In Russia the rise in the marriage-age from the time of Catherine II to Stalin, continuing at an even faster pace in the twentieth century with the disintegration of the exogamous community family, gives rise to a specific religious system: militant atheism. This system tries to destroy the father. Anti-religious atheism is nevertheless a typical manifestation of metaphysical anxiety, of a mystical conception of political life. In Islamic territory the rise in marriage-age, conspicuous in the cities, encourages Muslim fundamentalism — which most certainly corresponds to an increase in religious anxiety — but does not lead, as in Russia or in Catholic or Lutheran Europe, to a vertical authoritarian, bureaucratic conception of religion and of society.

Anxiety

The overall ideological balance sheet for the authoritarian family is far from depressing. Throughout the world, this anthropological form seems capable of ensuring the formation of stable, pluralist political systems, accepting a generally vertical organization of society but tolerant of individual differences. The authoritarian family structure, unlike its exogamous community counterpart, is not 'heterophobic': it is not afraid of differences and does not require society to be made uniform. It has an unfortunate tendency to perceive differences which do not exist and to combat ideological phantoms of its own creation. It defines them not as social heterogeneity, but as aggressive external forces. A perfect example of such an ideological creation is German anti-Semitism, produced by an extreme and particularly rigid authoritarian family structure. It remains true that Nazism is not typical of all authoritarian systems which are capable of great variation in the intensity of their xenophobic tendencies. Nazi paranoia is exceptional in time and space. To understand and explain it, the special characteristics of the German anthropological model which lead to a convulsive deviance in the tendency towards fratricide inherent in any family system practising primogeniture (or ultimogeniture) must be identified.

The ambiguity of male—female relations, a general trait of those anthropological types which strongly encourage an ideal of continuity of the family lineage, is in Germany taken to an extreme not found elsewhere. Lack of definition becomes instability. How can this unconscious, secret tendency of family organization be grasped? Quite simply by systematically measuring the frequency of illegitimate births in each family system.

Illegitimacy, the conception of children outside marriage ('natural' children in French), seems to be a virtually inevitable concomitant of exogamy. Seeking a marriage-partner outside the family group implies casual encounters and a relaxation of control over female sexuality. There are few reliable figures available for endogamous systems, but the little research which has been done suggests that a preferential marriage model does in fact exclude the very notion of illegitimacy. The figures available for Islamic countries show a negligible proportion of illegitimate births between 0 and 0.1 per cent. However, not all the exogamous types produce similar levels of illegitimacy. Even within the one family category not all the variants display the same proportion of 'natural' births.

The authoritarian family is doubly remarkable: both because of the high average level of illegitimacy rates and because of their variability, going from 0.6 per cent in Israel in the late 1960s to 27.3 per cent in Bavaria around 1850. The figures for the nuclear and exogamous community families are on average lower and more consistent. An exhaustive study of the evidence on European countries shows that the authoritarian family, in which there is a certain a priori ambiguity in male–female relations, has resolved this dilemma in different ways in various cultures. Two distinct models emerge from the statistics if one takes marital relations into account. First, an unstable model, with a high illegitimacy rate: this model applies to the German, Scandinavian, Scottish and Basque cultures. Second, a stable model, with a low illegitimacy rate: this type includes the Occitan, Breton, Irish and Jewish variants.

This subdivision of the authoritarian model produces a real sub-typology, unlike the differentiation which the analysis of age at marriage makes possible. The type of matrimonial relations in an anthropological system is a constant; and the indicator which reveals it – the illegitimacy rate – varies little over time. The geographic distribution of illegitimacy was far more stable between 1820 and 1980 than that of age at marriage. The differences between regions in 1980 are much the same as they were in 1850, despite individual changes. On the contrary, differences between the marriage-ages in various European countries have tended to decrease.

Identifying two variants of the authoritarian family – stable and unstable, corresponding to low and high levels of illegitimacy – allows us to localize and comprehend two of the most tragic phenomena of European history: the great satanic fear of the sixteenth and seventeenth centuries, and Nazi anti-Semitism. The witch-hunts and the Jew-hunts have often been compared by historians, the similarities between them being obvious, even to the point of cremation being used in both as a technique of elimination. But an anthropological comparison has never been made, although the two massacres arose from one and the same anthropological terrain: the unstable authoritarian family.

Table 13 Illegitimacy and family type in Europe in the mid-nineteenth century (percentage of live births)

Authoritarian family		Absolute nuclear family		Egalitarian nuclear family		Exogamous community family	
Bavaria*	27.3	Denmark	13.2	Northern France	6.8	Finland	7.6
Saxony*	15.0	England	7.3	Poland (1890)	6.1	Hungary (1870)	7.5
Austria*	14.5	Western France	4.7	Spain	5.9	Central-Mediterranean France	5.4
Alsace*	10.5	Netherlands	4.0	Romania (1870)	3.2	Russia	3.0
Sweden	10.3			Greece (1870)	1.3	Bulgaria (1890)	0.2
Norway	9.4					Serbia	0.2
Belgium*	9.4						
Prussia	9.1						
Scotland*	8.9						
French Basque country*	8.2						
Occitan regions (1860)	4.3						
Breton-speaking regions	3.1						
Ireland (1870)	2.1						
Israel (1968)	0.6						
Average	*9.5*	*Average*	*7.3*	*Average*	*4.9*	*Average*	*4.9*
Standard deviation	*6.7*	*Standard deviation*	*4.2*	*Standard deviation*	*2.2*	*Standard deviation*	*2.2*

*Major centres of witch-hunts.

Killing the mother

In the best studies four main centres emerge in the development of witch-hunts. They are separated by calm areas which escaped simultaneously from satanism and from the fires of repression. Central and southern Germany was the largest and most significant area of anxiety. The three others were Scotland, the Basque country and Flanders — an apparently heterogeneous collection but easily brought together by a single anthropological type, a particularly anxiety-prone version of a system which tends to create psychological tension: the unstable authoritarian family.

In each of these four areas the satanic and repressive fever developed independently. Around the largest — that part of the Germanic world bordered by Saxony, Alsace and the Tyrol — there was a penumbra, including Lorraine, Franche-Comté, Burgundy, Denmark and Poland, all nuclear family regions, where witch-hunts did take place but with less intensity. In Denmark, Lorraine and Burgundy, too, illegitimacy rates are high, a sign of instability in male—female relations and an anthropological trait normally accentuated by the authoritarian family, but which can exist elsewhere.

Recent studies in historical anthropology make it possible to grasp the similarity of structure between a typical witch-trial and the unstable authoritarian family. A trial generally involves an old woman (the witch), an adult male (the accuser), and a mythical male figure (Satan in one of his different incarnations). The age difference between the male accuser and his female victim is that between a son and his mother. For the witch is a mother-image, not merely a symbol of women in general, and a mother who is perceived as copulating with a stranger, Satan, whose identity as father or lover is uncertain. A witch-trial thus reflects a vertical perception of the family and reveals only in a minor way the clash between father and son which the classical analyses required. The principal conflict is between mother and son, transfigured by satanic ideology and diverted on to an inoffensive old woman picked out from the village. The killing of the mother, which is symbolic but which nevertheless finishes with a real murder, is characteristic of a system where female authority is strong but unconsciously resisted and where the shaping and education of the children can be very extensive because of the high status of women. Only maternal power can profoundly effect the shaping of children. And it is the mother rather than the father who ensures the transmission of the psychological mechanisms underlying respect for authority. Paternal power is a domestic abstraction, a symbol more than a fact, the threat of corporal sanctions for children and no more. In practice the father is neutralized by his activities outside the home, as much in rural societies as in urban ones. The woman, however, is always at the physical centre of the family unit.

In agnatic systems, which are strongly masculine, the status of the woman is affected by the cultural system; her authority over her own children is weakened. And because the father is more distant and cannot replace her in the role of education, strongly masculine systems are in practice weak, as far as training the children is concerned. On the contrary, systems which are more egalitarian in terms of male—female relations and which allow the mother more than hypothetical power have strong educational potential. This is confirmed by the fact that it was in authoritarian family areas that, between the invention of printing and the French Revolution, mass education developed, independently of industrialization and economic progress: in Scandinavia, Scotland and Germany. The Basque country and Béarn were also remarkable under the *ancien régime* for their level of cultural development.

Once again, however, the authoritarian family model takes two forms: when it is stable, as in Ireland, Brittany and the Occitan areas, it does not achieve particularly outstanding educational results. The isolation of the regions concerned, where witch-hunts did not occur, incidentally, reinforces this mediocrity. Female authority seems to be greatest in the unstable authoritarian system. It enables rapid educational advances but implies strong psychological tension, the result of a profound moulding of individuals.

The Germanic centre, in the sixteenth century, was the source of three cultural waves: the Reformation, the witch-hunts and the spread of literacy to the masses. They were as much the beginning of the modern period in Europe as the French Revolution or the English Industrial Revolution. Underlying this fundamental historical movement, which without admitting it tended towards universalism through literacy (expanding throughout Europe from its Germanic centre), may be seen a vertical, asymmetrical, particularist family structure in which the mother is always powerful but often unconsciously hated.

The authoritarian family functioned in this pathological way — producing the witch-hunts and mass literacy — only during a particular period, a vital but transitional one. The regions concerned subsequently settled down and became, in the eighteenth and nineteenth centuries, calm, pleasant, provincial societies, small German towns which rested for two centuries following these excesses.

In Catholic areas of Europe, which coincided increasingly with authoritarian family systems, the mother-figure was finally deified in the cult of the Virgin, the progress of which, from the Middle Ages to the nineteenth century, was one of the principal lines of development of Catholic theology. The Holy Family came to have the inevitable vertical anthropological structure to which Catholicism was adapting more and more. Christianity increasingly spoke about the father, less and less about the brothers. Jesus became an obedient son instead of a revolutionary brother. But whom did he obey? Mary? Certainly. God, his real father? Of course. Joseph? Perhaps. Strangely, the Holy Family with its two levels of paternity reproduces the ambiguity of the satanic model in which the presence of the true father is paralleled by the intervention of a demon.

Although saved by Counter-Reformation Catholicism, however, the Virgin, like the witch, was one of the great victims of the sixteenth century: one of the favourite themes of Protestantism was the rejection of the cult of saints and above all that of Mary, who was ejected from the Reformation theological repertoire with exceptional violence.

But Lutheranism, like Catholicism, did not escape anthropological determinism. Its distant, severe God is a father. And the very idea of predestination, by which certain children of the Lord are chosen independently of their good deeds on earth while others are rejected, is an ideological pastiche of the authoritarian family which passes on the inheritance to one son while condemning the others to social instability.

From the sixteenth century onwards, Catholicism and Protestantism were separate religions but were equally severe and vertical, playing, although sometimes in different ways, on the same anthropological keyboard. In places where other family systems were dominant, other ideologies would be born: English liberalism, the French revolutionary ideal, communism.

Bringing forth the monster

It still remains to explain the most monstrous phenomenon in the history of humanity: Nazism, born in an authoritarian family region. It is not just one form of totalitarianism among others but a distinct phenomenon, as different from Russian communism as from Anglo-Saxon liberalism. But in its essential features National Socialism was no more than it claimed to be: a diseased interpretation of social-democratic ideology, of statist, xenophobic principles which it took to their ultimate, most lunatic extreme.

It seems paradoxical to place peaceful, stable, Scandinavian social democracy in the same category as National Socialism, a brief, mad moment in German history. In order to overcome a natural resistance to this assimilation, one which is ideological rather than intellectual, I would wish to point out a historical fact and to offer a fundamental correlation.

The historical fact: Germany was the birthplace of the social-democratic ideal which derives, through Lassalle, from the Prussian conception of state socialism. In 1914 German social democracy was the strongest in the Second International. It had all the characteristics typical of social democracy throughout history: respect for the parliamentary system and for public liberty but a desire for state intervention. Although unaware of the fact, it already respected private property and contested Marxist tradition on this score. It was highly bureaucratic and in control of its trade unions.

The correlation: before coming to power Nazism was an electoral mutation; in 1932 the NSDAP (German National Socialist Workers' Party) won a third of the votes cast. Of all the political parties in the Weimar Republic it was the most national, the least regionalized. However, a systematic analysis of the correlation between the NSDAP vote by district and the major German groupings in the period before it developed, in 1928 – nationalist Right, Social Democrats, Catholics – shows maximal geographic coincidence between social democracy and National Socialism. Systematic use of coefficients of correlation enables us to avoid two complementary myths: that National Socialism was a hysterical mutation of the German Right; that Nazism was a nationalist version of totalitarian communism. The maximal correlation is with social democracy, while that with the Right is high, that with the Communist Party low, and that with the Catholic *Zentrum* negative.

However, electoral figures do not accurately mirror support for the party: analysis of the geographical origins of its leaders gives the reverse picture. Unlike the voters who were mostly in the Protestant north, Hitler and the initial leaders of the party came from the Catholic south. The key to the strength of the

Nazis may well lie in this polarization, in the coexistence of two nuances of the unstable authoritarian family, one providing the leaders and the other the mass following.

The south, where Catholicism exercises a stabilizing influence on the population, nevertheless produces, because of its late marriage-age, a higher level of marginality and of individual deviance: in Catholic areas there are many more unmarried adults and many more illegitimate children, distinct categories but ones which derive from the same exceptionally rigid matrimonial model. Furthermore, in Bavaria marriage was not available to everyone; the community had to give its consent and refused it to the poor. The Protestant north was better at integrating individuals into the family but was quicker to transfer allegiance from God to the state. It provided the electoral support and the bureaucracy of the Nazi movement.

The combination of paranoid individualism with submission to bureaucratic authority, the very essence of Nazism, is thus mirrored in a geographical dualism and in the Prussia/Bavaria pairing. The concentration-camp mechanism is a form of organized sadism which has adopted the basic rules of administrative rationality. In cultural terms Nazism creates a painful synthesis of the southern Baroque and the Prussian statist traditions.

The existence of two anthropological blocs belonging to a single general type — the unstable authoritarian family — and differing only in their matrimonial model, is not a coincidence

Table 14 Origins of the German National Socialist Workers' Party

Party	Coefficient of correlation
SPD (Social Democrat Party)	+0.64
DNVP (nationalist Right)	+0.57
KPD (German Communist Party)	-0.25
Zentrum (Catholic)	-0.69

Between 1928 and July 1932 the NSDAP went from 2.6% to 37.4% of the vote. A few coefficients of correlation between the Nazi vote in 1932 and votes for other parties in 1928 give a measure of the affinity between Nazism and various other groups (35 districts).

Source of original electoral figures: A. Milatz, *Wähler und Wählen in der Weimaren Republik* (Bonn, Bundeszentrale für Politische Bildung, 66, 1965).

but arises from the very size of Germany, geographically and demographically. Its authoritarian family model is not one among many: in quantitative terms it represents 80 per cent of Europe's authoritarian family systems. The unit formed by Austria and the two Germanies represented 87 million people around 1970; Belgium represented 10 million, Sweden 8.5, Scotland 5, Norway 4, Israel 3.5, Ireland 3.

There are certainly nuances within the Belgian, Israeli, Scottish, Swedish and Norwegian groups; but these have not been able to take the form of total opposition between two blocs identifiable by their religious labels: Protestants and Catholics. More generally, an ethnocentric system containing 3 or 4 million people will not produce the same ideologies as a bloc with nearly 90 million. Germany was for several decades the principal power on the European continent: demographically, culturally and economically. The cultural narcissism of the Basques, the Irish, the Jews, the Swedes and the Norwegians is, in terms of world history, fairly inoffensive and even picturesque. That of a great power is much less so: it suggests superiority rather than simply difference. Only Japan is comparable to the Germanic world in its demographic bulk — not in its duality, for it is much more homogeneous than Germany. Since the mid-nineteenth century, however, isolated and held back by its peripheral location, Japan has had to face the need to catch up with the West, a situation, incidentally, which it has been handling with ever increasing success.

Thus Germany is not one authoritarian model among many but *the* authoritarian model, just as Russia before the emergence of China *was* communism. Germany, however, because it did not expound a universalist ideology, has never been considered the general incarnation of an ideological type.

This analysis of Nazism does not legitimize it, any more than the anthropological dissection of communism legitimized that particular political system: National Socialism never won more than a third of the votes cast, the vast majority of the German people having experienced Nazism as a nightmare which led, as far as they were concerned, to six million deaths. The revelation of an anthropological basis is thus not a condemnation of Germany, any more than it is a criticism of the social-democratic ideal of which National Socialism was only a misshapen form.

The logic of social phenomena must be clearly distinguished from political morality. Logic leads us to note an anthropological similarity between social democracy and Nazism but tells us nothing about the respective moral qualities of these two ideologies. Above all it says nothing about legitimacy. Unlike Nazism, social democracy — a stable, moderate version of the authoritarian model — often has been and is in many countries legitimized by a liberal electoral process.

In fact most anthropological systems can take two forms, hysterical or stable. Violent phases always coincide with periods of cultural transition: the advent of mass literacy at the time of the witch-hunts, urbanization and industrialization in the case of twentieth-century Germany.

A similar ideological analysis reveals within communism the existence of both hysterical and stable forms: Stalinism was attended by a period of modernization, Brezhnevism coincided with one of stabilization. What distinguishes the community type from the authoritarian model is that neither of its forms involves legitimization through a free electoral process. What unites them is the difficulty both systems have encountered in achieving modernization without extensive bloodshed. Communism and socialism are both produced by hard, vertical family systems which bring together parents and children in complex households. The nuclear family systems which insist on the fluidity of relations between parents and children overcome more easily the ordeal of mental, industrial and urban upheaval.

4

The two forms of individualism

Characteristics of the egalitarian nuclear family:	Characteristics of the absolute nuclear family:
1 equality of brothers laid down by inheritance rules;	1 no precise inheritance rules, frequent use of wills;
2 no cohabitation of married children with their parents;	2 no cohabitation of married children with their parents;
3 no marriage between the children of brothers.	3 no marriage between the children of brothers.
Principal regions: northern France, northern Italy, central and southern Spain, central Portugal, Greece, Romania, Poland, Latin America, Ethiopia.	Principal regions: Anglo-Saxon world, Holland, Denmark.

Until the beginning of the twentieth century, the individual was the hero of the social sciences and of political thought. He was at the heart of eighteenth-century English liberal thought. He remained an essential element of French sociological theories of the late nineteenth century. But in the twentieth century, with the rise of Germany and then of Russia and with the diffusion of their social science and their ideologies, the hero disappeared, making way for sociological constructions which stressed the non-existence of consciousness and the importance of collective forces in determining events. At the crossroads of the two modes of thought, Durkheim tried to reconcile in his interpretation of suicide the action of individual will and that of social forces. He took further than anyone else a latent nineteenth-century idea, that of the progressive emergence of the individual, an atom freed from the rigid structures of traditional rural society, from the extended family of the past, stepping hesitantly towards an ill-defined personal and social future. Durkheim's individual believes himself to be free but is simply 'anomic', without laws or goals. For this very reason he is in anguish, consumed by a collective, destructive, suicidal force. The level of the propensity towards self-destruction, measured each year by the suicide rate, depends on the country's degree of development. Nevertheless Durkheim remains close to the individualistic thought of the Enlightenment, whose optimism he simply reverses. The individual represented progress and hope; he continues to represent progress but yields morally and sociologically to morbid temptation. The rapid rise of suicide rates in most of the European countries between 1800 and 1900 is a gauge of the spread of this pessimistic individualism.

Developed in France and England, the individualist model was offered to the world. Its universal acceptance presupposes an evolutionary hypothesis. In the Middle Ages the individual did not exist. He emerged in the West during the Reformation and the French Revolution. Henceforth Russia and the rest of the world have only to await the disintegration of their traditional cultures and the appearance, in hundreds of millions, of the individual, a wonderful elementary social particle whose amazing energy, once freed, sets history in motion.

In recent years England, which has done more than any other nation to define the rights of the individual, has dealt a severe blow to this evolutionary model. At Cambridge in the late 1960s an encounter between historians and anthropologists led to a direct examination of the English family system in the past. Peter Laslett, with the help of household lists, has thus studied household composition as far back as the sixteenth century, and Alan Macfarlane has extended the analysis back to the thirteenth century by reinterpreting medieval documents about inheritance customs. The result of this research is clear: extended families have never existed in England where, at least since the Middle Ages, the nuclear model has been the dominant form. The evidence is convincing, but this is not the first time that a hypothesis concerning the consistency of family structure over long periods of time has been postulated. Le Play, who generally rejected evolutionary models, accused the Gauls of the Paris basin (one wonders where this intuition came from) of having favoured an unstable family model, in other words a nuclear one.[1] According to Le Play, this explained their incorrigible unruliness! What the research conducted in England in the 1960s and 1970s shows is that the individual, in the sociological sense of the word, has always existed in certain regions of Europe.

---

[1] *L'Organisation de la famille* (Tours, Mame, 1875).

Underlying the attachment of English and French thinkers to individualism is a shared anthropological determinism: the nuclear family, which emphasizes the mutual independence of children and parents and tries to make both into individuals, in city and country alike, in 1450 just as much as in 1900.

Dislocation

The dislocation of traditional English and (northern) French societies by a complex process of urbanization, industrialization and the spread of literacy, has been comparatively less painful than in cultures dominated by a family ideal that emphasizes the complementary qualities of parents and children. The rural exodus separates the generations and erodes the core of complex families of the exogamous community and authoritarian models. It has no effect on a system dominated by nuclear households, where the early breakdown of domestic groups is socially acceptable and prepared for by an apprenticeship in individual autonomy from childhood. Urbanization in England started early and was soon complete. By comparison with Germany and Russia which developed later, the process in England seems to have been an easy one. It occurred in a peasant society which was already very flexible.

It would be wrong, however, to imagine an idyllic, effortless transformation, although in the case of nuclear family systems the upheaval among the large numbers of people who are shifted into a modern environment — literate, urban and industrial — is largely temporary. The example of Durkheim's primary indicator, suicide rates, is significant. Everywhere in Europe during the nineteenth-century period of modernization, the frequency of suicide increases. In England the increase is remarkably slow. In the north of France it is rapid but is followed, in the middle of the twentieth century, by a sharp decrease to a less spectacular level. In countries with a complex family structure, like Germany, Sweden, Hungary, Finland and Austria, the suicide rates level off in the twentieth century but remain high.

Political expressions of the moral disturbance created by dislocation are equally transitory in a country like France. Countries with an egalitarian nuclear family structure derive from their egalitarianism a slight but definite leaning towards communism, not comparable with that of exogamous community family countries but still not negligible. The capitals and major towns of egalitarian nuclear family regions are often centres of substantial communist implantation: this was true of Paris in 1921 and is the case in Athens today. But this political geography, the result of dislocation, is temporary. It is already breaking down, as is clear from the collapse of the French Communist Party in the Paris region since 1978. Once the urbanization process is complete the stabilization of the population makes the communist integrating mechanism redundant. In the case of Paris these movements of growth and decline in suicide rates and in communism are parallel. They follow one another a generation apart: suicide rates began to decline after 1945, the French Communist Party after 1978.

Impossible totalitarianism: Cromwell and Robespierre

France and England did not wait for the arrival of communism before having their revolutions, destroying the monarchy and replacing it with a power that did not depend on heredity. The process was not at all straightforward, not without struggle and violence. England had a civil war in the seventeenth century, before France, and, as in France, the culmination of several years of revolutionary strife was the establishment of a dictatorship. But Cromwell's power, like that of Robespierre 150 years later, had two fundamental characteristics: it was temporary and it respected private property. The English Commonwealth lasted a few years and Robespierre's dictatorship a few months. In both cases the people were required to conform to a particular moral and ideological order, not an economic one. Never did the French and English Revolutions question the right of individuals to independent activity within society. On the contrary, on an economic level the English Revolution was eager to diminish the power of the state, while the French Revolution specialized in despoiling one branch of the *ancien régime*, the church. England quickly established the principle of constitutional monarchy which has remained stable since the eighteenth century. France, on the other hand, moved into a period of political instability in the nineteenth century: she grew accustomed to seeing Paris overthrow the regime every twenty years, but never questioned the economic and cultural independence of civil society from the state. When despotism appeared under Napoleon I, Charles

X or Napoleon III, or in Paris under the Commune, it did not culminate in the totalitarianism of either Left or Right.

From this point of view nineteenth-century France irresistibly reminds one of a sauce which refuses to thicken. In Germany the 1918 Revolution which destroyed the monarchy led within fifteen years to the establishment of a totalitarian regime. In Russia the process took a year. France, after the convulsions of the Commune, the culmination of popular insurrections in Paris, produced a parliamentary republic, a model of respect for liberty and of individualistic temper. Undoubtedly, revolutionary thought has always embodied a penchant for totalitarianism. But in both France and England the mechanisms of total power broke down in the face of a nuclear family structure which was incapable of renouncing individualistic values or of allowing men to be absorbed into the state machine.

A quick glance around the world reveals that nuclear family systems everywhere are incapable of producing totalitarian ideologies or political forms which seek and achieve the total absorption of civil society by the state. Here a clear distinction must be made between totalitarianism and dictatorship, the latter by definition being neutral towards the workings of civil society. If one accepts this criterion one must also admit that the very concept of dictatorship presupposes social conservation. The two political models which emerge from developments in English and French history — liberalism and (non-totalitarian) dictatorship — occur, separately or consecutively, wherever the local anthropological base is nuclear.

The Anglo-Saxon world — England, the United States, Australia, New Zealand — is uniformly liberal. The Latin world displays a preference for phases of liberalism and dictatorship in quick succession: France in the nineteenth century; Spain; Greece (southern if not strictly Latin); Latin America in the twentieth century, a nuclear family region where the army realizes its full political potential. Nevertheless, being Latin is not the essential ingredient in this mixture of social liberalism and political dictatorship. Between the wars, independent Poland, close to the Latin world in its family structure, followed a similar type of political behaviour, combining social individualism with a military regime à la Pilsudski.

Thus the political facts confirm the inability of individualist family structures to produce totalitarian social systems. They also reveal the existence of two political models: one liberal, the other oscillating between extremes of anarchism and militarism. However, if one stops thinking of legitimacy in terms of universal suffrage, both the liberal and the anarcho-military systems can be seen to have one vital thing in common: governmental instability. The electoral model ensures a rapid turnover of presidents or prime ministers in the United States and in England. The succession of military coups in Latin America produces a series of governments following one another with equal rapidity. And let us not forget nineteenth-century France: thanks to periodic revolutions she changed regimes more frequently than twentieth-century Sweden has changed governments. The individualist temperament thus expresses in two different ways its aptitude for replacing the government in office — by free elections or by force. Its use of force, however, is unstable and anarchistic and does not give rise to a totalitarian settlement.

The essential difference between the liberal and anarcho-military models arises from the distinction between the two nuclear family models: absolute and egalitarian. But before moving on to analyse the relationship between liberalism and the absolute nuclear family, and the link between anarcho-militarism and the egalitarian nuclear family, I would like to emphasize a number of other characteristics which are shared by the two individualist family models and which are expressed by similarities in economic and social behaviour.

The control of the working class

The proletariats of authoritarian or exogamous community family regions have simple trade-union histories, determined by the political structure of the country. Communist and social-democrat traditions give the party priority over the trade union. Ideally, a disciplined working class serves as an economic arm guided by a political brain embodied in the organization's intellectuals and bureaucrats. From this point of view there are few differences between German social democracy and Russian Bolshevism.

The proletariats of the individualist world are less easily controlled. In England the Labour Party was originally the political wing of the trade unions, a complete reversal of the Germanic social democrat model. The Latin countries of Europe, from the second half of the nineteenth century onwards, gave birth to an impressive number of anarchist or anarchist-type ideologies which quickly infiltrated the working class and prevented a take-over of the unions by the various political bureaucracies: French anarcho-syndicalism, Spanish and Portuguese anarchism.

Socialist parties appeared in France, Italy and Spain, distinguishable from the start from their northern European counterparts by their organizational impotence, their unruliness and their inability to give life to their collectivist ideology which therefore remained purely doctrine. Ill-suited to individualist mental structures, collectivist dogma could not seize the imagination and had little power as an ideology. The tension between the individualist unconscious and the socialist conscious was resolved around 1900 in France, Spain and Italy through verbal revolutionism, and by taking up radical positions critical of the reformism of the Germanic social democrats. Nevertheless, it was the latter who unresistingly accepted socialist discipline as a life-style. But here again the north—south opposition is simply a convenient approximation: what matters is the contrast between authoritarian and nuclear family structures. England falls on the Latin side: the Labour Party is just as undisciplined and anarchical in its behaviour as are its Latin counterparts. It is distinct from them merely in its rejection of violence and in its respect for classic liberal forms. Its greater power derives more from the size of the British working class, which at the end of the nineteenth century represented over half of the active population, than from the organizational talents of its leaders.

In all nuclear family countries working-class militancy takes a similar form: an irrepressible penchant for spontaneous strikes, a preference for mass action decided at grass-roots level without the agreement of the union leaders. It is a living tradition: all the countries which towards the end of the 1960s were affected by massive strikes of this kind had nuclear family structures: Italy, France and England, which invented the 'wild-cat' strike organized at base by shop stewards elected on the shop floor.

There remains the Polish working class, marvellously undisciplined, which succeeded in re-creating from below an organization independent of the communist system imposed by a foreign army. The action of the Polish proletariat and of the Solidarity movement is the latest expression of an age-old individualism, capable of surviving forty years of communist bureaucracy.

Poland against the communist order

Poland is the only nation in central Europe where there is a nuclear and not an authoritarian or exogamous community family system. This difference undoubtedly explains the peculiarity of Polish history. The nation and its state were undermined in the eighteenth century by aristocratic rebellion, then split up and absorbed by Prussia, Austria and Russia, regions with a dense and disciplined family structure. Poland has none of the neurotic anxiety characteristic of Eastern Europe and of most countries with a dense family structure; the Polish suicide rate is abnormally low for the region: 12.5 per 100,000 inhabitants during the 1970s compared with 34.0 in East Germany, 40.5 in Hungary, 23.0 in Bohemia, 25.0 in Finland. The Soviet Union does not publish a breakdown of mortality by cause of death, but certain anomalies in age-specific mortality rates in Russia suggest a very high suicide rate, between 30 and 50 per 100,000 population.

From an anthropological point of view Poland is particularly close to northern France, another egalitarian nuclear family region also in contact with the Germanic and authoritarian cultures of northern Europe. This is clearly the reason for the historical affinity between two nations which, despite having no common border, have remarkably similar egalitarian and individualist cultures from which some curious convergences have resulted. For example, a French reader cannot help thinking, on reading a science-fiction novel by the Pole Stanislas Lem, that his rationalist, individualist stories could quite easily have been written by a Parisian essayist of the eighteenth century.

Around 1970 Polish individualism discovered its historic mission: to undermine the Soviet regime from the inside. A planned, bureaucratized economy can never work properly because on principle it denies the idea of the quality and the value of work. It treats the working population as an undifferentiated quantity which can be divided and multiplied. Studies of Eastern Europe show just how accurate were those thinkers at the turn of the century who wrote of the theoretical and practical impossibility of creating an economy which was both socialist and developed. But an empirical approach to the communist economies leads to another complementary observation: something like a law of unequal dysfunctioning. None of the countries under Soviet influence achieves the level of efficiency of the poorest

Western nations; but there are some spectacular differences in the degree of inefficiency of the various popular democracies. The Hungarian and East German economies reach an almost acceptable level of productivity. The Czech, Russian and Bulgarian economies seem to display a trend towards a fall in the rate of growth, but also towards stabilization in stagnation. With Romania we approach the grotesque. In Poland we find it, immersed in a surrealist economy: the third largest producer of coal in the world, she is unable to heat properly her own thirty million inhabitants. Poland is particularly unsuited to socialism, a result of the individualist character of its family and cultural system.

Hungary and Bulgaria, exogamous community family countries, have more or less succeeded in adapting to bureaucratic planning. The German Democratic Republic and Czechoslovakia, dominated by authoritarian family structures, have absorbed the principle of vertical social organization. Poland — and to a lesser extent Romania, where the nuclear family structure has been quite strongly influenced by the Russian, Bulgarian and Hungarian models — has simply been unable to submit to the will of the state and the party.

Economic control

Strangely, this law of unequal dysfunctioning is also to be found in the West, reversed as a law of differential efficiency. State intervention in the economy, which increased dramatically following the 1929 crisis, created fewer problems in countries with an authoritarian family structure — Scandinavia, Germany — than in countries with a nuclear culture such as those in the Anglo-Saxon world, where resistance to attempts at vertical, bureaucratic integration came from independent economic sectors. Members of authoritarian societies accept unquestioningly an economic discipline which appears irrational and despotic to individualist temperaments.

The crisis of the Anglo-Saxon economies in the 1960s and 1970s followed a period of unprecedented bureaucratization of international capitalism. This development fitted in fairly well with the statist traditions of Sweden or of Prussia, but in the United States or England it faced a far more libertarian conception of the economy. The political effect of this cultural resistance became clear around 1980: it is expressed in neo-liberal doctrines calling for the dismantling of the bureaucratic state, such as those of Margaret Thatcher and Ronald Reagan, whose programmes have no equivalent in the 'Western' world. There is, for example, nothing similar in Germany, Sweden or Norway, despite the arrival in power of bourgeois parties in the two Scandinavian authoritarian family countries: towards 1979 public expenditure exceeded 60 per cent of the gross domestic product in Sweden and 50 per cent in Norway.

In the United States and Great Britain, where the struggle against the state in a sense expresses their historical tradition, the very principle of central government action in the economic sphere was not accepted in the 1930s without a struggle. It needed Keynes, whose thought was as much political as it was economic, to convince people of the need for the state to take regulatory measures. Swedish social democracy and German national socialism had no need of theoretical support from Keynes in order to initiate, from the mid-1930s, counter-cyclical policies of public works and of maintaining aggregate demand. What Keynes provided in the Anglo-Saxon countries was the idea that such policies did not undermine the rights of the individual or of property. Use by the state of money taken from 'nowhere' was no longer seen as theft but as a neutral technique for restoring full employment. Such respect for individual rights worried the Germans and the Scandinavians much less. Keynesianism is a scientific theory but its motivation is ethical and not merely technical.

Abandoning the gold standard and putting more money into circulation has had varying effects on the different capitalist economies. In individualist systems – the United States, England, France, Italy, Spain – the absence of a strongly disciplined mentality created a tendency towards irresistible increases in inflation. In the case of the anthropologically authoritarian models – Japan, Germany – the existence of rigid vertical structures made more efficient monetary stabilization possible.

Equality versus liberty

Although similar in their individualist sensibilities, England and northern France differ in their attitudes towards equality: stressed by the family system of the Paris basin, it is ignored by that on the other side of the Channel. The opposition of these two anthropological systems fits perfectly the ideological

Table 15 Dominant family structure and inflation rates in the OECD countries in 1980 (percentages)

Absolute nuclear family		Egalitarian nuclear family		Authoritarian family	
United States	13.5	France	13.6	Japan	8.0
United Kingdom	18.0	Italy	21.2	Germany	5.5
Canada	10.1	Spain	15.5	Austria	6.4
Denmark	12.3	Greece	24.9	Belgium	6.6
Netherlands	6.5	Portugal	16.6	Sweden	13.7
Australia	10.2			Norway	10.9
New Zealand	17.1			Ireland	18.2
Average	*13.2*	*Average*	*18.4*	*Average*	*9.9*
Weighted for population:	*13.6*	*Weighted for population:*	*17.3*	*Weighted for population:*	*7.6*

OECD = Organization for Economic Co-operation and Development.

polarity of the eighteenth century: England ardently supported liberty, France liberty and equality. But the latter is trapped by the determinism of family structures in an insoluble contradiction.

The concepts of liberty and equality are in fact partially contradictory. Free individual development presupposes the emergence of differences between men. One could even say that true individualism necessarily involves the acceptance of these differences. The egalitarian ideal rejects this heterogeneity. On an anthropological level the contradiction provokes family quarrels which come to a head with the division of the paternal inheritance. The principle of equality no longer applies after the separation of the brothers.

On a political level, the simultaneous existence of liberal and egalitarian aspirations in France in the nineteenth century lay behind the political instability of that period. France rejected both totalitarianism and inequality; she sought a levelling of conditions but would not allow the state to put this into practice. The Third Republic achieved a kind of synthesis at the end of the century, its ideology succeeding for a moment in perfectly reflecting the family system by placing the school at the centre of the political apparatus. The Republic proclaimed and wanted to achieve equality of opportunity. It was a question of giving each individual an equal start: after this some could be promoted, preferably according to personal merit. This is an exact transposition of the familial mechanism which requires equality between the sons in dividing up the inheritance, but later tolerates a divergence of fortune without thinking that fraternal solidarity should continue beyond adolescence. A precise reflection of the anthropological base of northern France, this synthesis had more impact on people's minds than any other doctrine or ideology. Even today, equality of opportunity is an ideal shared both by the secular elements of the Right and by the Communist Party.

Experience shows that such an ideological system rarely functions harmoniously. In France it coincided with the achievement of widespread literacy, a brief moment in the history of nations. More often, coexistence between the principles of liberty and equality is not peaceful and ends in some form of Bonapartism, or military power. This was the case in France following the end of the Revolution, which did not succeed in producing either stable totalitarianism or a stable liberal, constitutional regime. It was the case in the twentieth century in Greece, in Latin America, Spain and Italy (the model being complicated in the last two countries by the presence of a minority of dense family structures), where individualism and egalitarianism clashed and produced cyclical instability, an oscillation between two political poles, one liberal and the other military.

Feminism and machismo

The principle of symmetry between brothers is not without consequences for male–female relations, which are different in the two nuclear models (absolute and egalitarian). In its two variants the nuclear family always fits in with systems of bilateral parentage, giving equal weight to paternal and maternal roles. Women participate in the division of the inheritance (they are generally excluded in the case of the exogamous community family). This is to be expected: a nuclear household is simply the association of one man and one woman who are in a situation of exclusive dialogue, implying some degree of equality. But paradoxically, the absolute variant, which has no interest in the principle of symmetry, has in practice taken equality between the sexes further than the 'egalitarian' family. The principle of equality between brothers implies an a priori idea of masculine solidarity. It reinforces an inequality between the sexes which is seen as natural by all societies. The absolute nuclear family, on the other hand, is indifferent to equality between brothers and to male solidarity. It allows the conjugal bond to develop to its logical – egalitarian – conclusion and leads to the most feminist anthropological system in the world, that of the Anglo-Saxon countries.

The absolute nuclear family is a stable structure without internal contradictions. The egalitarian nuclear family accepts a contradiction between the principles of solidarity within the couple and inequality of the sexes. It leads to the machismo of the Latin countries which affirms the primacy of the male in a nuclear, bilateral, family system. Machismo rejects on a theoretical level a solidarity between the sexes which operates on a practical level. This contradiction engenders the tension and violence characteristic of the Latin countries, stressing at one and the same time the individual, equality between men, the inequality of the sexes, and solidarity within the couple. This violence can take individual forms – injuries and murders – or socialized ones – military coups and liberal revolutions.

An examination of the ages at marriage of husband and wife

Table 16   Age difference within couples at marriage in nuclear
family regions (first marriages only)

Country and date	Age difference (years)	Family type
England (1970)	2.1	Absolute nuclear
Poland (1971)	2.4	
Northern Italy (1975)	2.8	
Spain (1965)	3.2	
Northern France (1955)	3.4	Egalitarian nuclear
Southern Italy (1975)	3.8	
Corsica (1955)	4.9	
Calabria (1975)	5.2	

shows that the difference, an indication of inequality, is greater in egalitarian nuclear systems (though never comparable to that of exogamous community models) than in absolute nuclear systems. There is one exception to this rule: Poland, an egalitarian nuclear country but one where the age difference between husband and wife is very slight. (Poland deviates from the egalitarian nuclear model in the same way that Russia deviates from the exogamous community model: by having a matriarchal bias within a system which in general terms proclaims equality between brothers and male superiority.)

The absolute nuclear family, which produces a lower level of violence and encourages co-operation within society, is also culturally more dynamic than its egalitarian counterpart. Its practical acceptance of female authority allows an in-depth training of children and more rapid educational progress. In this respect it is comparable with the authoritarian family which also accepts maternal power.

Nevertheless, one structural characteristic is common to both the egalitarian nuclear and the authoritarian models which are otherwise complete opposites: the existence of a measure of ambiguity in the status of women. The authoritarian family proclaims a masculine ideal of family continuity, but in practice tolerates strong female authority. The egalitarian nuclear family simultaneously seeks solidarity within the couple and inequality between the sexes. However, the tension lies between different family members in each case. In the egalitarian nuclear system it exists between husband and wife; in the authoritarian system it arises between a man and his mother.

Weakening vertical family ties, nuclear models are in general less anxiety-producing than authoritarian or exogamous community systems. They tend to coincide with low suicide rates, suicide being least common in the case of the egalitarian nuclear family where maternal authority is reduced. The stresses produced in this anthropological variant by the ambiguity of matrimonial relations are not easy to fit into classic psychoanalytical patterns, which are themselves derived from a vertical family system.

The New World: disorder in matrimonial models

From an anthropological point of view the New World is not an original civilization. It is a large-scale replica of the systems from which it emerged – the Anglo-Saxon and Iberian systems. The United States more or less reproduces the English model, familial and political liberalism having been integrally transported across the Atlantic Ocean. Brazil duplicates the egalitarian nuclear system which dominates central Portugal. Hispanic America as a whole transposes to the new continent the principal family structures of Spain: nuclear and egalitarian. The political forms of Latin America are not fundamentally different from those of the Iberian peninsula. Caudillo-ism waxes strong on both sides of the ocean.

Anglo-Saxon liberalism and Iberian anarcho-militarism have nevertheless taken on extreme characteristics and on the other side of the Atlantic have become almost caricatures of their original forms. This radical evolution of political practices corresponds to an anthropological deviation which is the same in the absolute nuclear systems of North America and in the egalitarian nuclear forms of South America. In both cases the transplantation, while not affecting the nuclear nature of the system, is accompanied by a relaxation of the matrimonial bond which is manifested in the North by a spectacular increase in the frequency of divorce, and in the South by the generalized practice of cohabitation outside marriage, which also implies that marriages are highly unstable. This increased tension engenders a specific pathology which is expressed by a rise in violence. In the New World as a whole, levels of homicide reach levels which are ten, thirty or even fifty times greater than the equivalent levels in Europe. There is a homothetic transformation: the absolute nuclear family in its destabilized form in the United States does not produce the same level of violence as the egalitarian nuclear family in its destabilized form in the South. Because England was from the start less violent than Spain, the United States is three times less violent than Mexico: 11 murders per 100,000 population in the USA, compared with 43 in Mexico (less than one in the European continent as a whole in the mid-1970s).

These homicide rates are among the highest in the world and correspond to individualist cultures where psychological conflicts are translated into extroverted aggression rather than into neurotic or suicidal introversion. On a global scale the suicide and homicide rates are in negative correlation: they appear as complementary phenomena, interchangeable but distinct: individual aggression corresponds to nuclear family systems, suicide to vertical family systems. In both cases the instability of the matrimonial bond, embodied in the divorce rate, is a decisive aggravating factor.

The carrying out of personal vendettas is of course to be found – socialized and transformed by ideology – in the political traditions of the United States and Latin America where political assassination is to differing extents a well-established tradition. Assassinating the president is almost a custom in North America. The Hispanic and Portuguese regions of the South can afford a systematic liquidation of political activists owing to a level of violence three times greater. But this brutality never leads to totalitarian stabilization, something the nuclear family is incapable of.

During the 1970s Latin America as a whole entered a phase of increased violence, both private and political, with little distinction between personal revenge and ideological executions. In Brazil, Argentina, Guatemala and El Salvador perverse political forms have appeared, decentralized techniques of eliminating opponents by effecting their disappearance or their assassination. Political science has not succeeded in comprehending this politico-ideological form. It is neither the result of totalitarianism nor of classic dictatorship. But the large-scale intervention of activitists – right- and left-wing – in the process is one of the major characteristics of the phenomenon.

Today, the modernization of Latin-American society through literacy and urbanization is almost complete, a century later than in northern Europe. The demographic transition, that is to say the fall in birth-rates, reached its peak in Argentina and Spain in the 1930s, and in Chile during the 1960s. It is beginning today in Central America, from Mexico to Costa Rica. This transformation implies — in Latin America just as in Russia or in England — the development of political and social consciousness among the masses and an accentuation of the fundamental political traits associated with the anthropological system in each region. This is why mass violence succeeds the military violence of the nineteenth century.

Nevertheless, it is doubtful whether this hysterical phase will lead to the installation of communist regimes, as in Cuba. The exogamous community family form is alien to the continent as a whole. There are perhaps a few notable exceptions in Central America — primarily among the Mexican Indians — which would be worth classifying if one sought to foresee the evolution of Nicaraguan-style regimes. But it is unlikely that Indian family systems, most of which are not community forms, would triumph even in this region over the generally individualistic character of social relations.

Central America does not display the usual symptoms of vertical authoritarian or exogamous community family systems, which alone are able to engender totalitarianism of the classic European type. The few examples of suicide rates which are available are very low: 4.4 per 100,000 population in Costa Rica (1977), 3.4 in Guatemala (1972), 1.7 in Mexico (1975), 2.6 in Panama (1975). Around the same time the frequency of suicide was over 15 per 100,000 on the island of Cuba.

Towards anomie

Latin America has not eliminated the Indian populations which in certain countries constitute an important part of the local anthropological base. In countries like Peru, Bolivia and Paraguay, the Indian family tradition can be considered the dominant one. For the most part it corresponds to the anomic model which I will study in detail in chapter 7. But it should be noted that the matrimonial disorder of the Spanish egalitarian nuclear structure brings it close to the anomic variant. The fragility of the conjugal bond is common to both systems. In both cases it leads to the re-establishment of ties between adult generations, an abandoned woman often returning to live with her parents. In such cases we find, in a theoretically nuclear system, complex units where the link between generations is effected through the woman.

The few studies of urban families that have been carried out, like the work of Oscar Lewis on the Sanchez family in Mexico

City, highlight in what is theoretically an egalitarian nuclear environment another characteristic trait of the anomic family: a relaxation of the incest taboo.[2] Sanchez at one stage of his life marries the sister of his son's wife. This only breaks the rule against alliances between those related by marriage, but it is still outlawed by the Catholic tradition. The Sanchez family also reflects in its conjugal behaviour a third, African-type component of the Latin American family: a barely disguised form of polygamy. Sanchez kept several women in different apartments.

This well-known study by Oscar Lewis concerns only one family and therefore has no statistical value, but it does reveal a complex model which lies at the intersection of three anthropological systems: Spanish, Indian and African. These three traditions have two things in common: a low level of parental authority and a marked instability in matrimonial relations. Their fusion is not a theoretical impossibility.

The example of Latin America shows that there is no absolute opposition between the (exogamous) nuclear family and the anomic family. Examples can be found of each stage in the transition from the complete anomie of the Cambodian and Aymara systems, which allow marriage between children who share one parent, to the Iberian egalitarian nuclear system which seeks, in line with Catholic tradition, to avoid marriage between cousins. Between these two extremes may be found an infinite range of more or less imperfect nuclear families: Mexican, Brazilian, Thai, Filipino, Paraguayan, Burmese, Malay and Indonesian. In all these cases, there is a link between the collapse of the nuclear norm and the relaxation of the exogamy requirement. An unbroken scale leads from the least disordered egalitarian nuclear system of South America, that of Argentina, to the most anomic South-East Asian model, that of Cambodia.

The instability of marriage in Latin America is not a recent phenomenon: it is structural and not the product of a particular time. In the twentieth century, however, the long-term trend is towards stabilization through a progressive decrease in the frequency of unmarried cohabitation which shows up in all the successive Brazilian, Venezuelan, Costa Rican, Columbian, Peruvian and Guatemalan censuses. Latin American countries are incapable of producing reliable statistics on age at marriage, but it is likely that the fall in the frequency of unmarried

---

[2] O. Lewis, *The Children of Sanchez* (London, Penguin, 1964).

cohabitation may be interpreted as a rise in marriage age (marriage taken here in the *de facto* rather than the legal sense, meaning a stable monogamous union, independent of official recognition). The continuous spread of contraception can only correspond to a strengthening of the bond between husband and wife and to a growing sense of parental responsibility. The feverish political activity in Latin America today therefore coincides on an anthropological level with a stabilization of matrimonial behaviour. Nevertheless, it is doubtful whether such matrimonial behaviour, closer to traditional European models, will lead to a less turbulent political scene: Argentina, where the demographic transition was largely complete by the 1930s and where unmarried cohabitation has never been as widespread as in the tropical and subtropical parts of the continent, remained in disorder in 1980. It is an example of a society where the family unit is quite stable but where anarchic violence still rages on a political level. Once again, the transition to modernity fails to destroy the basic anthropological traits of a political system. The oscillation of Latin American countries between left-wing liberalism and military dictatorship is not yet over.

The sword without the cross

Since the coming to power of the military usually coincides with non-authoritarian family structures — not characterized by a strong tie between parents and children — in practice the sword rarely cohabits with the cross, a fact which undermines a traditional French ideological myth. The strength of religious sentiments arises from a vertical family structure, the opposite of that which produces military power.

In Latin America, Africa and South-East Asia, the army takes control of atomized societies with a weak family structure, whether the model be nuclear, anomic or an African unstable system. Religion in its later European form — ecclesiastical, bureaucratic and monotheistic — takes hold particularly strongly in authoritarian family systems. Produced by different anthropological bases, the powers of the church and the army are not destined to overlap. Latin America, which is remarkable for its military coups, is also notable for its weak clerical framework. In order accurately to perceive the phenomenon of religion we must free ourselves from the republican preconception which associates religion with backward societies and secularization with progress. The most

Table 17   Secular clergy in various countries (according to census statistics)

Country and date	Number of secular clergy, per 10,000 inhabitants
Peru (1945)	1.8
Paris basin (1975)	5.2
Germany (1971)	6.5
Austria (1971)	6.7
Spain (1970)	7.0
France (1975)	7.5
Aveyron and Lozère (1975)[a]	23.0
Ireland (1966)[b]	31.5

[a] French départements with the largest proportion of clergy.
[b] All clergymen included.

devout societies, which are of authoritarian family structure, are to be found without distinction among the developed (Bavaria) and the underdeveloped (Ireland) countries. Conversely, the dechristianized world may be underdeveloped (Peru) or highly developed (the Paris basin).

Today, countries with a nuclear family tradition are neither particularly devout nor particularly atheistic. In general, attitudes held are close to agnosticism or to secularity. These countries show little concern for the father-image, and are tempted neither to worship this image as do countries with an authoritarian structure, nor to reject it like the exogamous community systems. Nuclear family regions have not always been unreligious. What they cannot accept, however, is the authoritarian character which the great European religions, Lutheran and Catholic alike, have taken on since the Wars of Religion. Individualism rejects these creeds of submission. Medieval Christianity which combined all types of religious belief was in some places ambitious and arrogant, its cathedrals aspiring to touch the sky rather than submit, when it tried to penetrate the divine mystery through scholastic debate in a metaphysical version of the radical-socialist café.

From the sixteenth century onwards, nuclear family regions diverged into individualist beliefs, most clearly represented in institutional form by the English and American sects. The rejection of clerical authority was heightened in egalitarian nuclear family countries by a latent machismo which strengthened their rebellious spirit. The priest lost his prestige in two ways at once: his paternal authority and his privileged dialogue with women, striking characteristics of Counter-Reformation Catholicism, were rejected together. The confessional, where a woman exposes her emotional and moral problems to an unmarried man, is theoretically incompatible with the ideals of a masculine society. The husband tends to see the church, symbolically or physically, as a rival for the attentions of his wife. Conversely the existence of a matriarchal bias in any family system is for Catholicism a valuable, even indispensable, trump card. The reaction to dechristianization in the egalitarian nuclear regions of northern France in the nineteenth century was a reinforcement of the clergy's hold on the more feminist authoritarian family regions on the fringes of the nation.

The exception that proves the rule is Poland, where the egalitarian nuclear family deviates from its normally macho leanings. The matriarchal bias of the Polish system allows the survival of a deformed Catholicism concentrated on the cult of the Virgin Mary and imbued with anarchist sentiments.

In countries with an egalitarian nuclear family structure — the dominant tradition in northern France and Latin America — anticlericalism is not the same as atheism. It is a refusal to accept the authority of the priest rather than a negation of religion. Politically it is expressed not in Soviet-style anti-religious propaganda but in a desire to separate church and state, a separation achieved in Brazil since 1889 but not until 1905 in France. Anticlericalism is born of individualism: atheism arises from the destructive pressure which the exogamous community family exerts on the individual.

Latin universalism

It is almost tautological to say that individualist systems are not noted for their stringent disciplinary measures. Even when they are egalitarian and predisposed to adopt a symmetrical vision of social space which implies equality between men and between peoples, they do not forcibly try to reduce the anthropological differences within the national unit. In the Hispanic, Italian and French family systems there is not the same desire to reduce differences, to seek ethnic homogeneity, that is characteristic of the Russian and Chinese systems, both of which have long been dominated by a powerful tradition of forced assimilation. What characterizes present-day Latin and Greek cultures is their ability to ignore differences and to live with them in peace. The French attitude in this respect is typical, and quite different from that in Germany where despite an almost completely uniform authoritarian anthropological base there exists a capacity for producing ideological obsessions with differences and with race. France is a quite separate example of tolerance in diversity: an egalitarian nuclear bloc in the centre (45 per cent of the population) defines and unifies the nation, but coexists easily and without anxiety alongside other anthropological groups on the fringes of the national territory: authoritarian groups (33 per cent of the population), exogamous community groups (15 per cent), and absolute nuclear groups (7 per cent).

Universal man, dear to the French national tradition, is not an anthropological mean but any member of an administrative and linguistic community who disregards anthropological differences. Unlike Soviet and Chinese universalism, which like a steam-roller tries to crush cultural differences, French universalism is a welcoming ideology. Developing ahead of the Mediterranean Latin countries and more articulate on an ideological level, France formulated her universalist message as early as 1789. This in no way betrayed the traditions of other countries with an egalitarian nuclear structure, where integration creates few problems. Brazil is a good example of a tolerant country, but Greece, Italy, Argentina and Mexico are fundamentally similar in their attitudes and little marked by xenophobia.

This universalism, welcoming rather than destructive, often creates problems of internal structure in egalitarian nuclear family countries, for frequently anthropological minorities exist which have been accepted and allowed to settle. Unlike Russia and China, countries such as France, Spain, Portugal, Italy and even Greece, although small, are anthropologically heterogeneous. Large authoritarian and exogamous community groups live there intact. This anthropological diversity does not cause racial or ethnological conflicts. Instead, family differences are transposed onto an ideological level: each system produces its own vision of the world and of politics, propelling some people towards egalitarian individualism, others towards respect for authority, and yet others towards communism. Parisians, Bretons, Limousins, Lorrains, Provençaux, Basques and Francs-Comtois live together without too much difficulty, accepting each other as different provincial cultures, but clashing on an ideological level since 1789.

The decline of French individualism

At the end of the eighteenth century when the individualist and egalitarian ideology of northern France asserted itself, everything was straightforward. Regions with a complex family structure, located for the most part in the south and west of the country, were politically inactive because of their cultural backwardness. Only the part of France to the north of the Saint-Malo/Geneva line could read and write. This region dominated the rest and imposed its beliefs on the provincial elites as a whole, producing the Declaration of the Rights of Man, Robespierre, then Bonaparte. Literacy, which after the Reformation came from Germany in a slow, continuous wave, advanced evenly towards the west and the south. It finally reached the provinces and the complex family structures which were situated in the most backward part of the country: 1848 was a turning point. Since then the story of French individualism has been one of decline. In the twentieth century the Third Republic was devoured by the rise of anti-individualist ideologies: socialism, Catholicism, communism. History textbooks — which concentrate on the National Assembly, the resurgence of the Right, the penetration of the Socialist Party and then of the Communist Party — see this movement as chronological. In fact it is a geographical development and corresponds to the ideological activation of the dense family regions on the fringes of the nation.

Provinces where the family structure is authoritarian and the marriage age high (in the Basque country, Brittany, Rouergue, Savoy, Alsace) send conservative, Catholic deputies to the National Assembly. Authoritarian family regions where the marriage age is low (Aquitaine, Nord) form socialist bastions. Exogamous community family zones develop a special affection for the Communist Party (Berry, Limousin, the Mediterranean coast). The centre-west, an absolute nuclear family region (Basse Normandie, French-speaking Brittany, Anjou, Maine) which might have evolved according to the English model, was driven by the republican and predominantly egalitarian dynamic of the overall system towards the Catholic Right. The political history of France is largely a pseudo-history: it seems to happen chronologically but in fact happens geographically.

The Paris basin at the heart of the egalitarian nuclear system alone continues to embody the old ideal of liberty and equality and also, it must be added, the practice of instability. Only in this region do the voters sometimes change their minds, pushing the national majority to the Right, then to the Left: Gaullist in 1958, in 1981 the Paris basin sent a left-wing majority to the National Assembly. This must be contrasted with the fact that for a century none of the peripheral provinces has changed its allegiance.

The fall in age at marriage which became clear between 1945 and 1970 ensured a political change in the authoritarian family regions. It led the traditionally Catholic areas away from the Right and towards socialism.

The decline of individualism has not only had negative effects on the French political system. Paradoxically, the authoritarian family has tempered a Latin-American tradition, which created an alternation of liberal revolutions with *coups d'état*. In practice the conservative blocs on the fringes of the nation have played a stabilizing role, setting the strength of the family and the clergy against the secular military power. The end of the nineteenth-century revolutions came when the Catholic Right installed itself in the Third Republic. The equilibrium of French political forces, made up of a central, egalitarian, individualist bloc balanced by authoritarian groups on the fringes of the system, could indeed be worse. Spain and Italy, for example, have not been so lucky. The distribution of anthropological groupings in these two countries has allowed them to slide almost into totalitarianism.

Spanish Francoism: 'Caudillismo' and Catholicism

In its anthropological composition Spain is not very different from France. Two-thirds of its population have an egalitarian nuclear family system, the other third an authoritarian model. The exogamous community and absolute nuclear variants which are present but weak in France do not occur in Spain. However, the spatial distribution of anthropological groups on the Iberian peninsula is different from that in France. The authoritarian regions in Spain are all together in the north in the most culturally developed part of the country. To the south they touch the centre of the Spanish political system. More advanced economically and more compact geographically than their French counterparts, they have considerable influence on the ideological, political and religious structure of Spain. In the Basque country, in Catalonia and in Galicia, the most industrialized regions, the authoritarian family underpins forces which are centrifugal because of their ethnocentricity. In the landlocked north of the country the marriage age is high. The authoritarian family thus gives Catholicism mass support which, combined with the military tradition of the egalitarian, individualist areas, produces that exceptional, incomparable union of sword and cross: Francoism. The existence of two blocs, authoritarian and egalitarian nuclear, each with a compact geographical base, made the Spanish Civil War possible. In July 1936, at the beginning of the insurrection, the nationalists controlled only one vast zone between Galicia and Aragon centred on Burgos and Salamanca, together with the southern tip of the country where the army of Morocco was based. If we add the Basque country and Catalonia to these areas we reproduce the map of the authoritarian family in Spain.[3] The struggle for Madrid, which is situated at the meeting-point of the authoritarian zones of the north and the egalitarian nuclear regions of the south, was symbolic of an anthropological confrontation.

Portuguese Salazarism is not very different from Francoism in its basic principles: it links the same traditions. Like Spain, Portugal is divided anthropologically into northern and southern belts. The Catholic regions are located in the north, as in the rest of the Iberian peninsula. Salazarism, which dates from the 1920s, is like Francoism something other than a traditional dictatorship: both contain a rigid, ordered element which is characteristic of Catholicism and of the authoritarian family, reacting against the egalitarian, disordered individualism in the rest of the country.

Italy: fascism, Catholicism and communism

The existence of a rigid, totalitarian core is clearer still in Italian fascism which took hold of a country whose family structure is largely egalitarian nuclear but whose central region is dominated by the exogamous community family form. Tuscany and Emilia-Romagna, areas of dense family structure, are situated in the centre of Italy, cutting it in two. Furthermore they dominate the nation culturally through their universities which are the most important on the peninsula: Bologna and Florence have defined the language and law of Italy. The ideological weight of the community systems therefore greatly exceeds their relative demographic importance, which is not overwhelming.

[3] Cf. G. Hermet, *L'Espagne de Franco* (Paris, A. Colin, 1974), p. 74.

Fascist totalitarianism was a synthesis — non-racist and mildly socialist, but unsystematic and fragile — of contradictory aspirations arising from the egalitarian nuclear and exogamous community family models. The egalitarian nuclear family produced civil and military indiscipline. The exogamous community family provided an aspiration to order and to socialism. There is a demonstrable ideological link and partial anthropological continuity between fascism and Italian communism: in 1922 the active strength of the *fascii* (the grass-roots fascist groups) was greatest, in relation to the population, in Tuscany and Emilia where the communists were triumphant after the war.[4] The collapse of the fascist synthesis in 1943 allows us to distinguish ideologically its different anthropological components: the community family regions turned to communism, the egalitarian nuclear regions to Christian democracy.

Italian Christian democracy is not conventional political Catholicism. In Italy, the administrative heart of world Catholicism, there is no correlation between the strength of religious implantation and the Christian democrat vote. The south, which is not very Catholic, is Christian democrat. The north is also Christian democrat but is no more Catholic than communist Tuscany. Only Venetia sometimes proves the classic association of the number of priests with the strength of the right-wing vote. The coefficient of correlation between the number of priests and the Christian democrat vote in Italy is negative.

In Italy, as in Poland, Christianity is a form of defence against communism but does not succeed in wiping out the latent individualism of a culture dominated by a nuclear family model. The Christian democrat and communist parties have tended to grow in strength since the war, and minor movements within the Italian political system have been progressively absorbed.

Christian democracy spreads out from its Venitian bastion, the Communist Party from its bastions in Emilia and Tuscany. Their expansion has caused a continuous and worsening deformation of the two major Italian ideologies, both of which have deviated in parallel towards an individualism incompatible with the original ideals of Counter-Reformation Catholicism and Marxism-Leninism: Christian democracy was unable to prevent the majority of the country, which it supposedly controls, from returning a 68 per cent vote in favour of abortion in the referendum

---

[4] J. Buron and P. Gauchon, *Les Fascismes* (Paris, Presses universitaires de France, 1979), p. 32.

Table 18   Italy: some correlations

	Coefficient of correlation
Secular clergy per 100,000 population in 1955 Christian democrat vote in 1946	−0.20
Secular clergy per 100,000 population in 1955 Female marriage age in 1975	+0.46
Percentage of complex families in 1971 census (type D families, i.e. non-nuclear) Communist vote at Senate elections 1976	+0.44

The coefficients are not very significant from the point of view of statistical theory. They concern only twelve administrative units, the major regions of the peninsula.

of May 1981. As for the Italian Communist Party, every day its penetration into southern Italy seems to detach it further from the Moscow-based Communist International. Southern individualism carries it away from the disciplined Tuscan artisans and Emilian rural labourers.

Since its anthropo-geographical trajectory is the opposite of that of the French Communist Party (the PCF), the Italian Communist Party is moving away from totalitarianism towards individualism. The PCF on the other hand, originally based in Paris (an individualist region but one with a large uprooted population), later spread into the community family areas of southern and central France, gradually pulling away from its anarchist origins. The ideological inversion of the CGT (communist-led trade union), the citadel of anarcho-syndicalism at the end of the nineteenth century and today the incarnation of working-class discipline, is significant from this point of view.

The decline of individualism in Europe

In the eighteenth century two individualist powers dominated political thought in Europe: France and England. The cultural progress of the nineteenth and twentieth centuries has modified the ideological equilibrium of the continent just as it has transformed the balance of ideological forces within France. The growth of literacy in complex family regions has activated and sustained anti-liberal ideologies.

The egalitarian nuclear family of the Paris basin has finally been challenged by the authoritarian and community structures of the peripheral provinces. The cultural development of these regions has been achieved without any major demographic disturbances to accentuate further the changes in the respective ideological weight of the different provinces. 'Authoritarian' regions are in no way behind the egalitarian nuclear centre of the country as far as the spread of birth control is concerned. Their relative demographic weight is not increasing. But their cultural activation through literacy has integrated them into the national system, whose individualism, as a consequence, has been diluted.

If the whole of Europe is examined and not just France, a double expansion by complex family systems has to be analysed, and particularly that of the exogamous community family. First, there has been an increase in the ideological weight of complex family systems because of the spread of literacy, which since the end of the nineteenth century has reached countries east of Germany. Second, there has been an increase in the demographic weight of these systems arising from the population explosion in Eastern Europe, almost exponential in the case of Russia. These phenomena together ensure throughout Europe an increase in collectivist ideas and in communist ideology.

Table 19   The demographic weight of the various family types in Europe at different periods (as a percentage of the European population)

Family type	1200	1500	1800	1975
Authoritarian family	32	30	30	26
Egalitarian nuclear family	29	34	30	25
Absolute nuclear family	9	9	9	12
Exogamous community family	30	27	31	37

Europe from the Atlantic to the Urals, European Turkey excluded.

Source of population figures by country: C. McEvedy and R. Jones *Atlas of World Population History* (London, Penguin Books, 1978).

The French and English individualist systems have lost their hold on the continent. Around 1800 the egalitarian nuclear, authoritarian and community family models were roughly equivalent in size demographically, each accounting for about 30 per cent of Europe's population (from the Atlantic to the Urals). By about 1975 the exogamous community family had risen to 37 per cent, the authoritarian family had fallen to 26 per cent, and the egalitarian nuclear family to 25 per cent. This demographic decline was accompanied by a decrease in the strength of the individualist (nuclear family) and of the Christian democrat and socialist (authoritarian family) ideologies. These three were to some extent obliged to form alliances in order to resist the pressure of their great competitor, communism. A century earlier such an alliance would have seemed an aberration, egalitarian individualism (a lay, republican ideology) then seeing its principal enemy as Catholic authoritarianism. A different demographic evolution could have led to a different ideological balance and to other alliances.

Ethiopia and the Sudan: Marxism-Leninism
as a fashionable ideology

Ethiopia is one of the poorest countries in the world. Economically it is in no way comparable to countries like France, Spain and Italy. But because its family system is in general terms identical with those of the Paris basin and the Po valley, Ethiopia has to evolve politically along familiar lines: not in the same way as Russia, despite Mengistu's tactical alliance with Moscow.

The historical centre of Ethiopia, whose religion has survived Muslim pressure for over a thousand years, is Christian and therefore fiercely exogamous in its matrimonial sentiments. Household structure is nuclear and the inheritance system egalitarian, daughters being included in the division of successions along with sons. Egalitarian nuclear and bilateral, the anthropological structure is that of the Île-de-France. An individualist system, it does not lend itself to the creation of stable communism, however much the revolutionary regime seeks to demonstrate its support for Marxism-Leninism in order to satisfy the USSR which provides military and logistical aid.

If the institutional and economic activity of the new government is analysed point by point, setting aside the usual bloody and spectacular aspects of the revolutionary process, it must be admitted that Colonel Mengistu has not exceeded the goals attained by the French Revolution in 1793 and that he has even been far more moderate in religious matters: agrarian reform is in practice distribution of land and not collectivization; while a *modus vivendi* has been quickly established between the regime and the church.

Attitudes towards religion and towards the peasants are, more than the nationalization of industry, an indication of communism, which seeks to destroy the rural and metaphysical anthropological base of a country and not simply to emancipate the proletariat. Judged by these criteria, the Ethiopian revolution was essentially non-communist. Politically, it has like the French Revolution given birth to a military government rather than to a one-party state. The killings which led to the stable control of the system by a part of the army were no more numerous than those in France during the Terror and the September massacres.

Whatever pressure the Soviet Union brings to bear, and whatever those in power may desire, the Ethiopian revolution cannot result in communism. The country is currently disrupted by modernization, the urbanization process, and the beginnings of mass literacy. But the disturbances caused by these transitions will not produce total paralysis. An ideology is not simply a doctrine, but the building of doctrine into a corresponding anthropological and mental structure. There is a doctrine in Ethiopia: Marxism-Leninism; but the anthropological and mental structure (the exogamous community family) is not there to support it. In the long term the Soviet Union is playing a losing hand. It has laid its bets on an anthropological system unsuited to communism.

However the alliance between revolutionary Ethiopia and the Soviet Union is not simply an agreement between governments. The two systems communicate ideologically through two factors which their respective anthropological systems have in common: the principle of equality between brothers, and exogamy (the USSR, faced with a strategic choice between Muslim Somalia and Christian Ethiopia, chose Christianity and hence exogamy).

In our analysis of the electoral performance of the Western communist parties, we have already seen a partial affinity between Marxism-Leninism and the egalitarian nuclear family (see chapter 2). Unfortunately, the absence of elections in Ethiopia makes it impossible to evaluate the ideological impact of communism, as we did for the European countries. A slight geographical detour enables us to get round this gap in electoral sociology. Neighbouring Sudan (in theory an Islamic country but one whose eastern region is ethnologically similar to Ethiopia) recently witnessed two politological miracles which allow us to evaluate the exact propensity for communism of anthropological systems in this part of the world. The first miracle: the English liberal tradition lasted long enough for free elections to be held. The second miracle: an American political scientist gathered and analysed, in a remarkable study, the electoral performances of the different parties.[5]

The Sudanese Communist Party is indeed the largest, possibly the only, major communist party in Africa. Before its elimination by the army it had won 17 per cent of the vote in the Khartoum province in 1965 and nearly 19 per cent in 1968. This result is very close to that of the French Communist Party, which at the same time was gaining roughly 20 per cent of the vote in the egalitarian nuclear family region of the Paris basin — a high score when compared with absolute nuclear family countries. However,

---

5   P. F. Bechtold, *Politics in the Sudan* (New York, Praeger, 1976).

this is not enough if one thinks in terms of permanent and long-term communism. In both Paris and Khartoum two supplementary phenomena combine together to swell the communist potential: a temporary anxiety caused by upheaval, and a kind of fashion related to the strength and prestige of the Soviet Union. The USSR is today the only aggressive universalist system which is globally active. France is small and weakened, in terms of egalitarian beliefs, by the integration of authoritarian family regions into the national system during the nineteenth century.

Only Anglo-Saxon America can match the strength of the Soviet Union. Its technological superiority allows it to maintain a strictly military balance of power without too much effort. But the United States is ideologically at a disadvantage in its ambiguous attitude towards universalist ideals. It has difficulty understanding abstract, ideological solidarity between the peoples of the world.

The Anglo-Saxon world and universalism

The absolute nuclear family does not define relations between brothers a priori. It is indifferent to principles of equality and inequality in family relations, and has no clear attitude towards the principles of symmetry and asymmetry in social relations.

An egalitarian culture seeks equality between peoples. An inegalitarian culture tends to decree them superior or inferior. The absolute nuclear family is vague in its choices, a hypothesis confirmed by the history of the Anglo-Saxon world which has never aligned itself either with Russian and French universalism or with the German cult of difference. For a long time the favourite diplomatic stance of both the United States and Great Britain was indifference to the world: the splendid isolation of the English, the isolationism of the Americans. The essence of the system lies in a scarcely formulated but simple idea: live and let live, without trying either to destroy or to integrate other cultures.

On the level of race relations this attitude led the English emigrants to practise, in their contacts with Blacks and Indians (especially in America), all kinds of more or less official forms of apartheid; the Spanish and Portuguese, on the other hand, did not hesitate to take Black or Indian wives, thus creating the racially mixed societies of Latin America. But Anglo-Saxon racism is not aggressive: it is an acute awareness of difference which does not lead to a desire for murder. It is capable of evolution. After 1850 it deviated and was led to discover universalist values.

There are two important moments in this history, two decisive turning-points, and it seems that in both cases Anglo-Saxon culture was able, because of its indifference, to exercise a real choice between alternatives and escape the predeterminism of anthropology. The first turning-point was the American Civil War. A single culture was divided into two parts, one racist and the other abolitionist. The latter won and began a continuous cultural evolution towards an ever more militant anti-racism. The second turning-point, which did not concern America whose mind was already made up, was the question of anti-Semitism. England chose to align with the French and Russian universalist systems, in opposition to Germany. In England it is likely that the arrival on the political scene of the masses, who in practice (although not in theory) had an egalitarian inheritance system, contributed to push the system off course, since the noble practice of primogeniture which was so strong between 1750 and 1850 and had considerable racist potential was progressively eliminated from people's consciousness during the following century.

Anglo-Saxon universalism is not a 'natural' tendency, as in France or Russia, and is not determined by a clear anthropological structure. It results from a conscious effort to recognize the equality of others.

Soviet—American rivalry

Nevertheless, it is not at all certain that the universalist deviation of the Anglo-Saxon world will be a permanent one. With each generation the doctrinal system is questioned by a latent anthropological structure which has no clear-cut attitude towards equality between brothers and between men.

Anglo-Saxon Americans, despite their power, are less able to manipulate Third World peoples than the Russians, who are always ready to link arms with former colonials so long as they agree to wear the appropriate ideological label. In the long term, however, it is unlikely that the USSR will retain its seductive power over the egalitarian nuclear cultures of Central America or the Horn of Africa. The Ethiopian and (probably) the Nicaraguan family models are, like those of northern France, individualist as well as egalitarian. One part of them will be attracted by Anglo-Saxon individualism.

French culture of the years 1945–80 is typical in this respect. Parisian intellectuals are simultaneously fascinated by the Soviet political system and by American cultural life. For communism is not simply a dictatorship, even of the proletariat. It is also a rejection of abstract art, of pop music and of hitch-hiking. It is a culture, in the anthropological sense, which stresses obedience and denies the existence of the individual. The contradiction was resolved in Paris towards the end of the 1970s, when the Soviet model was finally perceived to be intolerable. The problem will be resolved elsewhere.

5

Endogamy

Characteristics of the endogamous community family:

1 equality between brothers established by inheritance rules;
2 cohabitation of married sons with their parents;
3 frequent marriage between the children of brothers.

Principal regions: Arab world, Turkey, Iran, Afghanistan, Pakistan, Azerbaijan, Turkmenistan, Uzbekistan, Tadzhikistan.

There is no clear, precise, decisive difference in character between the theologies of Islam and Christianity. Both are monotheistic and universalist. They share the same biblical tradition. Yet for nearly 1,400 years the opposition between these two sets of beliefs has been one of the major ideological conflicts in the world. The confrontation between them is the key to medieval history; it reappears today in other forms: in Iran, for example, where a rekindled Islam seeks to rebuff a formally dechristianized West.

Indeed the breath-taking expansion of Islam in the seventh and eighth centuries AD, from Arabia to Spain and the Caucasus, remains largely a mystery. Especially as the conquest quickly ground to a halt: an invisible frontier blocked the Muslim faith. The small kingdoms in the north of the Iberian peninsula, in Armenia and Ethiopia, set their different types of Christianity against Islam. The unshakeable resistance of these tiny states contrasts with the inability of the immense Persian and Byzantine Empires to defend their religious and cultural autonomy. Islam defeated giants but capitulated before dwarfs. Islamic history is in some ways similar to that of communism, which also set part of the world on fire only to stumble against invisible frontiers which we now know to be anthropological: Marxism-Leninism and its soldiers of the faith stormed only exogamous community family areas. The different ideologies — atheistic, secular and religious — being similar in nature, it is not surprising that we can detect beneath Islam's theological appearance an anthropological reality: the endogamous community family.

The ambiguity of the Koran

From Morocco to Pakistan, from Saudi Arabia to Afghanistan, a single family form dominates, its unique trait being preferential marriage between paternal parallel-cousins. Typical of the Muslim world and not simply of the Arab one, this characteristic can be observed in Afghanistan, Iran, Pakistan and among the Berbers of Algeria or of Morocco. Nevertheless, endogamous marriage was not invented by the Muslim faith. Paradoxically, the Koran contains only exogamous prescriptions, forbidding marriage between close relatives. The taboo, however, is minimal and not extensive: 'You may not marry your mothers, your daughters, your sisters, your aunts, your nieces, your wet-nurse, your foster-sisters, your grandmothers, the daughters of your wives to whom you are guardian, unless you have not lived with their mothers. You may not marry your daughters-in-law, nor two sisters. If a crime is committed, the Lord is forgiving and merciful.'[1]

Although strict concerning taboos on blood relations (particularly forbidding marriage with two sisters), the Koran does not outlaw marriage between cross- or parallel-cousins. It is this type of union which enables the community family to close in on itself, by allying the children of two brothers. Moreover, that which is permitted in Muslim lands is practised to the maximum, unlike in France where marriage between first cousins is now permitted but rarely occurs (it was forbidden by Catholicism and later accepted, in theory, by Protestantism and secular culture).

The division of the Mediterranean

The paradoxical process by which a taboo becomes an endogamous preference allows us to explain the expansion of Islam. Invented by the Arab world which practised systematic patrilineal endogamy, the Muslim religion moved into all the surrounding regions where exogamous prescriptions were weak or non-existent. It did not

[1] Chapter 4, 26–7.

Table 20 Preferential marriages in Muslim countries (male choices as a percentage of the total number of male marriages in the country)

Country/peoples and date	Paternal parallel-cousin	First cousin	Any relative
Negev Bedouin (early 1960s)	9.1		60.0
Druse (late 1950s)	13.3		
Kurds (early 1950s)	29.0		
Baluchis of Pakistan (1970s)		64	
Turkey (Taurus) (1970s)		16	
Turkey (Istanbul area) (1970s)			31.0
Lebanon (Beirut area) (1960s)	11.0		38.0
Iran (northern villages) (1960s)	10.2	22.8	31.5
Iran (Tehran) (1960s)	6.5	19.6	25.1

create an endogamous model but regulated and organized one by eliminating only the most extreme forms of incest: the marriage between brother and sister of ancient Egypt, that between brother and sister of Zoroastrian Iran, and that between half-brother and half-sister of ancient Palestine. Islam stops in the West, in southern Spain, at the limits of the area once under Carthaginian rule, Phoenician in anthropological terms.

From the beginning Christianity chose an exogamous ideal. In *The City of God* Augustine developed an evolutionary idea of the incest taboo, according to which the prohibitions gradually became more extensive.[2] In fact Christianity simply inherited the Roman kinship prohibitions which forbade marriage between first cousins. The story of the kidnapping of the Sabines is a typical exogamous foundation tale.

The conversion of the northern barbarians to Christianity from the sixth century onwards marked the beginning of an extension of the exogamous ideal, which was apparently more strictly applied among the Germanic peoples than among the Romans. Even today penal legislation covering incest, while moderate or non-existent in Latin countries — France, Italy, Spain — in northern Europe and particularly in Germany betrays a phobia and abhorrence of sexual relations between close relatives. Between 1950 and 1955, 400 people were sentenced each year in West Germany for breaking the incest laws. There is nothing in the French criminal code on the subject: it punishes only when an adult takes advantage of a position of authority over a minor, whether it be as father or guardian.

The movement of the fiercely exogamous Germanic peoples, then of the endogamous Arabs towards the Mediterranean, therefore polarized a situation which was originally extremely diverse. The Christian world embodied the ideal of exogamy, the Muslim world that of endogamy. Two monotheistic forms of universalism confronted each other, trapped by an anthropological difference. Christians and Muslims saw each other as savages, incompatible with one another because of their sexual and family morality.

Islam abroad

Islam was a major military and cultural power before the technological breakthrough of the West. Because of its power

---

[2] Ed. by D. Knowles (London, Penguin, 1972), p. 623.

it had a certain ability to spread into regions with different anthropological substrata. In areas on the edge of the endogamous community world but outside it, Islam was able to win widespread conversions under pressure: in the Balkans, the Sahara, the upper Nile valley, in central Asia, Black Africa and Indonesia. In this outer circle one notes the existence of a Muslim religion which is distinct from its specific anthropological base, grafted onto different family types: exogamous community in Albania, Bosnia and among the Kazakh of central Asia; egalitarian nuclear in Sudan and Ethiopia; anomic in Malaysia and Indonesia; unstable systems in Africa. But in each case Islam, while retaining almost all its fundamental theological characteristics — monotheism, universalism, pilgrimages to Mecca — relaxes its hold on customs and morality. The words of the Koran are disregarded in the area of inheritance, for example. Women, instead of receiving half as much as men, inherit an equal amount in Malaysia and Indonesia, while in exogamous community family countries they are totally excluded from the succession.

A doctrine which does not coincide with its familial counter-part cannot become an ideology. On its own it is unable to win complete acceptance. Once removed from its anthropological vector, a religion loses its strength and its ability to resist other doctrines. This is very clear in the case of Islam, invulnerable to communism in its endogamous community bastions but easily rebuffed when it appears on foreign terrain. Albania and part of Bosnia which are Muslim but have an exogamous community system, were easily infiltrated by Marxism-Leninism. The Indonesian anomic structure allowed an atypical form of communism, powerful and unstable but unique in the Muslim world, to appear alongside Islam. In Sudan and Ethiopia (where some Islamic communities still remain) the presence, in certain regions, of egalitarian nuclear family structures allowed the development of various Marxist movements among social groups which were officially Muslim.

Red Islam

The distinction between two forms of support for Islam — doctrinal and anthropological — is crucial in considering the future of Soviet Islam and hence of the USSR. Both forms exist there, which suggests a future split in Muslim attitudes towards the Russian policy of assimilation.

The Islam of the Kazakhs and the Kirghiz is superficial because it is exogamous. But the Muslims of Azerbaijan, of Turkmenistan, of Tadzhikistan and of Uzbekistan are less unusual and practise preferential marriage. The Russians will perhaps succeed in digesting exogamous Kazakhstan, where they already represent over half the population. The Kazakh family system is not fundamentally different from that of their conquerors: an exogamous community family, in this case including an anti-feminist bias which is absent from the Russian system. As a general rule, the monotony of family structure in the USSR is in contrast to the diversity of peoples and languages: Balts, Georgians, Armenians, Kazakhs and Kirghiz are not very different from the Russians in their family organization, and these similarities may explain the relative success of the Russian policy of conquest and assimilation. The only heterogeneous and probably unconquerable areas are the group of Muslim republics of the Caucasus and central Asia. Nevertheless, around 1970 they represented a population of twenty-four million.

Black Islam

Africa is often seen as the area where Islam is expanding. Islam is sometimes held to be more capable of converting the Black continent to monotheism than is Christianity. Statistical studies of this are hardly convincing, based as they are on fragmentary local material. To explain this hypothetical expansion an anthropological factor is put forward: Islam's tolerance of polygyny, which is widespread in Africa and which Christianity rejects outright. But it is an over-simplification to believe that Muslim polygyny and African polygyny are the same. Having several wives — a conjugal arrangement allowed in most non-christian cultures — is still a minority phenomenon in Islam, a privilege of the rich which affects at most 5 per cent of the population. African polygyny is a popular phenomenon, based on specific demographic and familial features: very wide age differences between husband and wife, and the passing on to the son of the father's wives, as an inheritance. This practice, which is indispensable for really widespread polygyny, is forbidden by the Koran. Strict on taboos of affinity, it specifies: 'You shall not marry the wives of your fathers.'

Unlike Islam, Black Africa, often lax in matters of affinity, is on the whole rigorous as far as prohibitions of consanguinity are concerned. Endogamous marriage is rare if one excludes a few regions in West Africa (Senegal for example) and peoples like the Peuls. Black Islam, whose existence and extent are not in doubt, has not met its anthropological counterpart in Africa. It is superimposed, as in Albania, Kazakhstan and Java, on a different family structure, one capable of producing in the course of modernization specific ideologies independent of the Muslim faith and capable of overwhelming it.

Homogeneity of the central core

In its central, endogamous core Islam has one advantage over Christianity: it is more homogeneous — not simply through the accidents of history but also through the make-up of its anthropological terrain. The common denominator of Christianity is a single rule: exogamy. The universal Church is silent on inheritance and on the cohabitation of the generations. In practice, from the beginning several family types — admittedly all exogamous — accepted Catholicism. Islam is more precise and specific: it sets out rules of inheritance which are adapted exclusively to the endogamous community family. Apart from its exogamous and anomic fringe, Islam is perfectly homogeneous from an anthropological point of view, unlike Christianity which covers nuclear — egalitarian or absolute — authoritarian and exogamous community family systems. The difference explains the relative doctrinal cohesion of Islam through the centuries and Christianity's marked tendency towards fragmentation and internal religious wars. Orthodox, Protestant and Catholic Christians end up belonging to completely distinct and autonomous religions. Nor should we forget the other 'religious' attitudes of anticlericalism and atheism, born in the Christian homes of the egalitarian nuclear and exogamous community families.

The divisions within the Muslim world are less acute. They do not correspond to fundamental differences of theology, rites or organization. The pilgrimage to Mecca illustrates the success of Islam's quest for unity, despite the Shiite split, for example. But it is the presence in Arab and Berber North Africa, in Egypt, Kurdistan, Afghanistan and Iran of an identical family structure — endogamous community — which is the principal reason for this success, rather than an autonomous theological dynamism.

The horizontal nature of human relations

Endogamous marriage profoundly influences relationships of authority within the community family. The household remains all-powerful but the father is eclipsed and replaced as the regulatory mechanism by custom. In the endogamous community family there is no balance between the strength of vertical father–son relations and that of horizontal brother–brother relations. The power of the fraternal bond surpasses all others, particularly the paternal tie. The inheritance system set out by the Koran clearly shows the weakness of vertical relationships within the family. Inheritance is not, as in the various European law codes, a simple transmission of patrimony to the children. In Koranic law it is divided into a large number of parts and spread over the whole family group. The arithmetic of these successions enthrals Muslim jurists and gives them their *raison d'être*. It would probably require a lifetime's work and practice to master the rules given in the chapter on *Women* but a few fundamental principles can be deduced. Inheritance can occur in every direction: downwards by transmission to the children; upwards by transmission to the parents (a sixth if the deceased has only one son); laterally by transmission to the brothers and sisters. Each succession requires complex calculations by fractions. Such a system can only function thanks to the endogamous mechanism which in practice continually recycles the same patrimony within the same family. In certain extreme cases the undivided, endogamous nature of the family turns the whole idea of succession into pure abstraction.

A closed, horizontal system, the endogamous community family is probably the anthropological environment which more than any other in the history of humanity integrates the individual. Ideally, one's wife is a cousin, one's father-in-law an uncle, each nephew a potential son-in-law. The absence of any mechanism to centralize authority allows the release of tension. Psycho-social surveys carried out in Tunisia or Turkey, for example, show that the Muslim family is one of those least torn by internal conflict, the father in no way being seen as a threat by the children. In such a context the psycho-analytical concept of parricide is totally inoperative: atheism is thus inconceivable.

The signs of social disintegration dear to the pessimistic sociologists of the late nineteenth century – illegitimate births, suicide – are at their lowest, on a world-wide scale, in Islamic lands. In the nineteenth century Gaillard, a Catholic priest, social reformer and author of a treatise on illegitimate births, noted the rarity of abandoned children in Muslim countries, a fact which he nevertheless refused to attribute to Islam. The endogamous system requires the absolute control of women, making casual encounters and conceptions not followed by marriage impossible. The few figures available are almost insignificant: 0.3 per cent of births in Tunisia were illegitimate in 1965, 0.2 per cent in Algeria (1965), 0.0 per cent (*sic*) in Egypt and Syria (1967 and 1955 respectively). At the same time, the average number of illegitimate births in the Christian West was roughly 7 per cent of all births, a figure characteristically high for an exogamous culture.

The difference between Islamic and Christian societies is just as great in the case of suicide, which is very rare in Muslim countries. Here too the statistics are few and unreliable, but still evocative: 0.2 per 100,000 inhabitants in Jordan in 1976, 0.7 in Iran between 1965 and 1971. The Western average at this time was nearly 14 per 100,000 population. The endogamous system, strongly structured by the community family framework, minimizes psychological tension and conflict between individuals. Unlike its opposite, the exogamous system, it produces little anxiety.

More than any other civilization Islam limits the necessity of exchanging women between families, which Lévi-Strauss perceives as the anxiety-producing mechanism *par excellence*.[3] Islam's solution to the problem of exogamy is a theoretical limit (and probably one that cannot be exceeded), which gives women a specific status and implies an ideal of negation.

The Muslim woman: physical protection and social negation

I am not concerned here with judging Islam or with portraying it as essentially anti-feminist, in the great European Christian tradition. Formulated in vague, general and moralizing language, 'the oppression of women' is simply a slogan without any sociological substance. In many ways the condition of Muslim women is better than that of Indian or Chinese women. They are

[3] *The Elementary Structures of Kinship* (London, Eyre and Spottiswoode, 1969), conclusion.

not threatened at birth with infanticide, like their sisters in China or north India. Nor are they, as these are, excluded from the inheritance, although the fraction they receive is admittedly half that of their brothers. In the following two respects the Muslim woman is protected. In theory by the Koran, for it is presented as a doctrine which seeks to improve a woman's position. In practice, by the psychological system of the endogamous community family: in such an anthropological structure the wife is not a dangerous and potentially hated stranger but a cousin who must be loved and protected. Because she can marry within the family, the daughter in Islamic lands is not, like her Chinese and Indian sisters, a threat to the patrimony which must be eliminated by infanticide or by an exclusion rule. The exogamous community family, when it is not tempered by a matriarchal bias as in Russia, is a far greater threat to women's lives than Islam.

Protection is not equality. On occasion it is even the opposite. Muslim women are physically protected so that they can be more easily destroyed socially. They do not participate in religious ceremonies. They are often veiled. They have no role in society, the endogamous system being physically embodied in a separation of the sexes. In economic life (apart from domestic tasks), women in Muslim countries play a smaller role than anywhere else in the world. They account for less than 20 per cent of the working population. A wide age difference between husband and wife (an average of 6.4 years) reflects the inequality of the sexes in a demographic sense: the woman is kept in the position of daughter rather than of wife.

There is nevertheless a cultural price to pay for the social elimination of women. Destroying the potential for female authority means retarding the development of education. Even so, the position of Muslim countries is no worse from the point of view of mass literacy than that of the exogamous community systems which have a very strong agnatic bias, such as north India and even China. On a cultural level the 'physical' (China, India) and the 'social' (Islam) destruction of women have more or less the same effect: a tendency towards long-term social stagnation. The centuries-long relapse of China, India and the Muslim world after a spectacular initial expanding phase was no doubt due to this very same cause: the refusal to integrate women into the normal functioning of society.

Table 21 Age differences within marriage in Muslim countries

Family type	Country and date	Average age difference (years)
Endogamous community family	Bangladesh (late 1970s)	7.7
	Iran (1966)	7.0
	Rural Morocco (1967)	7.0
	Egypt (1969)	6.2
	Pakistan (late 1970s)	5.5
	Jordan (late 1970s)	4.7
Anomic family	Indonesia (late 1970s)	4.4
	Malaysia (late 1970s)	3.5
	Muslim southern Philippines (1973)	2.6

Endogamy against the state

The idea of the state, as Max Weber showed, runs parallel with that of depersonalizing human relations. The establishment of abstract, rational norms of individual behaviour which depend neither on the family nor on friendship allows the bureaucratic machinery to be created and operated. Despite his encylopaedic and global preoccupations, however, Weber never stopped believing in evolution. In his view, depersonalized bureaucratic relationships were a stage which followed the feudal or patriarchal personalization of power. The state was a moment, the concrete administrative incarnation of a tendency towards rationalization. This Weberian intuition can, however, easily be adapted to a model which is anthropological rather than evolutionary. Certain family types lead easily to the depersonalization of power; others are totally unsympathetic towards it. This is the case with Islam, whose endogamous community structure poses an insurmountable obstacle to the construction of the state in the Western, Chinese or Japanese sense of the word.

An exogamous system requires a priori the establishment of a relationship between two individuals who are strangers to each other: a husband and a wife. Its opposite, endogamy, rejects the creation of a household on the basis of a casual human relationship. Exogamy leads to the development of the state; the exogamous choice of a partner serves as a model for bureaucratic relations which create links between individuals who do not know each other. Endogamy, on the other hand, leads to societies without a state. In Muslim countries, the western-style state is superimposed on a social structure which it cannot catch hold of or control, because society is overlaid with a network of invulnerable family bonds preventing the creation of impersonal bureaucratic relations.

Islamic tradition recognizes two fundamental institutions: religion and the family. Unlike its Western counterpart, it has never tried to create an autonomous central administration, either secular or religious. In Europe, on the other hand, the idea of the state dominates. Up to the Reformation in northern Europe and the Revolution in France, the bureaucratic machine was duplicated, there being two laws and two centralized administrations. The Catholic church, as much or even more than the royal state, embodied the idea of bureaucratic depersonalization. The church was an administration composed of celibates, opposed to the very idea of family relationships. Islam, on the other hand, believes in genealogical transmission of religious functions and conditions; it rejects the notion of a bureaucratic and depersonalized religious system. It is also remarkably decentralized and anarchic in its clerical organization.

Ibn Khaldun sets out in his *Mugaddimah* (An introduction to history) a conception of political organization which is completely foreign to that in the West, despite their common use of the family line to determine a prince's right of succession. Ibn Khaldun does not distinguish the state from the clan. The strength of a political power depends on the vitality of a clan at a particular time, which according to Khaldun cannot last for more than four generations. In his view the idea of lineage includes an element of degeneration: '[Nobility] reaches its end in a single family within four successive generations' because the son is not worthy of his father.[4] Hence the dynastic alternations which make up the political history of Islam.

The weakness of the state within Islamic society makes the Muslim world a politically fragmented one. It has been unable to create an empire like that of the Romans, the Chinese or the Russians. Even the Arab world, which apart from its religious homogeneity has a certain unity in its written language, has not achieved political centralization. The ideal of fraternal solidarity allows us to understand the fundamental contradiction of Muslim culture, which more than any other in the world combines an aspiration to unity with a tendency to fragmentation.

The hypertrophy of the fraternal bond, whose ultimate result is marriage between the children of two brothers, leads to this ambiguity. It produces an acute sense of equality between men and of the unity of humanity through equality between brothers. But it also provokes, on a familial and no longer an ideological level, an endogamous introversion which gives Muslim society the appearance of a series of juxtaposed families rather than of a community of individuals. Such is the structure of the community of Muslim believers (Ummah) which contrasts with the European idea of the nation as a collection of individuals rather than of families.

Socialism without the state

The ideological perception of Islam by the West has until now been a negative one. The Muslim faith is defined in opposition to

---

[4] *The Mugaddimah*, translated from Arabic by Franz Rosenthal, abridged edition (London, Routledge and Kegan Paul, 1967), p. 105.

Anglo-Saxon liberalism, to French-style individualism and to communism, with little understanding of its ability to resist these supposedly modern ideologies. Once the working of the endogamous community family is understood, Islam's solidity no longer looks like a challenge to modernity but like a permanent anthropological phenomenon.

Islam is doubly unaware of the individual. It rejects the Western individual, the psychological atom deified by the French and Anglo-Saxon systems who escapes both the family and the state. But it also rejects the communist notion of an individual escaping from his family into the state. Islam recognizes only two levels of integration: the family and the community of believers, the Ummah. The concepts of nation, state, and political party are imported. The two great ideological variants produced by Islam between 1960 and 1980 – Arab socialism and religious fundamentalism – cannot be understood in Western terms. The religious fundamentalism of the 1970s is straightforward in so far as it does not try to apply Western terminology to ideological conceptions peculiar to Islam. Arab socialism, which dominated the 1960s, is, on the other hand, ambivalent: it applies European verbal categories – party, state, nation, socialism – to an ideologico-anthropological base to which they are totally alien.

Islam is egalitarian, universalist, anti-racist. It derives from its community family source an authentic 'socialist' aspiration to mutual assistance and collectivism. What is missing that prevents it from creating political systems with the coherence and efficiency of social democracy or communism? – quite simply a sense of the state. Arab socialism is a unique attempt to build socialism without the state, or to be more precise and less derisive, an effort to construct socialism in a culture without any special aptitude or a tradition of centralized, bureaucratic administration.

Socialism in Algeria, Syria, Iraq, Egypt – before the liberal, capitalist impulse provided by Anwar Sadat – went through the motions of state socialism without any real conviction: nationalizing large and even small industries, controlling overseas trade. In this respect there is no ambiguity: Algeria, Syria and Iraq can be defined as countries with socialist economies, at least in the industrial and urban sectors. But social organization has not followed suit: family loyalties cut horizontally across the vertical edifice of the state, undermining the system and producing what in conventional administrative terms is called corruption. In reality it is no more than the adaptation of a particular anthropological type to the transplantation of a rational but imported administrative structure.

Above all, Arab socialism lacks the spirit of discipline which is present in the communist and social democratic models. The authoritarian and exogamous community families contain a strong vertical element, a father—son bond which provides society with a model for the relations of command and obedience necessary for the smooth operation of a bureaucratic system. Islam, which takes on the horizontal brother—brother bond, one of complicity rather than of obedience, cannot put its collectivist theories into administrative practice.

The comparison between Soviet state communism and Muslim socialism without the state allows us to distinguish two elements which in communism are logically distinct: a collectivist aspiration also found in the Muslim faith; and a need for discipline which is totally absent from Islam.

The definition of socialism

We can now locate more precisely, thanks to anthropology, the concepts of socialism and communism whose definition is one of the unsolved problems of contemporary political science. All socialist ideologies correspond to complex family structures. Only the light, nuclear systems — absolute or egalitarian — and the anomic ones if they are not too dense in practice, escape the temptation of socialism. On the other hand the authoritarian, exogamous and endogamous community families, and (as we shall see) the asymmetrical types, always produce a certain aspiration to socialism, trying to reproduce in ideology the enclosed anthropological structure. Socialism is the desire to re-create the wide but circumscribed community of a dense family, the *Gemeinschaft* as Tönnies would have put it.

Socialist ideologies are distinguishable by their other components, which are also derived from the family system: communism is egalitarian and authoritarian; social democracy is inegalitarian and authoritarian; Arab socialism is egalitarian, but while still not liberal is not authoritarian in the European sense.

In order to understand the Muslim concept of authority one must get away from the Christian opposition between liberty and authority and introduce a third element to describe the way power is exercised in the Muslim family and in ideological systems derived from it. Preferential marriage creates a disembodied form of authority, strong but at the same time non-existent, which on a doctrinal level corresponds to a deep respect for custom, without producing blind obedience to modernizing bureaucracy.

The nuclear family leaves the individual free to choose a marriage partner. The authoritarian and exogamous community families give the parents the right to organize unrestrainedly the individual lives of their children. The endogamous community family leaves such organization to custom, depriving parents and children equally of their freedom of choice.

The story of individuals serves as a model for the history of nations. History is made by individuals in nuclear family countries, by the government (a parental symbol) in authoritarian systems. It is defined by custom and thus eliminated in the case of endogamous anthropological systems. Islam's historical passivity can be seen to derive from its fundamental anthropological mechanism.

Arab socialism and social democracy both accept religion to a greater or lesser degree, a fact which distinguishes them clearly from communism. Indeed militant atheism depends on a conjunction of two anthropological variables, strong paternal authority and strong solidarity between brothers, which allows them to unite to destroy religious faith. The authoritarian family, the basis of social democracy, includes only one of these variables: paternal authority. The endogamous community family – the basis of Arab socialism – contains only the other, fraternal solidarity. The Muslim father is too easy-going to be hated or rejected, either in human or divine form. The Islamic god is too forgiving for anyone to want to annihilate him.

Fundamentalism and marriage age

The revolutionary movements of the Arab world, socialist in the 1960s, most frequently became religious fundamentalist in the 1970s, as in Iran where the Islamic revival ended up destroying the monarchy.

But does fundamentalism develop by chance? It is certainly not a phenomenon related to cultural backwardness, associated with the most traditional religious practices. There is no statistical relationship, for example, between the frequency of pilgrimage to Mecca in each country and the strength of the fundamentalist movement. However, other correlations prove to be highly significant: they show the religious revival to be a phenomenon of modernization rather than of regression.

European authoritarian family countries progressed from religiosity to socialism, through the fall in age at marriage and

Table 22 Conventional Muslim faith: pilgrimages to Mecca in 1975

Country	Pilgrims x kilometres per inhabitant[a]	Pilgrims per 1,000 inhabitants[b]
Libya	50.3	20.0
United Arab Emirates	21.3	14.8
Yemen (Arab Republic)	10.6	14.7
Algeria[c]	9.4	2.8
Turkey	6.9	3.0
Kuwait	6.2	6.1
Malaysia	6.1	1.1
Jordan	5.9	5.5
Syria	4.5	3.7
Nigeria	4.1	1.3
Senegal	3.7	0.8
Iran	3.3	1.9
Tunisia	3.2	1.2
Mauritania	3.2	0.6
Morocco	3.1	0.6
South Yemen (People's Democratic Republic)	2.7	2.9
Indonesia	2.2	0.4
Lebanon (Muslim)	1.3	1.7
Somalia	1.6	0.9
Egypt	1.5	1.2
Pakistan	1.2	0.5
Iraq	1.0	0.8
Sudan	1.0	1.1
Ghana	0.9	0.2
Afghanistan	0.8	0.3
Uganda	0.5	0.2
Bangladesh	0.2	0.04

The absence of any statistical relationship between conventional faith (measured by the frequency of pilgrimage to Mecca) and the strength of fundamentalism is obvious. Algeria, Syria, Tunisia and Egypt are scattered throughout the table. Iran, where fundamentalism has triumphed, appears in the centre, perfectly average in its traditional religious behaviour.

[a] Annual number of pilgrimages multiplied by the number of kilometres between Mecca and the capital of the country concerned, divided by the number of inhabitants.

[b] Annual number of pilgrims divided by the population of the country and multiplied by 1,000.

[c] Italics indicate countries marked by fundamentalist disturbances in 1980–1.

Source: *Statistical Yearbook*, Saudi Arabia Ministry of Finance and National Economy, Central Department of Statistics (Riyadh, 1969–, 1975 edn), pp. 229–30.

the decline of mysticism, without witnessing violent atheism. On the whole the evolution of the Muslim countries has been the reverse: from the socialism of the years 1965 to 1975 to an increasing religious fundamentalism which nevertheless does not question the collectivist ideals of Arab socialism. One again finds, in the case of the Muslim world, an oscillation between two poles, one socialist and the other religious. Here also the key factor is age at marriage, which as it rises leads from mysticism to socialism, as happened in most Muslim countries between 1960 and 1980.

Once again we must avoid a priori doctrinal judgements which link religion and backwardness, secularization (or atheism) and modernization. The rise in marriage age which occurred in most of the underdeveloped world between 1940 and 1980 was a phenomenon of progress, linked with growing literacy, urbanization and a general modification in economic and sexual behaviour. This rise did not lead to a decline of religiosity but to an increase. In Japan, the shining example of modernization, the growing strength of the Komeito, the political wing of a Buddhist sect, can be linked with a rise in urban celibacy rates.

Russian atheism, which considers itself a modern movement, is the ideological counterpart of a rise in age at marriage and of the breakdown of the exogamous community family, and can be seen as a reinforcement of a negative religious sentiment bearing on the non-existence of God and of an after-life. The situation is similar in Muslim countries where the growth of education, the rapid spread of cities and the problems of food supply — all factors in the uprooting of traditional rural society — lead to a rise in age at marriage, and to mysticism.

The lack of political and demographic data for the Arab world makes an exhaustive study of this correlation impossible, but it is clear that powerful fundamentalist movements develop in areas of rapid change because it is in these places that the marriage age is rising. Iran, where fundamentalism has become the dominant political force, is a perfect example. Because a rise in age at marriage is a necessary part of the process of modernization, fundamentalism will eventually threaten all Muslim countries. Between 1980 and 1982 strong religious movements could already be seen to be coinciding with a relatively high marriage age.

A comparison between Morocco — one of the Muslim countries least affected by fundamentalism — and Iran — where the Islam revival has triumphed — is significant from this point of view. The average marriage age of women in rural Morocco in 1967 was 15.5 years; in rural Iran in 1966 it was 18.2 years.

In other countries where fundamentalism is strong but not dominant, like Egypt and Tunisia, the marriage age is high — for the Arab world of course. In countries like Syria and Algeria where 'Arab socialism' is still in power, the geography of fundamentalist uprisings coincides clearly with that of high marriage age. In Syria the Hama, Aleppo, Homs and Latakia provinces were particularly affected by religious risings between 1980 and 1982: they form the western part of the country, where the proportion of men and women married before the age of twenty is lowest. The same geographic overlap occurs in Algeria in the region between Bejaia and Annaba, where the two centres of fundamentalism are located in the region of late marriage which lies between Algiers and the Tunisian frontier.[5]

The rise in marriage age, which is clear in most urban centres, implies a modification of the behaviour associated with models of preferential marriage. On the basis of the surveys available, admittedly not numerous, it seems that the frequency of endogamous unions is falling only slowly, even in the cities: 31.5 per cent of marriages in one northern Iranian village are between cousins; 29.2 per cent in the suburbs of Tehran; 25.1 per cent in the capital itself.[6]

Most striking is the change which is taking place in the distribution of consanguine alliances. In the countryside the wife is chosen, in 61.5 per cent of endogamous marriages, from among the family of the husband's father. In the city the proportions are reversed: in 53.8 per cent of cases the wife belongs to the family of the husband's mother. The urbanization process produces a matrilateral swing in the kinship network. The endogamous model holds good but is modified, reflecting the growing importance of the wife and the mother in the urban environment. Even in Islamic areas modernization leads to an increase in female power. Hence the anxiety of Muslim and Iranian men who were fighting, alongside Khomeini, to some extent against the Shah and to a large extent for the *chadar* (female veil), in other words against the liberation of women which the former sovereign supported.

The uprooting of traditional society which led in Europe to

---

[5] *Statistical Abstract 1981, Syrian Arab Republic*, pp. 88–9; *The Population of Algeria*, CICRED, World Population Year 1974, p. 46.

[6] *The Population of Iran*, CICRED, World Population Year 1974, pp. 21–2.

a massive rise in suicide rates and to the growth of revolutionary (and sometimes totalitarian) movements, in the anthropological system represented by Islam produces a specific form of anxiety whose basic characteristics are religious. The ritual obsessions provoked by modernity are fairly typical in a Muslim context: reinforcement of dietary, pictorial and sexual proscriptions, for example. They are, however, accompanied by political character-istics which have no equivalent in European modernization. Fundamentalism's inability to produce a strong, stable and unitary government is notable. Only a vertical, exogamous family structure could have prompted this sort of social discipline. In a country like Iran violence is remarkably decentralized, hardly less so than in Latin America. In the years following the overthrow of the monarchy the Iranian revolutionary authorities were scarcely in control of the situation. They could not even ensure their own safety: twice in 1981 the government was blown up and decimated. The unstable and multidimensional nature of post-revolutionary Islamic political struggles reflects, in the domain of political action, the natural fragmentation of a society atomized by family loyalties and incapable of producing an impersonal, abstract bureaucracy. The violence itself is typical of a 'macho' society and in that sense reminiscent of Latin America.

The unbureaucratic character of the Iranian revolution, whose violence unlike that of Bolshevism does not lead to the application of statist principles, does not imply an absolute difference in nature between the two phenomena. The symbolism of fundamentalism is religious and reactionary. That of communism is scientific and industrial. But in both cases the same unconscious wave of modernization drives the people to rebellion: growing literacy, a rise in marriage age, urbanization. In Iran the percentage of illiterates, which is over 83 per cent among men over sixty-five, by 1970 had fallen to 26 per cent in the fifteen to twenty age group. A transitional spasm, the Islamic revolution with its anti-Western symbolism should not make us forget one fundamental phenomenon: it coincides with a cultural transformation which is as deep as that which took place in Russia between 1900 and 1940.

Post-Islam

Preferential marriage may well be threatened by modernization, even if the most recent figures do not indicate a marked shift in this direction. Nevertheless, we can try to outline the new family system which such a modification would give rise to. The absence of any strong vertical, authoritarian element in the endogamous community family ensures that the breakdown of the preferential marriage model will not simply lead to the development of an exogamous community type. Held together by warm fraternal relations rather than by filial obedience, the endogamous community family cannot, as a complex household form, survive the breakdown of the preferential marriage model. The resulting structure would take an imperfect nuclear form, but with strong horizontal ties. The principle of fraternal solidarity would only disappear with regard to endogamy, which in no way implies the complete disappearance of the corresponding feelings. Wide age differences between husband and wife would remain, creating a single conjugal core but one even more afflicted by machismo than the Latin American nuclear family. The result: an imperfect nuclear family which would separate husband and wife while maintaining very strong fraternal ties. Such a structure already exists: in Corsica and in much of southern Italy, in places where the age difference within the couple is four years or more.

The disappearance of the regulatory mechanism of custom affords both liberty and anxiety. The Corsican or Calabrian model, a system without a father-figure or any kind of strong authority, based on fraternal relations which are no longer taken to their logical endogamous conclusion, inevitably produces great psychological tension which is directed laterally: in the form of conflict between males and between men and women. Such a culture is characterized in the political and social sphere by violence and vendettas. It has no place in mainstream political conflicts in France. Corsican political life does not obey the rules of stability and discipline characteristic of continental France. The influence of clans is all-pervasive, typifying a horizontally extended family structure and disrupting the normal play of relations of authority and subordination by introducing fraternal solidarity. In all these respects Corsican political life, anarchistic and unauthoritarian, is very close to that of Islam. It remains, at the end of the twentieth century, the great failure of French Jacobinism which did not succeed in mastering (either ideologically or culturally) an overly exotic anthropological terrain.

It is no doubt possible to link the Lebanese Christian family system with this exogamous but horizontal and deformed version of the Muslim anthropological type. The political effects of this structural imbalance are the same in Lebanon as in Corsica or southern Italy — violence, vendetta, anarchistic terrorism — aggravated and ideologically rationalized by a religious conflict and by contact with a neighbouring but openly endogamous family system.

The disappearance of preferential marriage therefore does not mark the end of the Muslim family system. There remains solidarity between brothers, extended also to cousins, a basic anthropological structure which influences a wide area of the Christian Mediterranean. Such mixed or deformed systems may represent the future of Islam, if the endogamous mechanism is indeed destroyed by the process of urbanization — but even this is far from certain.

6

Asymmetry

Characteristics of the asymmetrical community family:

1 equality between brothers laid down by inheritance rules;
2 cohabitation of married sons and their parents;
3 prohibition on marriages between the children of brothers, but a preference for marriages between the children of brothers and sisters.

Principal region: southern India.

The caste system must be considered here as a twentieth-century ideology. Nothing allows us to push it back, a priori, into a theoretical past created by Western ideals of modernity. The small amount of historical data available indicates, furthermore, that the divisions between the various groups in India have increased during the last four centuries. The power of the high religious castes has on several occasions been consolidated by foreign invasions — first Muslim then English — which destroyed the resistance of the native politico-military castes, the only ones whose prestige could defy that of the groups specializing in religious worship.

Simple and complex structures

Two remarkable books on the caste system have been written in France, Célestin Bouglé's *Essais* and Louis Dumont's *Homo Hierarchicus*, neither of which has really come to grips with the mechanism of creation and reproduction in Indian society, a society which classifies and separates men from each other, which is obsessed with the fear that physical contact is contaminating, and which enforces marriage within a particular human group, the caste (in practice the sub-caste). Bouglé and Dumont concentrate on the ideological superstructure of the castes, but fail to see that the dynamic and determinant element in the system is to be found at a more modest, solid and dense infrastructural level, the family group. They do not perceive the difference between a family ideology — the caste system — and the interpersonal family nucleus which produces it. The family, which gives rise to political liberalism in England, to social democracy in Germanic Europe, and to communism in Russia and China, in India produces and reproduces, with each generation, the caste system. Here as elsewhere, the simple (the family) engenders the complex (ideology), and not the other way round.

The influence of Durkheim, which has strongly affected both British and French anthropology, has not always been beneficial. It has certainly helped ethnologists, thanks to its capacity for dealing with the abstract, to avoid exoticism, the endless description of pottery, music, cuisine and colour. Firmly attached to a conception of society as a solid but invisible structure, anthropologists have been able to seek out, throughout the world, family systems invisible to the naked eye. But on a theoretical level the Durkheimian obsession with a global, supra-individual structure leads to a number of aberrations. It implicitly leads the student of family systems to postulate that ideology determines family structure, a premise which leads nowhere. According to Louis Dumont the caste system ultimately derives from a fanatical attachment to the principle of inequality which India applies to all areas of social life, just as nineteenth-century France tried to introduce equality everywhere. This is a tautological conclusion: it is not an explanation but a definition of the caste system. Dumont's principal merit is his recognition that men can conceive of society in different ways, and particularly his recognition that the caste system falls into the same category and has the same ideological value as French egalitarian individualism. This is the outstanding intuition that makes *Homo Hierarchicus* a great work.

The importance of southern India

Nor has the coexistence of two distinct family systems within the Indian group facilitated an understanding of the caste system. Northern India controls the subcontinent politically but southern India dominates it culturally. This anthropological and geographical dualism, which results in the separation of political and religious functions, has considerably confused the issue: the north is less attached to the caste system than the south, yet is located in the upper part of the Indian hierarchical model. The south, politically inferior and treated with contempt because of the dark colouring of its inhabitants, is nevertheless the real home of the caste ideology. It is there that proscriptions on marriage and on contact with untouchables are most respected. Division into castes is most marked there. The south creates its own inferiority through its attachment to the principle of separating man from man.

The Aryan conquerors from the North did not have a caste system. They fitted into it, simply adding their own fairly banal typology, similar to that of medieval Europe, which recognized four *varnas* based on professional specialization — priests, warriors, merchants and others — and on colour.[1] The four great castes of theory — Brahman, Kshatriya, Vaishya and Shudra — have little practical importance in daily life: the basic endogamous groups are the sub-castes, small and localized, corresponding to specific occupations and regions rather than to nation-wide social categories.

The cultural primacy of the south takes several forms, not all ideological and religious. In southern states the literacy rate is higher and birth control is more widespread. During the late 1970's the birth-rate fell to 30 per 1,000 in Tamilnadu, Kerala, Orissa and Mysore, compared with 40 per 1,000 in Uttar Pradesh and Rajasthan, the states which surround the political centre, Delhi. In the south political participation is greater, as is shown by the relatively low abstention rates in the different elections.

The north is more populous, less literate, has a higher birth-rate and is less attached to the caste system, giving the impression of a sociologically amorphous and passive mass. The contrast between the two is most annoying for racist proponents of the Indo-European theory which portrays the inhabitants of northern India as cousins of the Aryan conquerors of Europe. The most European part of India, in terms of language and colour, is particularly notable for its backwardness in relation both to the subcontinent and to the rest of the world.

Exogamy plus endogamy

The basic original trait of the southern Indian family system is asymmetrical preferential marriage, which is based on two premises:

---

[1] In Europe, this scheme became trifunctional, distinguishing warrior, priest and worker.

an exogamous-type prohibition on alliances between the children of two brothers or two sisters, and an endogamous-type proscription on marriage between the children of a brother and a sister. The ideal partner is a matrilateral cross-cousin (mother's brother's daughter).[2] But in certain cases it can be a niece: a sister's daughter.

The two main aspects of this system — parallel patrilateral exogamy and cross matrilateral endogamy — are equally important. Their combination engenders the principal Indian ideologies, in particular the castes. The existence of an endogamous model on the family level explains that of an endogamous ideology on the social level. The matrimonial exclusivity of the family serves as a model for the matrimonial exclusivity of the caste. But in a more subtle way the matrimonial system encourages an asymmetrical perception of social space: not all individuals have equivalent positions, not all can be married, not all are equal. In this sort of anthropological and mental environment the idea of equality between men or between peoples seems particularly alien. Like the authoritarian family, whose structure is asymmetrical (without being endogamous), asymmetrical marriage works against the unity of the human race.

However, the principle of parallel patrilateral exogamy is ideologically just as necessary for the functioning of the caste system as the obsession with cross matrilateral endogamy. It prevents the community family from turning in on itself completely. In practice it imposes a recognition of others which does not exist in the Muslim system, endogamy being taken to its extreme in Islamic lands and carried out almost without distinction between the paternal and maternal sides, even if in theory the preferred alliance is between the children of brothers.

The Muslim world, fragmented by the social practice of endogamy, has not produced a caste system for two reasons. It is prevented from doing so by its resolutely symmetrical, egalitarian vision of social space; and it lacks the principle of order and discipline, one could almost say the statist principle associated with the exogamous community family. In India on the other hand, this principle of order does exist in an elementary form, determined by a community family block whose exogamy is parallel patrilateral and therefore appears to be complete from the point of view of the household, which only groups children with the same father. The caste is a mini-bureaucracy which can determine a priori the relationships between individuals who are

---

[2] Rather than a patrilateral cross-cousin (father's sister's daughter).

not related. It is also a depersonalized mechanism, less removed from Weber's bureaucratic rationalization than the Muslim ideologico-familial system.

Two kinds of racism

The idea of dividing up humanity underlies two great ideological systems which embody two extreme versions of what in everyday language is called racism: the caste mechanism and Nazism. In both cases the inequality of men becomes the basic principle of social organization. Furthermore, since the beginning of the twentieth century, the existence of the Indo-Ayrans has served to prop up European racist fantasies, a process encouraged by their belonging to the same Indo-European linguistic group as the Germans, the Latins and the Greeks. The proximity and conceptual interaction of the two most spectacular racist ideologies in world history necessitates a detailed comparison of the family structures which produced them: the asymmetrical community family and the authoritarian family. The detailed analysis undermines the idea that Nazi ideals and the caste system are related. It also requires us to refine or even to reject Louis Dumont's depiction of the concept of inequality as the key to the Indian social system. The caste ideology, powerful and still unconquered, is in many respects less radical and less inegalitarian than National Socialist ideology.

The family system of southern India lacks the conceptual simplicity of the German, Jewish, Basque and Irish authoritarian models. The Indian marriage mechanism relies on the existence of a community household which encourages association between brothers and imposes an egalitarian division of inheritances. Two contradictory principles − symmetry and asymmetry − meet in the Indian system, which is far less radical in its rejection of the brother than the authoritarian family, a system that practises fratricide and simple inequality.

The asymmetrical community family further multiplies the contradictions. Its community organization, with an egalitarian division of the patrimony, should lead it towards universalism. But it is diverted by an asymmetrical vision of matrimonial space which corresponds, furthermore, to a mechanism of endogamous restriction. The keystone of its peculiar complexity is the basic bond which gives the asymmetrical community family its structure: not the brother-brother relationship but the brother-sister axis. It is this bond between siblings of opposite sexes which is reinforced and extended by matrilateral alliances: marriages between the children of brother and sister.

This depiction of family relations certainly does not imply that ties between siblings of the same sex in India are insignificant. The kinds of polygamy observable in southern India amply demonstrate the importance of all horizontal relationships within the asymmetrical community family. Polygyny in this area normally follows a sororal pattern with a man marrying several sisters, a matrimonial form prohibited both by Christianity and by Islam. In certain regions in the south of the subcontinent, on the other hand, there are frequent examples of fraternal polyandry, several brothers marrying the same woman, a pattern which until recently was very common in Kerala and Ceylon. In its most extreme form, therefore, the family system of southern India leads to a complete rejection of affinity taboos: solidarity between sisters or between brothers is taken a long way. Even so it is not the fundamental bond, for it is the brother-sister axis which lends the system its specificity and which produces the caste system. Beyond fraternal polyandry, sororal polygyny and cross-cousin marriage, however, one finds the same relaxed attitude towards the incest taboo, reduced here to a minimum.

Absorption and separation

The position of the caste system with regard to universalism is more subtle than that of authoritarian ideological systems, which derive from a simple ideal of fraternal inequality. The authoritarian family does not define the status of the 'other', the outsider. It is purely and simply a mechanism of exclusion which demonstrates little aggression where small groups like the gypsies, the Jews, the Irish, the Swedes or the Basques are concerned, but which can lead to a desire for destruction of the outsider if the anthropological vector is a demographically powerful group like the Germans. The Nazi experience reminds us that absolute racism was invented and put into practice in Europe and not in the Third World.

Compared with National Socialism, the Indian model for relations between men and between peoples appears moderate. Hindu syncretism enables a diversity of religious and philosophical systems to coexist with one another. From one end of the Indian subcontinent to the other one finds an innumerable host of sects and religious groups, some prospering and some stagnating, but all combining to form what is conventionally called Hinduism. The central characteristic of this 'system' is polytheism, the indispensable ideological complement of the caste system which is also tolerant of diversity and differences. Throughout its history Hinduism has shown an astounding capacity for absorbing foreign gods and beliefs. These beliefs are not considered heretical and are digested by a theological system which does not as such exist, and which cannot be defined except by its very capacity for absorption. The mechanism signifies, unlike purely ethnocentric religious beliefs such as Judaism, the existence of a penchant for universalism. This bias exists in India, arising from the community nucleus within the family organization which conceives and puts forward a model for equality between brothers. In India only the marriage system produces an asymmetrical perception of social space. The fraternal cohabitation and egalitarian division of inheritance work in the opposite direction, towards symmetry and thus towards universalism.

The logic of metempsychosis

The principle of reincarnation, one of the great themes of Hinduism, logically contradicts the principle of separating families and men. The possibility of passing from one state to another in successive incarnations — from animal to human, from low to high caste status — denies the existence of the barriers which in daily life separate different socio-religious groups. Metempsychosis rounds off and at the same time attenuates the caste system, re-establishing the metaphysical unity of mankind and even of the living world. It fixes inequality within one lifetime and not in eternity. In this respect Hindu separation differs markedly from the ideological rejection of the 'other' which is typical of the authoritarian family. The latter places its exclusion mechanism in eternity.

In the case of the asymmetrical community family the central mechanism for creating ideology is located in the domain of matrimonial alliances: endogamous marriage isolates the family group and is transposed into an ideal of separation, absolute but symbolically limited in time by the principle of metempsychosis. With the authoritarian family the separation mechanism is found in the domain of descent: rejection of the brother produces a supposedly eternal lineage continuity. The sense of difference corresponding to this system can also be projected into historical eternity. The Japanese, the Jews, the gypsies and the Basques project their specificity into past centuries and millennia, into a unique history which overlaps with that of other men only through superficial contact or through conflict.

Like the exogamous and endogamous community families, the asymmetrical community family implicitly rejects the idea of lineage. It perceives the successive generations of a family in terms of cycles rather than as a historically continuous process. Its endogamous, asymmetrical mechanism gives it a spectacular appearance: fear of physical contact and the myth of untouchability are radical concepts for a European. But in many other respects the asymmetrical community family is less brutal in its rejection of the 'other' than the authoritarian family which breaks down the relationship of fraternity, particularly when it is fiercely exogamous as in the Germanic countries.

Development and the status of women

In southern India, as in the Germanic world, the principle of asymmetry produces (as far as relations between the sexes are concerned) a relatively favourable position for women, very different from those observable in strong agnatic systems — Chinese, Muslim, Tuscan — where equality between brothers seems to have as its corollary a low status for wives. In southern India the capital importance of the brother-sister bond implies a matriarchal bias in the family system. Infanticide of female offspring, frequent in northern India, disappears in the Dravidian regions of the south.

The southern states of Kerala, Orissa and Tamilnadu differ sharply in their attitudes towards infanticide from those states in the north, (Uttar Pradesh, Punjab, Rajasthan, Madhya Pradesh, Gujarat,) where the massacre of the innocents was traditionally extensive. In the 1971 census there were 1,019 women for 1,000 men in Kerala, 979 in Tamilnadu, but only 874 in the Punjab — an indication of the persistence of female infanticide in the north.

However, the exogamous community family of northern India is extreme in more ways than one. It is remarkable and unique in the world in its low average marriage age. Unions between children are undoubtedly the most surprising characteristic of this family system, distinguishing it from its theoretical neighbours in Russia, Tuscany and even in China. In north India the median marriage age falls to 15.1 for males, 13.0 for females. In the south on the other hand it is 24.8 for men and 17.7 for women.

The position of women in the south is ambiguous and relative: wives are not manipulated children as in the north. But the very

Table 23 Median marriage age in India *c*.1960

Region	Husband	Wife
South	24.8	17.7
West	19.7	14.3
East	19.6	14.7
Centre	19.1	13.2
North-west	18.4	15.2
North	15.1	13.0

considerable age difference between husband and wife — seven years on average — implies a relationship of submission and inequality. It is above all the primacy of the brother-sister bond which gives women in southern India a more enviable position than their sisters in the north.

The larger role accorded to women in the south explains the greater cultural dynamism of southern India. Kerala and Tamilnadu are ahead of the northern states in terms of literacy and are particularly in advance of the region surrounding the capital, Delhi. Everywhere increased female status produces the same results — cultural progress — whether it be a structural element of the German or Jewish authoritarian families, of the English absolute nuclear family, or of the Indian asymmetrical community family. All things being equal, an agnatic bias, on the other hand, slows down cultural development: here northern India, one of the most backward and impoverished regions in the world, is a perfect example. In destroying women it destroys itself and is condemned to a stagnant form of social equilibrium.

Rampant communism

Despite the extraordinary diversity of languages, rites and customs in India, one anthropological form is common to the whole subcontinent: a community family nucleus which is always exogamous as far as the agnatic group is concerned. Two variants divide India between them, building on this unchanging core. In the north there is bilateral exogamy, the marriage prohibition extending to the mother's family. In the south there is only partial exogamy combined with a system of preferential cross-cousin marriage on the maternal side. The collapse of this endogamous but asymmetrical matrimonial model would transform the southern Indian family into a simple exogamous community one. This has happened in the Mapuche regions of Chile where the disappearance of asymmetrical marriage was accompanied by a splintering of the community household. As one would expect this disintegration facilitated strong communist implantation.

A similar evolution is conceivable in southern India where asymmetrical marriage prevails: indeed the electoral tallies of the different Indian communist parties show that Marxism-Leninism is not a negligible doctrine in the land of castes. Paradoxically Hinduism, an apparently anti-universalist ideology which divides men from each other, is less resistant to Marxism-Leninism than Islam, which like communism is officially a universalist and egalitarian creed. The Indian state which is electorally resistant to communism is Gujarat. This state is not officially the most Muslim in terms of the declared percentages of practising devotees, but it is certainly that where the presence of endogamous community family forms — typically Islamic — is best attested.

Elsewhere in India the existence of a partially exogamous group assures communism some latent influence, an influence which is stronger in the south of the country where the caste system was created and is respected than in the north where prohibitions on pollution and on marriage within the group are less strictly followed. The probable cause: the superior cultural dynamism of the southern part of the Indian sub-continent, which affords women more influence in society. The greater role accorded to women within the Dravidian anthropological system produces a logical cycle which is complex and partially contradictory: the strength of the brother—sister tie leads to a preferential marriage model (protection against communism), but the latent feminism of the system increases its capacity for cultural and economic modernization and its propensity for spontaneous disintegration.

The two regions of maximum communist development in the subcontinent — West Bengal and Kerala — belong in terms of family structure to the Indian anthropological pattern. But each is in its own way an extreme case. While not altogether untypical, certain traits feature so prominently in them that they must be considered as specific cases and deserve separate analysis. In both states the electoral strength of the different communist parties — pro-Chinese and pro-Soviet — exceeds 30 per cent of the vote. Since the end of the 1960s Marxist coalitions took on the responsibility of government (after the 1957 and 1967 elections

Table 24 Communist vote, number of clergy, literacy ratio and sex ratio in selected Indian states

State	Communist vote 1962 (%)	Number of clergy per 10,000 inhabitants 1971	Literacy rate per 1,000 inhabitants 1971	Sex ratio 1971 (number women per 1,000 men)
Kerala	39.1	12.9	698	1019
Bengal	25.0	5.6	389	892
Andhra Pradesh	19.3	7.3	285	977
Orissa	8.0	8.6	305	989
Tamilnadu	7.8	10.4	454	979
Punjab	7.1	8.8	387	874
Bihar	6.3	3.3	234	956
Assam	6.3	5.4	346	901
Maharashtra	6.0	4.5	458	932
Uttar Pradesh	5.4	3.9	254	883
Rajasthan	5.4	7.0	226	919
Mysore	2.3	5.6	368	959
Madhya Pradesh	2.0	4.9	264	943
Gujarat	0.2	9.9	418	936

in Kerala, after the 1967 election in West Bengal). In the absence of federal control, West Bengal and Kerala would no doubt have been definitively transformed into communist regimes.

The case of West Bengal is relatively banal from the point of view of the general anthropological model developed in this book, and has been dealt with in the chapter devoted to the exogamous community family. The peculiar parricidal nature of its system of family relations brings it close to the Chinese model. It differs markedly from north-western India where the exogamous community family is deactivated by its cultural inertia, by the physical and social destruction of women, and by the cultural dominance of a caste ideology which comes from the south. The case of Kerala, on the other hand, is unusual. Well known to political scientists because of its leaning towards communism, Kerala is equally familiar to anthropologists thanks to its perfect matrilineal family systems. It remains to bring together political scientist and anthropologist, each possessing half of a truth, half of a particularity: communism in Kerala is an ideological product of the matrilineal system, or rather of its decomposition.

Kerala: matrilineal system and communism

Despite its rarity, the matrilineal family system of Kerala is only an extreme example of the general model which is typical of southern India: asymmetrical community. But the brother–sister tie there becomes so strong that it is never broken. Admittedly it does not lead to a conjugal union between brother and sister, but nevertheless it keeps them permanently within the same immutable household — the *Taravad* — where the brother in practice exercises paternal authority. The sister's husband is merely an intermittent visitor, and the patrimony is in principle passed on intact, but in certain cases may be divided.

This system differs from the African matrilineal systems, which also transmit the patrimony through the female line, in its strong domestic organization. In the African matrilineal system the maternal uncle remains a distant, theoretical authority. In Kerala traditional domestic organization is a stable system in which there is real authority. The negation of the father is accentuated in Kerala by fairly extensive polyandry, the 'visiting husband' being often not one but several individuals, each in turn enjoying the favours of their wife. This fragmentation of the paternal role eliminates ambiguity and places effective authority in the hands of the uncle and the mother.

Kerala's family system thus emerges as an extreme version of the southern Indian model, though inverted in certain respects. The brother—sister tie no longer simply produces matrilateral preferential marriage, but is perpetuated indefinitely, destroying the classic conjugal relationship. Corresponding to the sororal polygyny of south-east India is a form of polyandry, often fraternal, with several brothers sharing a single wife. Polyandry, which is fairly rare in the world, recurs a few hundred kilometres away in Sri Lanka (Ceylon), whose family system is in other respects quite different.

The multiplicity of castes and religious groups in Kerala makes it impossible to describe a truly general family model. The one just outlined is that of the Nayars, a particularly perfect and striking example of a matrilineally organized caste which is in a minority in Kerala, but which nevertheless represents the ideal form of the local family system. This exotic model is that of the most culturally developed state in India: the literacy rate in Kerala in 1971 was 70 per cent and increasing steadily. This state of 20 million people is rapidly progressing towards a European-type cultural balance. Once again 'exoticism' is not backwardness. Northern India, on the other hand, while far more unremarkable in its family structure and markedly more European from an anthropological point of view because of its respect for incest taboos, is notable for its high illiteracy rate. Only 30 per cent of the adult population could read and write in 1971.

Vertical household organization, striking in Kerala, is the domestic incarnation of the ideal of discipline and is one of the preconditions for the development of communism. Solidarity between brothers is another prerequisite, represented in this case not by the classic mechanism of the exogamous community family but by polyandry. Wife-sharing is even more significant than house- and work-sharing. The two main political traits of the exogamous community family are present here but displaced: the uncle replaces the father as the incarnation of authority. Equality between brothers is expressed through sharing a wife and not a piece of land.

As in the case of the exogamous community family, it is not the family system in its natural state that engenders communism, but its disintegration. The twentieth century has been an age of fragmentation for the matrilineal family systems of Kerala. Ordinary nuclear households have progressively replaced the compact, vertical, undivided *Taravads* of tradition. The biological father is taking the place of the uncle in the authority structure. This is the anthropological background against which the irresistible rise of communism in Kerala must be viewed: as in Russia, an anthropological revolution has accompanied the development of Marxism-Leninism in southern India. The party, or the state, tries to take over the weakening authority of a family organization which is being atomized.

However, communism in Kerala cannot be expected to be exactly identical to that in Russia, where the family system is after all markedly different. It is impossible to say how an autonomous communist regime in Kerala would have evolved, for the presence of the federal Indian government has prevented the establishment of any total, definitive power which could develop freely. One cannot say that it would have followed the trajectory of Russian communism, with a Stalinist and a Brezhnev phase. In fact an anomaly in Keralan communism is already obvious: the existence of two communist parties, one originally pro-Chinese and the other pro-Soviet. Worse still, they were able to co-operate in government, a phenomenon totally incompatible with the tradition of Bolshevik sectarianism. Was this an accident of history? This would be hard to believe, since in neighbouring Sri Lanka a similar heresy has been carried even further: to the extent of participation in government by both orthodox communists and Trotskyites. Such an arrangement would have provoked a reaction of fear and hysteria in any orthodox Stalinist. The capacity of warring bedfellows to coexist in government in both Kerala and Sri Lanka should be linked with the weakness of sexual prohibitions of affinity and with the system of polyandry. Where brothers can share a wife, communist parties can share a revolution. The communists of southern India have thus succeeded only partially in adapting to the ideological system laid down in Moscow, Peking, Paris and Rome. The anthropological specificity of southern India re-emerges in the form of incestuous political behaviour which would be unacceptable for a European who was brought up to respect the incest taboo in every detail.

Ceylon: approaching the ineffable

Ceylon does not really belong to the Indian cultural and anthropological sphere. Divisions among castes are weak; the family system (as far as the Singhalese — the non-Tamil majority

— of the population is concerned) is not of an asymmetrical community type. Polyandry brings Ceylon into line with Kerala, but is not combined with a domestic and matrimonial system precisely defined by custom: there is no preferential marriage, no *Taravad* on the southern Island. Inheritance is bilateral; men and women have exactly the same rights. Marriages between cousins are on the whole rare, if the few village monographs that have been written there are to be believed. However, the system of polyandry (which has been slowly disappearing since the mid-nineteenth-century) itself engenders a dense and extended family structure, but one whose socio-political effects are not of the classic type. This unique anthropological model can only produce unique political forms, just as strange and indescribable as the family system from which they emerge.

In Ceylon as in Kerala, anthropological exoticism is accompanied by considerable cultural dynamism: the literacy rate in Sri Lanka is among the highest in the Third World, 78 per cent in 1976. But is it really a Third World country? The demographic transition is taking place on the island, where the birth-rate had fallen to 21 per 1,000 as early as 1971. The suicide rate is remarkably high and almost European in this respect, falling somewhere between the rate in Sweden and that in France: 17.2 per 1,000 inhabitants in 1968, perhaps as a result of the disintegration of a family system which is dense because of polyandry. Sri Lanka has attained modernity, carried along by a family system which is unusual but sufficiently feminist and matriarchal to be capable of rapid progress. On a political level, modernization naturally has a destabilizing effect which nevertheless cannot be described in conventional political terms. No one has been able to situate, either politically or ideologically, the 1971 insurrection against a left-wing coalition government. Revolutionary and neutralist, spontaneous and violent, the 1971 rising which shook the most traditional area of the island, the Kandian region, where polyandry still existed at the beginning of the century, is easier to define negatively than positively. On 23 April 1971 the leader of the government, Mrs Bandaranaike, thanked an unlikely collection of countries for their help in suppressing the insurrection: the United States, Britain, the Soviet Union, Egypt, India, Pakistan, Yugoslavia, Canada, East and West Germany.[3] The whole world was in league against something ineffable, unclassifiable and worrying.

---

[3] *Le Monde*, 25–6 April 1971.

From a religious point of view, Ceylon belongs to Hinayana Buddhism and not to Hinduism. In its very ambiguities and uncertainties, the family system resembles the anomic model which dominates the Buddhist and Muslim areas of South-East Asia: the weakness of taboos on incest and the indeterminate nature of the household form are from this point of view equally typical. Belonging on the one hand to southern India, Ceylon also fits in with the anomic family model, which has produced the strangest and the least tangible ideological forms.

7

Anomie

Characteristics of the anomic family:

1   uncertainty about equality between brothers: inheritance rules egalitarian in theory but flexible in practice;
2   cohabitation of married children with their parents rejected in theory but accepted in practice;
3   consanguine marriage possible and sometimes frequent.

Principal regions: Burma, Cambodia, Laos, Thailand, Malaysia, Indonesia, Philippines, Madagascar, South-American Indian cultures.

Social anthropology, a Western science, is still not completely detached from the influence of Christianity, and occasionally has trouble accepting the existence of cultures for which prohibitions on consanguine marriage are not a major preoccupation. Marriage between cousins is conceivable for anthropology, accepted by Protestantism and just tolerated by Catholicism. But anthropologists refuse to imagine or to recognize unions between half-brothers and half-sisters, or even between full brothers and sisters.

The few known cases of marriage between brothers and sisters — Egyptian pharaohs, Inca emperors, Thai sovereigns — are treated as exceptions or rather as aberrations, and are generally interpreted as princely fantasy. Banal socio-economic analyses sometimes provide a way out for anthropologists who dislike being challenged in their beliefs: matrimonial normality takes refuge among the lower classes. Thus J. A. Mason, in his book on the ancient civilizations of Peru, develops a curious stratified model in which the degree of incest accepted increases systematically up the social scale. Among ordinary people, it is possible to marry a cousin, among nobles a half-sister, among the emperors a sister. Twenty pages further on the author himself casts doubt on this elegant construction, by revealing that Inca vocabulary made little distinction between sibling and cousin relationships.[1]

---

[1] J. A. Mason, *The Ancient Civilizations of Peru* (London, Pelican, 1968), p. 174.

Incest and social structure

Anthropology has in fact refused to prove the existence of true consanguine systems, in the name of moral rather than conceptual premises. The few village studies which have been carried out reveal that princely endogamous models are almost always reflected in popular practice. The most reliable Egyptologists, like Erman and Ranke, consider that marriage between brother and sister was common in rural and artisanal circles in ancient Egypt. A study carried out on a Cambodian village shows that marriage between half-brother and half-sister, which is tolerated in the royal family, is equally acceptable on the more modest social level of rice-growers. Even the Inca problem can be settled by reference to relatively recent ethnological material: the *Handbook of South American Indians* reveals that among present-day Aymaras (one of the ethnological components of the Inca empire) twins of opposite sexes are frequently or even systematically married. The author of this article in the *Handbook* detected three examples of such unions in a single district of a few thousand people.[2]

The official Catholicism of South America is an additional obstacle to objective, dispassionate analysis of anomic marriage systems. Although too weak to control anthropological practices, the church is strong enough to deny and mask local custom and to induce in the indigenous population a sense of guilt. Anthropologists working in South-East Asia do not have the same pretext: Buddhism has little interest in marriage practices and has never laid down rules for them. Its remarkable tolerance contrasts with Christian, Muslim and even Hindu attitudes towards marriage. But in Asia too incest is submerged in the ethnological subconscious. For example, one anthropologist working on a Burmese village first stresses the prohibition on marriage between close relatives, including cousins, and later, when methodically analysing the geographic origins of couples from several villages, reveals that among 64 married couples in the village of Thebeiktan 58, or 91 per cent, include a man and a woman born within the village.[3] Here we are confronted with a mathematical impossibility: such a small human group cannot respect strict prohibitions on

[2] J. H. Steward (ed.), *Handbook of South American Indians*, vol. 2, *The Andean Civilizations* (Washington, 1944), p. 544.

[3] J. and M. Nash, 'Marriage, family, and population growth in Upper Burma', *Southwestern Journal of Anthropology*, 19 (1963), pp. 251–66 (p. 261).

consanguinity unless it exchanges men and/or women with other villages.

The typical matrimonial system of the anomic family is more difficult to analyse than that of anthropological types which practise preferential marriage. The situation is one of anomie, absence of rules, not of preference for a particular type of marriage. Therefore the frequency of consanguine unions is not necessarily high in anomic systems, as it must be in an endogamous community system, for example. A flexible, faulty nuclear family, the anomic model does not prescribe rigid rules regarding marriage.

A final difficulty hindering an objective analysis of marriage in anomic family regions (and linked logically with the preceding one) is the existence of fine gradations in anomic behaviour. The gradations run from the virtual exogamy of the Philippines or Thailand to the hard-line incestuous models of the Cambodians and the Aymaras. Malaysia and Indonesia are somewhere in the middle: Islam has institutionalized marriage between cousins, which can be statistically observed owing to the very tolerance of the Koran.

As the evidence is insufficient, the two most convincing points of proof of the existence of an anomic family system are based on a consistency postulate rather than on direct observation. First, all the observed cases of extreme incest coincide with faulty nuclear systems: that is, they are flexible in their desire to separate brothers, sisters and cousins, or generations, whether we are dealing with Cambodia, Malaysia, Indonesia, Burma, with the Andean Indians, or even with ancient Egypt. Second, a specific social and political system always corresponds to this anomic family structure.

Geography

By an accident of anthropological history the anomic family systems are divided into two blocs which are completely independent geographically, linguistically and politically: Indian and especially Andean America, and part of South-East Asia. States which are as different in religious terms as Burma, Thailand and Cambodia (which are Buddhist) Malaysia and Indonesia (Muslim) and the Philippines (Catholic) have comparable family structures: faulty nuclear ones. Such religious variety is a clear result of the shifting, anomic character of this family type.

However, the religious divisions in East Asia are not unrelated to the family. The major metaphysical frontier on the continent, which divides *Hinayana* (Lesser Vehicle) Buddhism from *Mahayana* (Greater Vehicle) Buddhism, in practice separates the anomic family systems of the South which correspond to Hinayana Buddhism (Burma, Thailand, Laos, Cambodia, Ceylon) from the dense, vertical models of the North (the Vietnamese or Chinese exogamous families, the Japanese or Korean authoritarian families) which make up the world of Mahayana.

Family typology provides a good grid for interpreting the differences between these two doctrines that arise from the same faith. Mahayana, which coincides geographically with the larger and more compact family systems, recognizes that heads of families can reach Nirvana. Hinayana Buddhism, however, reserves salvation for religious virtuosos — to use Weber's expression — to monks removed from any family structure.

Madagascar, which is partly populated by people of Malaysian or Indonesian origin, can be linked with an anomic model tempered and deformed by the influence of an African component. Endogamous marriage between cousins, and more often between the children of first cousins, is extremely common there, but it is not really a preferential marriage model: it is not based on a systematically complex family structure. The households take different forms, sometimes nuclear and sometimes extended: inheritance rules are bilateral and thus do not discriminate between men and women. All this recalls the Malaysian model — in other words an anomic system.

Class endogamy

The absence of any exogamous rule produces the same results everywhere, in the absence of a preferential marriage model which concentrates loyalties and the social structure on the family. It induces elementary human units — one could say neighbourhood groups, whether they are real neighbours, inhabitants of the same village, or social neighbours, that is individuals who occupy a similar position in the social hierarchy — to turn in on themselves. In all the anomic family systems there is a recognizable tendency towards neighbourhood endogamy. Community endogamy is the notable characteristic of the South-American Indian cultures; but it is also observable in Madagascar or in anomic South Asia where social life is more sharply focused on an ideal of village solidarity and unanimity than anywhere else in the world, whether one is dealing with Cambodia, Indonesia or Burma.

The village is only the lowest social level in an economy of traditional agricultural type. At higher levels one encounters a tendency towards class endogamy. Most typical and most striking is the appearance of closed endogamous groups in noble and religious circles. It would be tempting to speak of castes if the term did not create confusion with the Hindu model, which is formalized and institutionalized, based on a preferential marriage model and on an asymmetrical community family framework. It is preferable to speak of isolates: Egyptian priests, Cambodian princes, Inca sovereigns, local Madagascan, Malaysian or Burmese communities have displayed at very different periods and social levels a striking tendency to form social and demographic isolates.

The general morphology of such societies cannot help but be segmented and despotic, the superior isolates basing their domination of the lower ones on the mystery of difference. Kings and priests, set apart from common mortals, frequently see themselves as incarnations of divine power. In such systems one can observe two frequent and recurrent phenomena which are at once economic and cultural. First, the construction of enormous and economically useless politico-religious buildings: the Egyptian pyramids, the temples of Angkor in Cambodia, of Borobodur in Java, of Machu Picchu in Peru — more temple-cities than religious sites, sheltering a whole isolate rather than a few religious professionals. The second typical phenomenon is a natural concomitant of any over-ambitious construction programme: the existence of a large population living in virtual slavery, sometimes officially viewed as a servile class. When the French colonists arrived in the nineteenth century 17 per cent of Cambodia's population were slaves. This sort of slavery differs from its Greek or Roman equivalent in that it is based less on conquest than on a natural tendency of the society concerned to break down into endogamous isolates.

The fragility of ancient political systems

Neighbourhood endogamy, local or social, thus has very different socio-political effects from the sort of endogamy associated with Muslim and Hindu preferential marriage, which does not lead to the state crushing society. The anomic family produces a power which appears strong, but which is not really comparable with the bureaucratic machines born of exogamous family models. Power, in an anomic system, involves the crushing of inferior groups which are enclosed because they practice endogamy, and at the same time atomized because of the amorphous nature of their family structure. In vertical family systems — authoritarian or exogamous community — power exists in people's minds rather than in the outside world: people are conditioned to obey through their education. They are nevertheless obliged by the exogamous structure to remain in contact with the whole society. In an exogamous system, society has a definite structure which is invisible and negative but independent of the state: a centrifugal force obliges individuals to leave their families, forcing them to interact with the wider social system.

The anomic family works in a completely different way: nuclear, unregulated, permissive in its techniques of education, it does not accustom its members to the principle of discipline. But it is incapable of structuring society negatively. On the contrary it defines a state of centripetal drift, with each individual being brought back into his group of origin by the absence of any exogamous constraint. State authority — if state it can be called — works from the outside on an individual who is not preconditioned by a family apprenticeship in obedience.

Thus one can distinguish two sorts of power, one which is centrifugal and which caps a society dominated by an exogamous principle (China, Russia), the other which is centripetal and which holds together a society characterized by anomic family structures (Cambodia, Egypt, Incas). These two variants both have a well-defined power structure, and both differ from the Muslim model in which familial endogamy and horizontal solidarity hinder the normal working of the state. Muslim society is, however, unlike the anomic world, strongly structured by precise family norms.

The simultaneous existence in history of centrifugal and centripetal states helps to explain the difficulties encountered in the interesting discussion on the Asiatic mode of production (AMP for the initiated), in which these two types of power could not be separated or identified because of the lack of analysis of the underlying family structures. The concept of the AMP combines all apparently despotic statist powers, whether they are based on an exogamous community family structure as in Russia and China, or on an anomic anthropological model as in Egypt and Cambodia. Study of the AMP in practice concentrates on

Egyptian, Assyrian, Inca, Cambodian, or Singhalese history but does not quite succeed in accommodating the distinct Chinese or Vietnamese cases. Based on the utilitarian postulates used by economists, fascinated by the problem of large-scale works, it cannot understand the essence of a form of despotism which is not specifically oriental and which arises not from a sense of discipline, but from the anthropological introversion of neighbourhood groups.

The state structures typical of anomic family regions display an unfortunate tendency to collapse at the slightest shock, under the blows of a few invaders, or even on occasion for reasons that are uncertain and obscure. The Inca empire was destroyed by a handful of Spaniards; Cambodia, so powerful in the tenth and thirteenth centuries, was finally engulfed by the Vietnamese and the Thais; the Javanese kingdom collapsed mysteriously in about AD 928. The fall of these centripetal states, all-powerful but fragile, each left several enormous architectural complexes to be overgrown by grass and brambles.

The anomic family basis of the centripetal states explains this exceptional fragility, this tendency for impressive state edifices to disintegrate and disappear. They are not the expression of a strong social structure, but the complement to a fragmented civil society. Their strength arises from the weakness of social organization. Such systems are poorly armed to defend themselves against the aggression of peoples who are better structured by an exogamous, centrifugal and conquering family system.

Anthropologists are wrong to deny the existence of hard-core, radical forms of incest, but it is true to say that societies engendered by anomic family forms are delicate, uncompetitive and permanently under threat of absorption or disappearance. There is a historical tendency for anomic, centripetal systems to contract and to be absorbed by other models. The most obvious instances of transformation do not proceed to the extent of adopting exogamous values, but involve a moderation and regulation of the inclination to incest through the principle of fraternity. For example, the Middle East from Persia to Egypt, which in ancient times practised radical forms of incest, was absorbed by Islam and subsequently adopted the structures of the endogamous community family.

Nevertheless, the fragility and the social inefficiency of the anomic family should not be exaggerated, especially where it occurs in its less brutal forms, as, for example, in Madagascar. On this huge and demographically heterogeneous island the anomic family, which produces endogamous communities (called *dèmes* by Maurice Bloch), is dominant. In the local hierarchy the groups of Asiatic origin stand higher than the African population.

Cultural dynamism

The incest taboo alone does not summarize either anthropology or culture. The fragility of those social systems which only faintly respect prohibitions on consanguinity does not prevent a certain cultural dynamism. The anomic family regions have become modernized fairly quickly, especially since the Second World War; indeed they have progressed much faster than more highly structured family systems such as those in India or in Muslim countries. Mass literacy is a fact in the Philippines, Malaysia, Thailand, Burma, Indonesia, Peru, Bolivia, Paraguay and Colombia. The fall in the birth-rate, an indication of the spread of birth control, is beginning in most of these countries, bearing witness to a cultural mutation which has no equivalent in Islamic and Hindu regions.

The relative cultural dynamism of anomic family regions poses no theoretical problems. It arises from the egalitarian nature of relations between the sexes, from the favourable status of women and respect for maternal authority that are characteristic features of all the nuclear family systems, of which the anomic family is simply a poorly regulated version. The family systems of South Asia — Burma, Thailand, Indonesia, the Philippines, Malaysia — accord women and men equal inheritance rights. In conventional anthropological terms they are clearly bilateral, unlike the systems of Vietnam and China where the exogamous community family excludes women from inheritance.

In the Indian regions of South America, and particularly in the Andes, the egalitarian nature of relations between men and women is not always obvious with regard to inheritance rules, which often exclude women; but it is clear in age at marriage and general matrimonial customs. The age difference between husband and wife is fairly small, in Peru, for example, as in Indonesia, Thailand, Malaysia and the Philippines, a sign of the relative equality between the sexes.

The nuclear family, even when flexible in its ideas, is based on an ideal of solidarity within the married couple which must have a positive effect on the status of women. Maternal power in turn

Table 25 The anomic family and cultural development

Country	Literacy rates (%)		Birth-rate per 1,000 inhabitants
	15–20 years of age	overall	
South Asia			
Burma	82 (1971)	60 (1962)	38 (1973)
Indonesia	82 (1970)	57 (1971)	37 (1971)
Malaysia	93 (1970)	60 (1970)	31 (1970)
Philippines	94 (1970)	83 (1970)	34 (1970)
Thailand		79 (1970)	34 (1970)
Cambodia			46 (1970–5)
Laos			45 (1970–5)
South America			
Bolivia	85 (1976)	63 (1976)	46 (1975)
Colombia	94 (1973)	80 (1973)	34 (1974)
Ecuador	87 (1974)	77 (1974)	42 (1974)
Paraguay	91 (1972)	80 (1972)	39 (1970–5)
Peru	88 (1972)	72 (1972)	40 (1972)
Sri Lanka	87 (1971)	78 (1971)	29 (1974)

Table 26   The anomic family and age at marriage in the 1970s

Country	Men	Women	Age difference
Cambodia[a]		21.3	
Indonesia	23.8	19.4	4.4
Java	24.0	18.8	5.2
other islands	24.6	21.2	3.4
Malaysia	26.3	23.1	3.2
Philippines	26.0	24.5	1.5
Thailand	25.0	22.5	2.5
Peru	25.7	23.2	2.5
Colombia	26.1	22.1	4.0
Sri Lanka	28.2	25.1	3.1

[a] Data is taken from 1961.

Sources: D. P. Smith, *Age at first marriage*, World fertility survey, Comparative studies, no. 7, April 1980, London; *The Population of Indonesia*, CICRED, World Population Year 1974; Yves Blayo, 'Les premiers mariages féminins en Asie', *Population*, July–October 1978, pp. 951–88.

implies a more effective and progressive form of children's education, and a greater cultural dynamism within anomic society as a whole.

Political ambivalence: individualism and communitarianism

The anomic family, an unperfect version of the nuclear family type, clearly does not produce, on a political level, Anglo-Saxon liberalism nor even French egalitarian individualism. Nevertheless, its general structure supposes the existence of an individualist, anti-authoritarian component, or even of a frankly undisciplined temperament. At the same time its propensity for creating endogamous, autonomous neighbourhood groups, in Indian America just as in South-East Asia, produces in political terms a strong attachment to communitarian ideas. This concept of community has no connection either with communism or with Tönnies' *Gemeinschaft*, both of which are sociological dreams derived from vertical, exogamous, community or authoritarian family systems. The communitarian ideal engendered by the anomic family, observable in both Indonesian villages and among the Quechua or Aymara populations of the Andes, is founded on an ideal of neighbourhood co-operation, rather than on a strong family structure.

The political culture of anomic family countries oscillates between two poles: individualism and communitarianism (which is not communism). The statist models of the past signify the victory of the communitarian tendency, fully embodied in the Inca system but clearly identifiable in the Egyptian or Khmer social structures. Around 1980 individualism dominated the anomic sphere of South-East Asia. It was evident in the militarization of power, a classic symptom of a system which is not particularly authoritarian and in which the sense of discipline takes refuge in a specialized institution, the army. In Burma, Thailand and Indonesia the army wields power directly or at least intervenes frequently in political life. The Philippines have a slightly different regime, since in this case a civil dictator enforces martial law. But this represents a nuance rather than a contrast. The political system of Malaysia is affected by the existence of two communities, Malay and Chinese, a situation which creates a particular tension: the ethnographic balance is a major political preoccupation and upsets the usual manifestation of ideological forces in an anomic family region.

Ethnographic duality also appears in Latin America where Hispanic and Indian cultures meet and sometimes mix. The Indian anomic model and the Castillian egalitarian nuclear model share a nuclear ideal and only differ significantly in their attitudes towards exogamy, on which of course the effective realization of the nuclear ideal depends. The communitarian aspirations of the Indian cultural base are, however, not found in the Hispanic system which is in practice far more individualistic. Until very recently the cultural pre-eminence of the European elites marginalized the political effects of the anomic family in what are, in demographic terms, predominantly Indian countries, such as Bolivia, Peru and Paraguay. After the conquest, the anomic family simply facilitated the grouping of the Indians into enclosed and easily controllable units, whether in traditional local communities or in the Jesuit community experiments in Paraguay in the seventeenth and eighteenth centuries.

The development of mass literacy on the continent as a whole, and especially in those nations with a large Indian population — like Peru where 91 per cent of young people between 15 and 20 can read, or Bolivia where the figure is 85 per cent — paves the way for a significant change in political culture. One can foresee a strengthening of communitarian tendencies. Curiously, Peru and Burma, which belong to the same anomic family model (in Peru only among the Indian population), have produced the first two socialist armies in the history of the world, and the corresponding military coups. In 1962 the Burmese army began to increase state control of the economy, leading to the proclamation in 1974 of a socialist republic. In 1968 the Peruvian army launched a less radical series of nationalizations, affecting not only foreign firms but also a large part of the press. The Peruvian socialist detour ended in 1980 with the return to power of the neo-liberals: it was thus a reversible process. The Burmese case was more radical: its military socialism implied much stricter state control of the economy, as well as the virtually complete political and commercial isolation of the country. Burmese socialism, nevertheless, differs from that of the Soviet Union in two vital respects: its driving force is the army rather than a communist party; and it is not at all anti-religious and does not attack Buddhism as a metaphysical system, even though it does try to limit the influence of the monks in the rapidly developing education system.

Neutralism

Most of the structural prescriptions of the anomic family are unclear, whether dealing with marriage, succession or co-residence between parents and married children. For example, it has an egalitarian inheritance system which is also a liberal one, in that the youngest daughter generally inherits the family house and the duty of looking after her parents in old age. Corresponding to this flexible attitude is a fairly undecided approach to symmetry or asymmetry in relations between brothers. In this respect the anomic family is very close to the absolute nuclear family, which applies no restrictions as far as the making of wills is concerned, but in general produces a more or less egalitarian distribution of parental property. In England and the United States this outlook results in a vision of fraternal relations which is neither symmetrical nor asymmetrical, and thus in a corresponding representation of social relations. Relations with the outside world are neither aggressive nor universalist. Indeed, isolationism seems to be the dominant characteristic of the Anglo-Saxon temperament in international affairs. With the same causes producing the same results, the anomic family, in a similar way, leads to a certain isolationism, and to an indifference towards the world, dramatically reinforced by the tendency towards communitarian endogamy, that is towards a closed social system. Burma has taken this model a long way: its neutrality is total and makes no concessions. Other states in the area have a marked tendency to ignore international affairs. Their alliances are defensive and pragmatic, often anti-communist for strategic reasons, but without any strong ideological conviction underlying their military commitment. Countries like Laos and Cambodia, before being absorbed by Vietnam, had an obvious neutralist temperament. Sri Lanka, although only partially subscribing to the anomic model, is another example of fierce neutrality.

Family structure and personality structure

To each family structure we can assign a corresponding personality structure, this term being used in the psycho-sociological sense of basic personality structure, rather than to refer to individuals. Therefore, to the authoritarian family corresponds an authoritarian personality, to the exogamous community family one which could be called a communist personality. The anomic family leads to a basic personality structure which is particularly interesting, but extremely difficult to analyse. Produced by a fluid family system, the anomic personality is easier to define negatively rather than positively. It is not authoritarian (as indicated by the absence of vertical family structuring); it has few sexual inhibitions (as seen in the absence of strong rules about incest, and in its generally feminist attitudes). In an anomic family system the individual does not base his perception of those who surround him on either egalitarian or inegalitarian conceptions, on principles of symmetry or of asymmetry.

To familial anomie there corresponds an individual state of anomie, reflected in a specific form of mental pathology. *Amok* is a furious homicidal state considered typical of Malaysia which lies in the centre of the Asiatic anomic family regions. It has become one of the classic concepts of cross-cultural psychiatry, which analyses variations in forms of mental diseases in different parts of the world. An individual suffering from amok kills indiscriminately and comes out of his trance-like state without any precise memory of what he has done in the preceding hours or minutes. It is a temporary delirium and, as all will agree, does not appear to follow any observable pattern, fitting in well in its

Table 27   The frequency of suicide and homicide in Asia

Country	Suicide[a]	Homicide[b]
Malaysia	5.3 (1973)	–
Philippines	1.1 (1974)	15.6 (1974)
Thailand	4.2 (1970)	–
Hong Kong	12.3 (1977)	2.9 (1977)
Singapore	9.7 (1977)	8.1 (1977)
Taiwan	13.6 (1967)	–
Japan	17.8 (1977)	2.6 (1977)

[a] Per 100,000 population, World Health Organization (WHO) category BE49 (Suicide and self-inflicted injuries).
[b] Per 100,000 population, WHO category BE50 (All other external causes).

general characteristics with the fluidity of anomic family relations. Unlike the authoritarian family, the anomic family does not produce stable psychotic systems that can anchor the personality in an ordered, long-term state of delirium. Amok is an exacerbated and spectacular form of the homicidal pathology typical of the nuclear family, which when it leads to violence tends towards homicide rather than suicide. The few figures available for countries like Thailand, the Philippines and Malaysia in fact demonstrate that homicide is common there and suicide rare. From this point of view, anomic South Asia contrasts with 'vertical' North Asia, authoritarian or community (China, Vietnam, Japan), where suicide is more frequent than homicide.

The suicide figures for Malaysia in particular afford an interesting comparison between anomic and community cultures, because they include on the same statistical grid most of the crucial anthropological variables for both the indigenous and the Chinese communities, while differentiating between them (see table 28). Here it is clear that the Malaysian anomic family, less dense than the Chinese community model, produces a lower frequency of suicide.

Buddhism and anomie

Malaysia is even more Muslim than Indonesia; it is clearly Islamic in the very high frequency of marriages between cousins, resulting in a harmonious combination of communitarian and familial endogamy. But it is Buddhism and not Islam which achieves the most characteristic ideological incarnation of the anomic family system. Hinayana Buddhism, because it believes in individual rather than collective salvation, extols the virtues of monastic wandering. It is well adapted to a nuclear, individualistic family structure. Vague in its conception of divinity – it does not affirm the existence of a god and is frequently considered to be agnostic or atheistic – it is quite obviously the product of a family structure that is not strongly vertical and that allows the father little authority. As a result the latter is unable to embody on earth or to project into the heavens a sufficiently powerful metaphysical image. But it is above all in its psychological conceptions that Buddhism emerges as a pure product of the anomic family.

More than any other religion, Buddhism sees itself as a theory of the personality, and a theory of its extinction. The effort to destroy the self which this religion preaches is based on an attempt to prove that the self does not exist. A sage, for example, will try to prove that 'I have toothache' is a typical case of conceptual confusion, and that it suffices to put the tooth and the other parts of the organism back into their logical position of mutual independence in order to isolate the pain in the tooth and to prevent it imposing on a self which in any case does not exist. The Buddhist conception of the personality, or rather of its non-existence, is not unconnected logically with the syndrome of disintegration of the self, that is to say with the homicidal fury called amok.

Amok in politics

The West recognizes, although it cannot explain, the existence of Muslim and Hindu ideological spheres, of Islamic fundamentalism

Table 28 Family structure and suicide rates in Malaysia

	% of households including at least two married couples (1970)	Suicide rate per 100,000 population (1973)
Malays	6.7	3.5
Chinese	15.7	7.6

Sources: *Census 1970, General Report*, vol. I, p. 463; *Vital Statistics* (Malaysia Peninsula), Kuala Lumpur, 1973, certified deaths only, tables 48.01 and 48.02.

and the caste system. It rejects and condemns, but nevertheless perceives, the politico-religious forces engendered by the exogamous community and the asymmetrical community family systems. But in the case of the anomic family even this level of recognition is not achieved. With this anthropological type we move out of the domain of what is explicable or unacceptable into the area of the ineffable. The anomic family is a shapeless thing, capable of absorbing Buddhism, Islam or Christianity, modifying them to suit its own needs. Is it then reasonable to look for logic or for constants in the political behaviour of regions which officially belong to different metaphysical systems? Burma, Thailand, the Philippines Indonesia, Cambodia, Malaysia, Laos, and even Sri Lanka do not in Western eyes have a distinct ideological history. In geopolitical writing they are described solely in relation to the two great ideologico-military blocs — liberal and communist — which have dominated world affairs since the Second World War.

The Singhalese insurrection of 1971 and the Thai rising of 1973 have been relegated by political scientists into a sort of conceptual purgatory: the Singhalese revolutionary movement is forgotten, no doubt guilty of failing to define itself sufficiently clearly in terms of the dominant Marxist-Leninist ideologies. The student wave which laid low the Thai government has also been lost sight of, and for the same reason. Yet behind these two incidences of collective violence one can see, as in the case of the French, English and Russian revolutions, a process of cultural modernization, a spread of literacy accompanied by the partial uprooting of the rural masses. Impossible to locate conceptually, these political explosions were nevertheless symptoms of an accession to modernity. Born on anomic anthropological soil, they arose naturally from an anomic ideological universe: in other words from a system without rules, and without any coherent, rigid formalization.

Nevertheless, two major political events related to anomic family systems have not been completely removed from the consciousness of the West. This is, first, because of the unprecedented level of violence each involved and, second, because initially at least both seemed to be reducible to the usual categories of Marxism-Leninism. The massacre of the Indonesian communists in 1965 and 1966 left 100,000 to 300,000 dead, according to the most reliable estimates; the genocide of the Khmer people, between 1975 and 1978, claimed several million lives. Interpretations of these events were poor:

the idea of an anti-communist trap was put forward for the first case, the degeneration of a communist movement for the second. Indignation was high, but did not prompt any global analysis: in one drama Marxism-Leninism played the role of the victim, in the other that of executioner. On two occasions this handsome ideology was used and deformed by an anthropological system which in the past had already deformed Islam and Christianity.

Indonesia: the communists massacred

The PKI — the Indonesian Communist Party — was in theory one of the most powerful in the non-communist world. However, its political stance, even before it was eliminated, was distinctly ambiguous: the official prop of the Sukarno regime in the early 1960s, it was rooted as much in the administration as among the people. Ideologically it wavered, being neither anti-religious nor truly revolutionary. On the eve of disaster its leaders elaborated a strange theory of power which as far as ambiguity was concerned went far beyond all Bolshevik mental contortions: that of 'the two aspects of state power'. It led to the idea that there existed in the state power of the Republic of Indonesia two 'aspects': one hostile to the people, taking in the compradors, capitalist bureaucrats and the landowners; the other a more popular aspect, including principally the national bourgeoisie and the proletariat. According to the two-aspect theory, a miracle was possible in Indonesia: the state could stop being an instrument by which the ruling class dominated other classes and could become an instrument shared by the oppressed and the oppressing classes.[4] This theory is quite a departure from orthodox Marxism-Leninism, but one can sense in this daring conception the vague anthropological form of the anomic family, which fails to set out a clear and precise attitude, either positive or negative, towards authority.

The subsequent history of the PKI clearly demonstrates that it was not a conventional communist party, and that it did not conform to the usual laws of evolution of the Marxist-Leninist phenomenon. Reports describing the 1965—6 massacres show that the elimination of the party was not a *putsch* organized by the state or by the army, but very largely a spontaneous, grass-

---

[4] Cf. *Le Monde*, 13 January 1967.

roots movement, with each local community eliminating its own communists, and each village tribunal organizing sessions of self-criticism and physical liquidation. Many reports emphasize the participation of communist militants themselves in this process of social extermination. The instability of opinion, the ability of 'communists' to deny their 'faith', is clear throughout.

The electoral history of the PKI shows, in a wider sense, that it had no stable geographic implantation, unlike its fellow parties in Chile, France, Spain, Italy, Greece and Czechoslovakia. The geographic stability of the different European political movements reveals profound, unchanging attitudes, whether communist, Christian democrat or social democrat. Such fidelity to communism, to Christianity or to socialism resists the suspension of free elective political processes. In his analyses of the Spanish referendum during the Franco period, Guy Hermet has clearly demonstrated that the political alignments preceding the civil war remained below the surface.[5] Support for the Left was no longer expressed in a socialist or communist vote, but through a rise in the abstention rate: the map of electoral non-participation in Spain in the 1970s reproduces that of the Left in the 1930s.

There is nothing equivalent to this stability in Indonesia, where shifts in behaviour are the rule and seem to be typical of many anomic family regions. In Thailand, a country with a high literacy rate, the average level of participation in ballots is barely 35 per cent and is lower in the cities than in the country. In Indonesia the electoral implantation of the PKI in 1957 was impressive but later disappeared without trace. Its bastions in central-eastern Java — corresponding to the least Islamic and most Hindu—Buddhist zones of the country — do not appear on the map of the manipulated elections of 1971 as areas of high abstention. The PKI, whose strength exceeded 50 per cent of the vote in 11 out of 80 Javanese districts, has literally evaporated. Because in certain regions it had a clear majority and was nevertheless finally savagely eliminated without massive army intervention, it seems legitimate to speak of an implosion of the PKI. The party was largely destroyed by its own activists and voters in a phenomenon of political amok, a homicidal fury in this case projected into the ideological domain, but characteristic of anomic family culture.

---

[5] L'Espagne de Franco (Paris, Armand Colin, 1974), p. 211.

Cambodia: from communism to cannibalism

The Cambodian phenomenon has made the most rational politologists return to anthropology. Starting from a Marxist-Leninist premises, it resulted in cannibalism. It was an extreme case in human history of the self-destruction of a society, going much further than Nazism or Stalinism in the direction of social implosion. The two great European forms of totalitarianism were aggressive, imperalistic phenomena — with Hitler carried out in the name of racist ideals, with the Bolsheviks in the name of universalist goals. Born of two exogamous social systems, they were driven by centrifugal forces. The Khmer revolution, produced by an anomic system practising community endogamy and tolerating marriage between half-brothers and half-sisters with different fathers (among both the upper and lower classes), obeyed a centripetal logic. It was not an explosion but an implosion. Between 1975 and 1978 Cambodia fell in on itself, cut itself off, denied the existence of the rest of the world, closed its embassies, and sent its urban populations back into the country.

There was strictly speaking no specific ideology underlying the Khmer Rouge movement, if by ideology one means a coherent vision of the future of society. The first manifestos of the KPNLF (Khmer People's National Liberation Front), which date from 1970, foresee only 'the creation of a new society freed from all the hindrances which through inhuman exploitation prevent the full development of the progressive working people'. Jean Lacouture, commenting on this quotation, emphasized that, 'the Khmer Rouge movement remains one of the most ill-defined in the world.'[6]

The Khmer Rouge phenomenon was a movement without a doctrine, floating in a state of ideological anomie. The perplexity of political scientists confronted by the Khmer syndrome, or by the Indonesian spasm, has its exact counterpart in the theoretical discomfort of anthropologists who have tried to describe the anomic family system in South-East Asia or on the Andean plateaux. Their writing often begins with an admission of perplexity. Jean-Francois Guermonprez, writing about Balinese society where the massacre of the Indonesian communists was

---

[6] *Survive le peuple cambodgien* (Paris, Seuil, 1978).

particularly extensive, aptly expresses this uneasiness when he states:

> None of the best proven concepts of anthropology or of ethnology seems altogether adequate to describe the Balinese situation accurately. The apparent absence of some profound and essential principles which constitute the basis of social organization creates a certain disarray latent in most of the works devoted to Bali. It is in this respect significant that the last chapter of a book on the kinship system is headed 'Do the Balinese have a kinship system?'[7]

Here the writer's conceptual uncertainty is particularly well expressed but it is also present, for example, in Gabrielle Martel's study of Lovea, a village near Angkor in Cambodia, an unregulated world without strict anthropological rules. The lack of well-defined family structure is paralleled, in Indonesia just as much as in Cambodia, by a lack of precision in ideological structure. The thesis that family and ideology are related is particularly strongly supported by an analysis of the anomic system, which allows us to establish a link between ideological non-being and anthropological non-being.

[7] 'L'organisation villageoise à Bali', in *Cheminements Ecrits offerts à Georges Condominas, Asie du Sud-Est et Monde insulindien* (Paris, Ecole des Hautes Etudes en Sciences Sociales, 1982), pp. 37–53 (p. 37).

8

African systems

Characteristics of African systems:
1   instability of the household;
2   polygyny.

Given the present state of anthropological knowledge no exhaustive, detailed analysis of the interaction between family structures and political systems in Africa is possible. Paradoxically, the Dark Continent, an area of fundamental importance in anthropological research, remains very poorly documented from the point of view of family structure. Above all, the states and the anthropological units do not coincide frequently enough for a precise study to be made of the influence of the family on ideology. The African states are recent constructions, artificial and colonial, and, in the vast majority of cases, taking in several peoples and systems. Their anthropological tissue is far more heterogeneous than that of even the most diverse of European political systems — France — which covers four family types, all of them exogamous.

However, the absence of state structure should not be seen as irrelevant, as a problem arising from historical coincidence. The absence in Africa of strong central bureaucracies on the European model, and of vast religious entities of the Muslim or Hindu types, is a major ideological fact which requires explanation. Given the present state of knowledge the analysis can only be very general, but there definitely exist characteristics common to all the different African anthropological systems, the study of which makes it possible to understand the fragmentation of states and religions on the continent.

Polygyny

A major trait distinguishes the African family models as a whole from their European, American and Asiatic equivalents: widespread polygyny, which is only one central element of a whole system. The numbers of men and women in any community being roughly the same, a proportion of polygamous marriages of 30 per cent or more of all unions implies the existence of peculiar demographic mechanisms. One of these is a wide age difference between husband and wife. Women marry much younger than men and on average have more years of married life: the excess of 'female married years' is what makes general polygamy possible. To create a demographic balance, remarriage has to be frequent. Often it is not a question of remarriage but simply of inheritance, a widow being automatically transferred as wife to the man designated by the rules of succession. This implies a certain weakness or even the non-existence of prohibitions on marriages between affines; a man can inherit wives from his brother and from his father, although naturally his own mother is excluded. This practice, which is fairly frequent in Africa, flagrantly contravenes both the Christian and the Muslim teaching on incest. Whereas Islam is lax over prohibitions of consanguinity by comparison with Christianity, it is nevertheless fairly strict concerning taboos of affinity: it forbids sororal polygyny and marriage between a man and his father's wife. Despite innumerable exceptions, Africa provides the inverse model of generally strong prohibitions surrounding consanguinity, combined with weak ones on affinity.

A fatherless world?

In Africa the transfer of patrimony — whether in goods or women — does not always follow the vertical lines usual among the sedentary populations of Europe and Asia. Succession is often horizontal rather than vertical, passing from an older to a younger brother rather than from father to son. This practice is particularly common in West Africa, on the coast and the hinterland of the Gulf of Guinea, the most densely populated area.

The principle of horizontal inheritance is implicit in Muslim law, for according to the Koran brothers can be included in the division of property. In West Africa it is an important part of social practice, clearly indicating that the primordial family relationship is that between brothers rather than that between father and son. Horizontal succession necessarily corresponds to a lax attitude towards paternal authority, which remains weak. The structure of the polygynous household, made up of several distinct sub-groups — each woman sharing a hut with her children — helps to dilute paternal authority. The father is everywhere and therefore nowhere.

Curiously, transplanting the West African family system to America via the slave trade forced the system to its logical extreme by 'decapitating' it. By suppressing the ideology of kinship which roofed the edifice, slavery completed the destruction of the paternal influence and presence. The black family of North or South America often retains only the elementary mother—child bond, the father being mobile or absent. American censuses distinguish between households whose head is a woman, according to skin colour: 25 per cent of 'white' households have a female head, and 41 per cent of black households.[1] It seems difficult to deny the existence of a link between the black family systems of America, decapitated from the point of view of paternal power, and the polygynous systems of West Africa, which while not formally questioning the principle of male dominance, in practice considerably weaken the authority of the father.

The slow rise of literacy

Without going into great detail which the inadequacy of data would render invalid, one can nevertheless point to one cultural consequence of the peculiar structure of the Black African family: a particular difficulty in socializing the children, the fragmented structure of the family not allowing thorough control over their activities in school or elsewhere. It follows that, from the point of view of literacy, Africa is the least advanced part of the Third World.

In North and South America the cultural development of communities has taken on a peculiar character, as it reproduces, within the very process of modernization, the matrilineal bias typical of West Africa and based on the fragmentation of the household, the primacy of the mother—child bond, and the absence of the father.

In most of the anthropological and social systems in the world, the spread of literacy is at first primarily among men, who learn to read and write before women. In Muslim countries men have

---

[1] *Statistical Abstract of the United States*, 1978, p. 44.

an enormous head start, while in exogamous community societies like China their advantage is considerable. In nuclear, authoritarian and anomic family systems their superiority is less marked in this respect, but nevertheless remains a fact. In the case of the African family models the situation is sometimes reversed, with women leading the way in the process of modernization: a phenomenon easier to observe in the United States or in Latin America than in Africa where education statistics are unreliable. In the US the illiteracy rate among the black population around 1959 was 28 per cent for men but only 23 per cent for women.[2]

The statistics gathered by Unesco, which illustrate the general trend throughout the world towards mass literacy, also reveal that women are ahead of men only in certain Latin American countries where people of African origin are numerous: in the Antilles where former slaves make up the bulk of the local population, and in the black 'protectorates' under South African control. Men are less literate than women in all the places where European influence on African culture has been strong. An exhaustive list of countries where the literacy rate among women was markedly higher than that among men between 1950 and 1975 would run as follows:

Dutch Antilles	Lesotho
Antigua	Martinique
Belize	Namibia
Botswana	Nicaragua
Brazil	Panama
Colombia	Philippines
Costa Rica	Puerto Rico
Cuba	Réunion
Dominican Republic	El Salvador
Guadeloupe	Seychelles
Honduras	Swaziland
Jamaica	Venezuela

Military regimes

Largely covered by non-vertical family systems with weak parental authority, African society does not respond well to discipline. It has trouble forming states; it is incapable of

---

[2] *Statistical Abstract of the United States, 1978*, p. 145.

producing European-type totalitarian systems, except perhaps in the East where there are a few more vertical anthropological models in the region corresponding to the states of Kenya, Tanzania and Uganda. The dominant political force is the army, which controls 60 per cent of Africa's political systems. Parties, even where there is only one and where they succeed in surmounting the problem of ethnic fragmentation, are empty shells which in no way represent the real stuff of power, unlike the Soviet Communist Party. The pre-eminence of the army is typical of light-weight, unauthoritarian family structures: it recurs even more strikingly in the case of the unregulated egalitarian nuclear family of Latin America, where the military actually control 80 per cent of the states. The military idea of discipline, artificial and superimposed on anarchistic societies, is for such anthropological models the only principle on which governments can rely.

Conclusion

The family hypothesis, which sees political and religious ideologies as reflections of latent anthropological values, is only deterministic in appearance. Admittedly, it largely deprives men of freedom to make their own history, and portrays them as acted upon rather than as initiators, as the unconscious vectors of norms which dominate them even as they believe they are changing the world or realizing a universal ideal. It makes the study of politics appear one of dreams, and turns *homo politicus* into a sleep-walker. But the family hypothesis does not lead to a historicist model claiming to reveal the meaning of human progress. It does not view liberty or servitude, equality or inequality, as rational and therefore universal objectives. On the contrary, it leads, in the last analysis, to the conclusion that human history is, as far as ideology is concerned, meaningless.

According to this interpretation, the family acts as the infrastructure: it determines the temperament and the ideological system of the statistical masses which make up sedentary human societies. But the family, varied in its forms, is not itself determined by any necessity, logic or rationale. It simply exists, in its diversity, and lasts for centuries or millennia. A unit of biological and social reproduction, the family needs no sense of history or of life in order to perpetuate its structures. It reproduces itself identically from generation to generation; the unconscious imitation of parents by their children is enough to ensure the perpetuation of anthropological systems. The duplication of family tissue, the arena of affection and pain, is an operation which like the genetic cycle of DNA-RNA does not depend on self-consciousness. It is a blind, irrational mechanism, but its power derives precisely from its lack of consciousness and visibility, for it cannot be questioned. Furthermore it is completely independent of its economic and ecological environments. Most family systems exist simultaneously in areas whose climate, relief, geology and economy are completely different. It is impossible to perceive any global coincidence at all between ecological or economic factors and family types.

The exogamous community family seems equally at home on the plains of Russia, in the Yugoslavian mountains and the Tuscan hills, in the cold regions of Finland and the subtropical provinces of south China or Vietnam. The authoritarian family flourishes both in sub-arctic zones (Scandinavia), continental areas (Germany), and in subtropical regions (south Japan). The absolute nuclear family (Holland, Denmark, but above all England) has easily adapted to North America without being fundamentally altered by a move of several thousand kilometres. This striking example of continuity is far from unique. Latin America reproduces the Castillian model; part of Madagascar retains, after centuries of separation, an anthropological system similar to that in Malaysia and Indonesia. The egalitarian nuclear family is to be found on the shores of the Mediterranean (Italy, Greece, Spain), on the northern European plain (Poland), and on the high plateaux of East Africa (Ethiopia). The asymmetrical community family coexists with the monsoon (in India) and also thrives in temperate regions (Chile). The anomic family is represented in the hot, humid, coastal regions of South Asia (Cambodia, Burma, Indonesia . . .) and on the cold plateaux of the Andes (Peru, Bolivia). Only the endogamous community family, which on an ideological level corresponds to Islam, more or less coincides with one climatic zone, the dry world extending from the Atlantic to central Asia across Africa and the Middle East. However, not all dry zones correspond to the endogamous community family: the American, Australian and South African deserts bear witness to that fact. Above all, the Middle East produced several thousand years ago one of the most durable authoritarian types: the Jewish family, structurally identical to the gypsy family and very similar to the Breton or Germanic models.

The geographic incoherence of the distribution of family types, which seem to be spread around the globe at random, is in itself an important point.[1] It makes us return to a concept

---

[1] This was written in 1982 and may have to be qualified: further research could lead to a partly different interpretation of the distribution of family types throughout the world. According to Laurent Sagart, a linguist with whom I have been working, some aspects of the geographical distribution of family types could be the outcome of a diffusion process. The hypothesis of a mutation spreading outwards from a centre located in central or western Asia would explain two important features of map 1. First, it would account for the almost perfect contiguity of all community family types. Second, it would account for the existence, at both ends of the old world, in

of which the social sciences are deeply suspicious, but a principle which is more and more accepted by geneticists: that of chance. Affective rather than rational, originating by chance hundreds of years ago and according to individual choices made in small communities, later expanding through the demographic growth of tribes and peoples, family systems perpetuate themselves simply by inertia. Not all family combinations are viable and not all have survived: the world of seven types (seven plus one if we include the African systems) described in this book does not seem very large if one considers the thousands of languages which coexist throughout the world. But this combination of anthropological types, coming down to us from an indeterminate past, has in the twentieth century played a trick on the ideal of modernity. It has seized and deformed it, in each region twisting it into a latent value-system which, put into an abstract, depersonalized form, has in one place produced the French revolutionary ideal, in another Anglo-Saxon liberalism, elsewhere communism, Muslim fundamentalism, social democracy, Buddhist socialism, and many other secondary forms.

At the heart of the ideological alignments which have determined the history of the twentieth century lies the family. But beyond this anthropological base, it is chance which makes the ideological history of the planet a process of aimless movement. This is a difficult conclusion for historians and sociologists to accept, for they have made determinism an article of faith, devoting themselves to the search for causes if they are modest, and to discovering the meaning of history if they are ambitious.

Such a conclusion obviously has ideological consequences. It implicitly attacks any belief in political or religious truth, because it emphasizes the existence of an unconscious anthropological substratum beneath each system of thought. This is not an unexpected result in the case of ethnocentric ideologies — German, Japanese, Basque, Jewish, gypsy, Irish, or in another sense the caste system — but, which is more surprising, it likewise reduces each of the universalist ideologies — French Jacobinism, the Russian Revolution, Islam — to a specific, particular anthropological core.

Europe and Japan (two peripheral regions), of very similar authoritarian family types. Sagart and I are at present working on a detailed explanation of the map of anthropological regions of the world presented in this book. No final conclusion has been reached at this stage of the research, but it is almost certain that a satisfactory explanation will require the combination of two complementary sets of factors: random phenomena *and* diffusion processes.

The family hypothesis reveals beneath the universalist systems anthropological particularities. But conversely, by picking out a single element of family structure — asymmetry — within the most diverse ethnocentric forms, it identifies a relationship between chosen nations and castes and restores them to their place of obedience to universal laws. This anthropological interpretation of political and religious thought particularizes universals, and universalizes the particular. Accepting such a representation of ideological life can lead only to a high degree of tolerance and to a measure of scepticism.

Bibliography

Abbreviations

HFPT: P. Laslett and R. Wall, eds, *Household and Family in Past Time*, Cambridge, Cambridge University Press, 1972.
LOE: F. Le Play, *Les ouvriers européens*, 2nd edn, 6 vols, Tours, A. Mame et fils, 1877–9.
FEW: R. Hill, R. König, eds, *Families in East and West*, Paris, Mouton, 1970.
CICRED: Committee for International Co-ordination of National Research in Demography.

FAMILY TYPES

Exogamous community family

Russia (European part of the USSR)

Benet S., ed., *The Village of Viriatino*, New York, Doubleday, 1970.
Chaliand G. and Ternon Y., *Le Génocide des Arméniens*, Brussels, Éditions Complexe, 1980.
Czap, P., 'Marriage and the peasant joint-family in Russia in the era of serfdom' in D. Ransel et al., *The Family in imperial Russia*, Illinois, University of Illinois Press, 1979.
Dunn S. P. and E., *The Peasants of Central Russia*, New York, Holt, Rinehart and Winston, 1967.
Hudson A. E., *Kazak Social Structure*, New Haven, Yale University Publications in Anthropology, 1938.
Le Play F., 'Charpentiers et marchands de grains des laveries d'or de l'Oural', *LOE*, vol. 2, chap. 4, pp. 142–78.
Le Play F., 'Forgeron et charbonnier des usines à fer de l'Oural', *LOE*, vol. 2, chap. 3, pp. 99–141.
Le Play F., 'Paysans et charrons des steppes à terre noire d'Orenburg', *LOE*, vol. 2, chap. 2, pp. 47–98.
Le Play F., 'Paysans, portefaix et bateliers émigrants (à l'abrok) du bassin de l'Oka', *LOE*, vol. 2, chap. 5, pp. 179–230.

Luzbetak L. J., *Marriage and the Family in Caucasia*, Vienna, St Gabriel's Mission Press, 1951.
Plakans A., 'Identifying kinfolk beyond the household', *Journal of Family History*, vol. 2, no. 1, Spring 1977, pp. 3–27.
Plakans A., 'Peasant farmsteads and households in the Baltic littoral, 1797', *Comparative Studies in Society and History*, 17, 1975, pp. 2–35.
Soviet census, 1970 (Migration and Households), Moscow, 1974, vol. 7.

Yugoslavia

Halpern J., 'Town and countryside in Serbia in the nineteenth century. Social and household structure as reflected in the census of 1863', *HFPT*, pp. 401–27.
Hammel E. A., 'The Zadruga as a process', *HFPT*, pp. 335–73.
Laslett P. and Clarke M., 'Houseful and household in an eighteenth century Balkan city. A tabular analysis of the Serbian sector of Belgrade in 1733–4', *HFPT*, pp. 375–400.
Lockwood W. G., 'Converts and consanguinity: the social organization of Muslim Slavs in Western Bosnia', *Ethnology*, XI, 1972, pp. 55–79.
The Population of Yugoslavia, CICRED, World Population Year 1974.

Bulgaria

Ilieva N. and Oshavkova V., *Changes in the Bulgarian Family Cycle from the End of the 19th Century to the Present Day*, pp. 381–92 in J. Cuisenier, *Le Cycle de la vie familiale dans les sociétés européennes*, Paris, Mouton, 1977.
Le Play F., 'Forgeron bulgare des usines à fer de Samakova', *LOE*, vol. 2, chap. 6, pp. 231–71.
The Population of Bulgaria, CICRED, World Population Year 1974.

Slovakia

Le Play F., 'Fondeur slovaque des usines à argent de Schemnitz (Hongrie)', *LOE*, vol. 4, chap. 1, pp. 1–67.
Stein H. F., 'Structural change in Slovak kinship: an ethno-historic enquiry', *Ethnology*, 1975, vol. XIV, pp. 99–108.
Vaclavik A., *Podunajska Dedina* (Monografia), Bratislava, 1925 (Croates de Slovaquie) (résumé in French).

Hungary

Az 1973 Évi mikrocenzus adatai, Census of 1973, Budapest, 1974, pp. 274–86.
'Az elsö magyaroszági népszámláláshoz 1786–1787', *Történeti statisztikai tamulmányok* (Potlas – supplement), Budapest, 1975.
Fel E. and Hofer T., *Proper Peasants*, Chicago, Aldine Publishing Company, 1969.

Le Play F., 'Iobajjy ou paysans des plaines de la Theiss (Hongrie centrale)', *LOE*, vol. 2, chap. 7, pp. 272—303.

Finland

Löfgren O., 'Family and household among Scandinavian peasants', *Ethnologia Scandinavica*, 1974, pp. 17—52.

Albania

Weekes R. V., ed., *Muslim Peoples. A World Ethnographic Survey*, Westport-London, Greenwood Press, 1978, pp. 19—22.

Central France

Biraben J. N., 'A southern French village: the inhabitants of Montplaisant in 1644', *HFPT*, pp. 237—54.

Dussourd H., *Les Communautés familiales agricoles du Centre de la France*, Paris, Maisonneuve et Larose, 1978.

Le Play F., 'Manœuvre-agriculteur du Morvan (Nivernais)', *LOE*, vol. 5, chap. 6, pp. 255—322.

Peyronnet J.-C., 'Famille élargie ou famille nucléaire? L'exemple du Limousin au début du XIXe siécle', *Revue d'histoire moderne et contemporaine*, XXII, 1975, pp. 568—82.

Central Italy

Herlihy D. and Klapisch-Zuber C., *Les Toscans et leurs familles. Une étude du catasto florentin de 1427*, Paris, Presses de la fondation nationale des sciences politiques, 1978.

Kentzer D. I., 'European peasant household structure: some implications from a nineteenth century Italian community', *Journal of Family History*, vol. 2, no. 4, winter 1977, pp. 333—49.

Klapisch C., 'Household and family in Tuscany', *HFPT*, pp. 267—81.

Le Play F., 'Métayer de la Toscane', *LOE*, vol. 4, chap. 3, pp. 121—82.

Northern Greece

Campbell J. K., *Honour, Family and Patronage. A Study of Institutions and Moral Values in a Greek Mountain Community*, Oxford, Oxford University Press, 1964.

Southern Portugal

Cutileiro J., *A Portuguese Rural Society*, Oxford, Oxford University Press, 1971.

Cuba and Central America

Analisis de las caracteristicas demograficas de la poblacion cubana, Censo de poblacion y viviendas de 1970. Dirección central de estadistica, Havana, 1973.

CELADE (Centro Latino-americano de demografia), *Cuba: el descenso de la fecundidad 1964–1967*, San Jose, Costa Rica, 1981.

Nelson L., *Rural Cuba*, Minnesota, University of Minnesota Press, 1950.

Nutini H. G., *San Bernardino Contla. Marriage and Family Structure in a Tlaxcalan Municipio*, Pittsburgh, University of Pittsburgh Press, 1968.

China

Baker H. D. R., *Chinese Family and Kinship*, London, Macmillan, 1979.

'China's new marriage law', *Population and Development Review*, vol. 7, no. 2, June 1981, pp. 369–72.

Fei Hsia-Tung, *Peasant Life in China. A Field Study of Country Life in the Yangtze Valley*, London, Routledge, 1939.

Gallin B., 'Cousin marriage in China', *Ethnology*, 11, 1963, pp. 104–8.

Granet M., *La Civilisation chinoise*, Paris, Albin Michel, 1968.

Hong Kong Population and Housing Census 1971. Main report. Census and Statistics Department, Hong Kong, 1972.

Huc Père R.-E., *L'Empire chinois*, Monaco, Édition du Rocher, 1980.

Pasternak B., *Kinship and Community in Two Chinese Villages*, Stanford, Stanford University Press, 1972.

The Population of Hong Kong, CICRED, World Population Year 1974.

Report on the Census of Population. Singapore, 1970, vol. 1, tables 11.2, 11.3 (household structure and ethnic origin).

Shau-Lam W., 'Social change and parent–child relations in Hong Kong', *FEW*, pp. 167–74.

Wolf A. P. and Chien-Shan Huang, *Marriage and Adoption in China, 1845–1945*, Stanford, Stanford University Press, 1980.

Wolf M., *Women and the Family in Rural Taiwan*, Stanford, Stanford University Press, 1972.

Vietnam

Hickey G. C., *Village in Vietnam*, New Haven, Yale University Press, 1964.

Phan Thi Dac Mle, *Situation de la personne au Vietnam*, Paris, CNRS, 1966.

Northern India (see *India*, asymmetrical community family)

Authoritarian family

Germany and Austria

Andree R. and Peschel O., *Physikalisch-statistichen Atlas des Deutschen Reichs*, Bielefeld and Leipzig, Velhagen und Klasing, 1878.

Bachofen J.-J., *Du règne de la mère au patriarcat*, Lausanne, Éditions de l'Aire, 1980.

Bardin M. et al., *Civiltà rurale di una Valle veneta*, Vicence, Accademia olimpica, 1976.

Berkner L. K., 'Inheritance, land tenure and peasant family structure: a German regional comparison', in J. Goody, J. Thirsk, E. P. Thompson, eds, *Family and Inheritance*, Cambridge, Cambridge University Press, 1976.

Berkner L. K., 'The stem-family and the developmental cycle of the peasant household: an 18th century Austrian example', *American Historical Review*, 77, 1972, pp. 398–418.

Census of the Federal Republic of Germany, 1970, part 8, *Bevolkerung in Haushalter*, Bonn.

Cole J. W. and Wolf E. R., *The Hidden Frontier, Ecology and Ethnicity in an Alpine Valley*, New York, Academic Press, 1974.

Evans R. J. and Lee W. R., *The German Family*, London, Barnes and Noble, 1981.

Golde G., *Catholics and Protestants. Agricultural Modernization in Two German Villages*, New York, Academic Press, 1975.

Khera S., 'An Austrian peasant village under rural industrialization', *Behavior Sciences Notes*, VII, 1972, pp. 29–36.

Khera S., 'Illegitimacy and modes of inheritance', *Ethnology*, XX, 1981, pp. 307–23.

Knodel J., *The Decline of Fertility in Germany*, Princeton, New Jersey, Princeton University Press, 1975.

Knodel J. and Mayres M. J., 'Urban and rural marriage patterns in imperial Germany', *Journal of Family History*, vol. 1, no. 2, winter 1976, pp. 120–61.

Laslett P., 'The stem-family hypothesis and its privileged position', pp. 89–112 in F. W. Wachter, E. A. Hammel, P. Laslett, *Statistical Studies of Historical Social Structure*, New York, Academic Press, 1978.

Le Play F., 'Armurier de la fabrique demi-rurale collective de Solingen (Westphalie)', *LOE*, vol. 3, chap. 4, pp. 153–203.

Le Play F., 'Compagnon menuisier de Vienne (Autriche)', *LOE*, vol. 5, chap. 1, pp. 1–59.

Le Play F., 'Mineur des corporations de mines d'argent et de plomb du haut Hartz (Hanovre)', *LOE*, vol. 3, chap. 3, pp. 99–152.

Le Play F., 'Mineur des gites de mercure d'Idria (Carniole)', *LOE*, vol. 6, chap. 1, pp. 1–33.

Le Play F., 'Tisserand de Godesberg (province rhénane)', *LOE*, vol. 5, chap. 2, pp. 60–102.

Sabean D., 'Parenté et tenure en Allemagne à la fin du Moyen Age', *Annales ESC*, 27, 1972, pp. 903–22.

Schreber D. P., *Mémoires d'un névropathe*, Paris, Éditions du Seuil, 1975.

Thompson L., 'Some limitations of the peasant concept', *Anthropologica*, Special Issue, 'Modernization and tradition in Central European rural cultures', pp. 59–82.

Tönnies F., *Community and Society* (Gemeinschaft und Gesellschaft), New York, Harper and Row, 1963.

Bohemia

Horska P., 'Fécondité illégitime et marché matrimonial dans les pays tchèques du XVIIe au XXe siècle', in J. Dupâquier et al., *Marriage and Remarriage in Populations of the Past*, New York, Academic Press, 1981.

The Population of Czechoslovakia, CICRED, World Population Year 1974.

Salzmann Z. and Scheufler V., *Komarov: A Czech Farming Village*, New York, Holt, Rinehart and Winston, 1974.

Belgium

Démographie de la Belgique de 1921 à 1939, Brussels, Office central de la statistique, 1943.

Helin E., 'Size of households before the industrial revolution: the case of Liège in 1801', *HFPT*, pp. 319—34.

Le Play F., 'Compositeur-typographe de Bruxelles (Belgique)', *LOE*, vol. 5, chap. 3, pp. 103—49.

Recensement belge de 1961, tome 6.1, *Recensement des ménages et noyaux familiaux*, Brussels, Institut national de la statistique.

Van Assche-Vancauwenbergh et al., *Cinq Etudes de démographie locale* (XVIIe—XIXe s.), Pro civitate. Collection 'Histoire', 8° series, no. 2, Brussels, 1963.

Van De Walle E., 'Household dynamics in a Belgian village', *Journal of Family History*, no. 1, 1976, pp. 80—94.

Norway and Sweden

Alström C. H., 'First-cousin marriage in Sweden 1750—1844', *Acta Genetica et Statistica Medica*, 1958, pp. 296—369.

Barnes J. A., 'Land rights and kinship in two Bremnes hamlets', *The Journal of the Royal Anthropological Institute*, 1957, pp. 31—56.

Beauchet L., 'Formation et dissolution du mariage dans le droit islandais au Moyen Age', *Nouvelle revue historique du droit français et étranger*, Paris, 1887.

Gronseth E., 'Notes on the historical development of the relation between nuclear family, kinship system and the wider social structure in Norway', *FEW*, pp. 225—47.

Lehr E., *Eléments de droit civil scandinave*, Paris, 1901.

Le Play F., 'Fondeur des usines à cobalt de Buskerud (Norvège méridionale)', *LOE*, vol. 3, chap. 2, pp. 54—98.

Le Play F., 'Forgeron des usines à fer de Dannemora (Suède septentrionale)', *LOE*, vol. 3, chap. 1, pp. 1—53.

Sundt E., *On marriage in Norway*, Cambridge, Cambridge University Press, translated and introduced by M. Drake, 1980.

Scotland

Smith T. B., *Scotland* (The British Commonwealth. The Development of its Laws and Constitutions), London, Stevens and Sons, 1962.

White South Africans

Argyle J., 'The myth of the elementary family: a comparative account of variations in family households amongst a group of South African whites', *African Studies*, vol. 36, no. 2, 1977, pp. 105–18.

French Minorities: Bretons, Occitans, Québecois

Burguière A., *Bretons de Plozévet*, Paris, Flammarion, 1977.

Collomp A., 'Famille nucléaire et famille élargie en Haute-Provence au XVIIe siècle', *Annales ESC*, vol. 27, no. 4–5, 1972, pp. 969–75.

Fine-Souriac A., 'La famille-souche pyrénéenne au XIXe siècle: quelques réflexions de méthode', *Annales ESC*, 1977, pp. 478–87.

Gold J., *Communautés et cultures. Éléments pour une ethnologie du Canada français*, Québec, Éditions HRW, 1973.

Le Play F., 'Bordier dit pen-ty de la Basse-Bretagne', *LOE*, vol. 4, chap. 7, pp. 336–9.

Le Play F., 'Paysan basque du Labourd (France)', *LOE*, vol. 5, chap. 5, pp. 192–258.

Le Play F., 'Paysans à famille-souche du Lavedan (Béarn)', *LOE*, vol. 4, chap. 9, pp. 445–510.

Spanish Minorities: Basques, Catalans, Galicians

Iszaevich A., 'Corporate household and ecocentric kinship groups in Catalonia', *Ethnology*, XX, 1981, pp. 277–90.

Iszaevich A., 'Household renown: the traditional naming system in Catalonia', *Ethnology*, XIX, 1980, pp. 315–25.

Le Play F., 'Pêcheur côtier de Saint-Sébastien (Pays basque)', *LOE*, vol. 4, chap. 6, pp. 291–335.

Lison-Tolosana C., *Anthropologia cultural de Galicia*, Madrid, Sigle XXI de España Editores, 1971.

Ireland

Arensberg C., *The Irish Countryman*, New York, American Museum Science Books, 1968 (1st edn 1937).

Cullen L. M., Furet F., *Irlande et France. Pour une histoire rurale comparée*, Paris, Éditions de l'École des hautes études en sciences sociales, 1981.

Israel

Chouraqui A., *La Vie quotidienne des hommes de la Bible*, Paris, Hachette, 1978.

Della Pergola S., *Jewish and Mixed Marriages in Milan 1901–1968*, Jerusalem, Hebrew University of Jerusalem, 1972.

Lods A., *Israël, des origines au milieu du VIIIe siècle*, Paris, Albin Michel, 1949.

Zagouri A., *Le Régime successoral des Israélites marocains*, Paris, Librairie générale de droit et de jurisprudence, 1959.

Gypsies

Cohn W., *The Gypsies*, London, Addison Wesley Publishing Company, Reading, Massachusetts, 1973.

Quintana B. B. and Floyd L. G., *Qué Gitano! Gypsies of Southern Spain*, New York, Holt, Rinehart and Winston, 1972.

Stoyanovitch K., *Les Tsiganes. Leur ordre social*, Paris, Marcel Rivière, 1974.

Japan

Caudill W. and Weinstein H., 'Maternal care and infant behaviour in Japanese and American urban middle class families', *FEW*, pp. 39—71.

Dore R., *Shinohata: A Portrait of a Japanese Village*, London, Allen Lane, 1978.

Embree J. F., *Suye Mura. A Japanese Village*, Chicago, University of Chicago Press, 1939.

Hayami A. and Uchida N., 'Size of household in a Japanese county through the Tokugawa era', *HFPT*, pp. 474—515.

Hsu F. L. K., *Iemoto: The heart of Japan*, London, John Wiley, 1975.

Kitano S., 'Dozoku and kindred in a Japanese rural society', *FEW*, pp. 248—69.

Lebra T. S., *Japanese Patterns of Behaviour*, Honolulu, University Press of Hawaï, 1976.

Makino T., 'Juvenile delinquency and home training', *FEW*, pp. 137—51.

Nakane C., 'An interpretation of the size and structure of the household in Japan over three centuries', *HFPT*, pp. 517—43.

Nakane C., *Kinship and Economic Organisation in Rural Japan*, London, Athlone Press, 1967.

Norbeck E., *Takashima: A Japanese Fishing Community*, Salt Lake City, University of Utah Press, 1954.

Population Census of Japan, 1975, vol. 2, whole Japan (results of complete count tabulation). Bureau of Statistics. Office of the prime minister, 1977.

Smith R.J., 'Small families, small households and residential instability: town and city in 'pre-modern' Japan', *HFPT*, pp. 325—471.

Suenar M. 'First-child inheritance in Japan', *Ethnology*, XI, 1972, pp. 122—6.

Yokoe K., 'Historical trends in home discipline', *FEW*, pp. 175—86.

Korea

Choi J.S., 'Comparative study of the traditional families in Korea, Japan and China', *FEW*, p. 202—10.

Korea Statistical Yearbook, 1970, p. 355. Inmates of welfare institutions.

Lee M., 'Consanguineous group and its function in the Korean community', *FEW*, pp. 338—47.

Nam il Kim, Byoung Mohk Choi, *Preference for Number and Sex of Children and Contraceptive Use in Korea*, World Fertility Survey, no. 22, London, June 1981.

The Population of Korea, CICRED, World Population Year 1974.

Statistics on Population and Family Planning in Korea, vol. I, December 1978, Korea Institute for Family Planning, Seoul.

Yun Shik Chang, Hae Young Lee, Evi Young Yu, Tai Hwan Kwoj, *A Study of the Korean Population*, Seoul, 1974.

Absolute nuclear family

England and the Anglo-Saxon World (USA, Australia, Canada, New Zealand)

Anderson M., *Family Structure in Nineteenth-Century Lancashire*, Cambridge, Cambridge University Press, 1971.

Fletcher R., *The Family and Marriage in Britain*, London, Penguin Books, 1973.

Greven P.J., 'The average size of families and households in the province of Massachusetts in 1764 and the United States in 1790: an overview', *HFPT*, pp. 545−60.

Laslett P., 'Mean household size in England since the sixteenth century', *HFPT*, pp. 125−58.

Le Play F., 'Coutelier de la fabrique urbaine collective de Londres (Middlesex)', *LOE*, vol. 3 chap. 6, pp. 273−317.

Le Play F., 'Coutelier de la fabrique urbaine collective de Sheffield (Yorkshire)', *LOE*, vol. 3, chap. 7, pp. 318−63.

Le Play F., 'Fondeur des usines à fer à la houille au Derbyshire', *LOE*, vol. 3, chap. 9, pp. 400−36.

Le Play F., 'Menuisier de la ville de Sheffield (Yorkshire)', *LOE*, vol. 3, chap. 8, pp. 364−99.

Macfarlane A., *The Family Life of Ralph Josselin. A Seventeenth-Century Clergyman*, Cambridge, Cambridge University Press, 1970.

Macfarlane A., *The Origins of English Individualism*, Oxford, Basil Blackwell, 1978.

Marriage and Divorce Statistics, Office of Population Censuses and Surveys, London 1978.

Pinchbeck I. and Hewitt M., *Children in English Society*, London, Routledge and Kegan Paul, 1969.

Pryor E.T., 'Rhode Island family structure: 1875 and 1960', *HFPT*, pp. 571−89.

Williams W.M., *The Sociology of an English Village. Gosforth*, London, Routledge and Kegan Paul, 1969.

Willmott P. and Young M., *Family and Kinship in East London*, London, Penguin books, 1957.

Wrightson K. and Levine D., *Poverty and Piety in an English Village. Terling 1525−1700*, New York, Academic Press, 1979.

Denmark

Elkitt J., 'Household structure in Denmark 1769—1890', in S. Akerman, H. C. Johansen, D. Gaunt, eds, *Chance and Change. Social and Economic Studies in Historical Demography in the Baltic Area*, Odense, Odense University Press, 1978.

Johansen J.C., 'The position of the old in the rural household in a traditional society', *Scandinavian Economic History Review*, 24, 1976, pp. 129—42.

Johansen J.C., 'Some aspects of Danish rural population structure in 1787', *Scandinavian Economic History Review*, 20, 1972, pp. 61—70.

Holland

Kooy G.A., 'Rural nuclear family life in contemporary western society', *FEW*, pp. 270—317.

Le Play F., 'Pêcheur côtier, maître de barques de l'île de Marken (Hollande septentrionale)', *LOE*, vol. 3, chap. 5, pp. 204—72.

Van der Woude A.M., 'Variations in the size and structure of the household in the united provinces of the Netherlands in the seventeenth and eighteenth centuries', *HFPT*, pp. 299—318.

West-Central France

Le Bras H. and Todd E., *L'Invention de la France*, Paris, Hachette, 1981, pp. 118—19, carte I, 1, 6.

Le Play F. 'Le manœuvre-agriculteur du Maine', *LOE*, vol. 6, summary of monography, pp. 122—42.

Le Play F., 'Tisserand de Mamers (Maine)', *LOE*, vol. 6, chap. 5, pp. 193—227.

Egalitarian nuclear family

France

Blayo Y., 'Size and structure of households in a northern French village between 1836 and 1861', *HFPT*, pp. 255—65.

De Brandt A., *Droit et Coutumes des populations de la France en matière successorale*, Paris, 1901.

Dupâquier J. et Jadin L., 'Structure of household and family in Corsica, 1769—71', *HFPT*, pp. 283—97.

Jollivet M., Mendras H. et al., *Les Collectivités rurales françaises*, Paris, Armand Colin, 1971.

Le Bras H. and Todd E., *L'Invention de la France*, Paris, Hachette, 1981.

Le Play F., 'Bordier de la Champagne pouilleuse', *LOE*, vol. 5, chap. 7, pp. 323—71.

Le Play F., 'Bordier-émigrant du Laonnais', *LOE*, vol. 6, chap. 3, pp. 84—122.

Le Play F., 'Charpentier (du devoir) de Paris', *LOE*, vol. 5, chap. 9, pp. 424—78.

Le Play F., 'Chiffonnier de Paris', *LOE*, vol. 6, chap. 6, pp. 257–327.
Le Play F., 'Débardeur de Port-Marly (banlieue de Paris)', *LOE*, vol. 6, chap. 9, pp. 442–92.
Le Play F., 'Maître-blanchisseur de Clichy (banlieue de Paris)', *LOE*, vol. 5, chap. 8, pp. 372–423.
Le Play F., 'Manœuvre à famille nombreuse de Paris', *LOE*, vol. 6, chap. 7, pp. 327–72.
Le Play F., 'Tailleur d'habits de Paris', *LOE*, vol. 6, chap. 8, pp. 387–441.
Sutter J. and Tabah L., 'Fréquence et répartition des mariages consanguins en France', *Population*, 1948, pp. 607–30.
Yver J., *Égalité entre héritiers et exclusion des enfants dotés. Essai de géographie coutumière*, Paris, Sirey, 1966.

Switzerland (French-speaking)

Le Play F., 'Horloger de la fabrique collective de Genève', *LOE*, vol. 6, chap. 2, pp. 34–83.
Netting R.M., 'Household dynamics in a nineteenth century Swiss village', *Journal of Family History*, vol. 4, no. 1, spring 1979, pp. 39–59.

Poland

Barnett C.R., *Poland, Its People, Its Society, Its Culture*, New Haven, Human Relations Area Files Press, 1958.
Kula W., 'La seigneurie et la famille paysanne dans la Pologne du dix-huitième siècle', *Annales ESC*, 27, 1972, pp. 949–58.
The Population of Poland, CICRED, World Population Year 1974.
Rocznik demograficzny, Warsaw, 1980, pp. 60–3, 'Population and households by relationship to head of household in 1978'.

Italy

Banfield E.C., *The Moral Basis of a Backward Society*, New York, The Free Press, 1958.
Barberis C., *Sociologia rurale*, Bologne, Edizione agricola, 1965.
Pellizi C., 'Structures familiales en Italie', *Sociologie comparée de la famille contemporaine*, Paris, CNRS 1955, pp. 117–28.
Schnapper D., *Sociologie de l'Italie*, Paris, PUF, 1974.

Greece

Du Boulay J., *Portrait of a Greek Mountain Village*, Oxford, Oxford University Press, 1974.
Friedl E., *Vasilika. A Village in Modern Greece*, New York, Holt, Rinehart and Winston, 1962.
Kenna M.E., 'Houses, fields and graves: property and ritual obligations in a Greek island', *Ethnology*, xv, 1976, pp. 21–34.
Statistiques du mouvement de la population (Greece), Athens, 1940, pp. 20–31 (age at marriage).

Romania

Keefe E.K. et al., *Area Handbook for Romania*, Washington, 1972.
The Population of Romania CICRED World Population Year 1974.
Recensement de 1930, vol. IX, Bucharest, p. 17 (household by region).
Stahl H.H., *Les Anciennes Communautès villageoises roumaines*, Paris, CNRS, 1963.

Spain

Familias y Nucleos Familiares, segun la Composicion, el Tamane, y el Area geografica. 1976 Census, III: Caracteristas de la poblacion. Instituto nacional de estadistica, Madrid.
Freeman S.T., *Neighbours. The Social Contract in a Castilian Hamlet*, Chicago, University of Chicago Press, 1970.
Pitt-Rivers J.A., *The People of the Sierra*, London, Weidenfeld and Nicholson, 1954.
Le Play F., 'Métayer de la Vieille Castille', *LOE*, vol. 4, chap. 5, pp. 247–90.
La Poblacion de España, CICRED, World Population Year 1974.

Portugal

La Population du Portugal, CICRED, World Population Year 1974.
Anuario demografico, Portugal, 1961 (age at marriage, household structure.

Latin America

IX Censo general de Poblacion 1970. Resumen general, Mexico D.F., 1972, pp. 83–170.
Fabregat C.E., 'Familia y matrimonio en Mexico. El patron cultural', *Revista de Indias*, no. 115–18, Madrid, 1969.
Flanet V., *La Maîtresse mort. Violence au Mexique*, Paris, Berger-Levrault, 1982.
Hammel E.A., 'Some characteristics of rural village and urban slum populations on the coast of Peru', *Southwestern Journal of Anthropology*, 20, 1964, pp. 346–58.
Harris M., *Town and Country in Brazil*, New York, Columbia University Press, 1956.
Lewis O., *A Death in the Sanchez family*, London, Penguin books, 1972.
Lewis O., *The Children of Sanchez*, London, Penguin books, 1964.
La Poblacion de Argentina, CICRED, World Population Year 1974.
La Population du Brésil, CICRED, World Population Year 1974.
La Poblacion de Colombia, CICRED, World Population Year 1974.
La Poblacion de Costa Rica, CICRED, World Population Year 1974.
La Poblacion de Guatemala, CICRED, World Population Year 1974.
La Poblacion de Panama, CICRED, World Population Year 1974.
La Poblacion del Peru, CICRED, World Population Year 1974.
La Poblacion de Venezuela, CICRED, World Population Year 1974.

Ethiopia

Hoben A., *Land Tenure Among the Ambara of Ethiopia: The Dynamics of Cognatic Descent*, Chicago, University of Chicago Press, 1973.
Levine D.N., *Wax and Gold, Tradition and Innovation in Ethiopian Culture*, Chicago, University of Chicago Press, 1967.

Endogamous community family

Arab World

Ayoub M.R., 'Parallel cousin marriage and endogamy: a study in sociometry', *Southwestern Journal of Anthropology*, 15, 1959, pp. 266—75.
Barth F., 'Father's brother's daughter marriage in Kurdestan', *Southwestern Journal of Anthropology*, 10, 1954, pp. 164—79.
Bourdieu P., *Sociologie de l'Algérie*, Paris, PUF, 1980.
Camilleri C., *Jeunesse, famille et développement. Essai sur le changement socioculturel dans un pays du tiers monde (Tunisie)*, Paris, CNRS, 1973.
Charles R., *Le Droit musulman*, Paris, PUF, 1956.
El Akim T., *Un substitut de campagne en Égypte*, Paris, Plon, 1974.
Gaudefroy-Demombynes, *Les Institutions musulmanes*, Paris, Flammarion, 1921.
Germanos-Ghazaly L., *Le Paysan, le terre et la femme. Organisation sociale d'un village du Mont-Liban*, Paris, Maisonneuve, 1978.
Khuri F.I., 'Parallel cousin marriage reconsidered', *Man*, 5, 1970, pp. 597—617.
Le Play F., 'Menuisier-charpentier de Tanger (Maroc)', *LOE*, vol. 2, chap. 9, pp. 398—446.
Le Play F., 'Paysans en communauté et en polygamie de Bousrah (Syrie)', *LOE*, vol. 2, chap. 8, pp. 304—97.
Lewis I.M., *Somali Culture, History and Social Institutions*, London, London School of Economics, 1981.
Patai R., *The Arab Mind*, New York, Scribner, 1976.
The Population of Egypt, CICRED, World Population Year 1974.
La Population du Liban, CICRED, World Population Year 1974.
La Population du Maroc, CICRED, World Population Year 1974.
La Population de la Tunisie, CICRED, World Population Year 1974.
Randolph R.R. and Coult A.D., 'A computer analysis of Bedouin marriage', *Southwestern Journal of Anthropology*, 24, 1968, pp. 83—99.
Roberts R., *The Social Laws of the Quran*, London, Curzon Press, 1925 and 1980.
Tabutin D., *Mortalité infantile et juvénile en Algérie*, Paris PUF, 1976, cahier de l'INED (Institut National d'Etudes Démographiques), no. 77.
Tillon G., *Le Harem et les Cousins*, Paris, Éditions du Seuil, 1966.
Valensi L., *Fellahs tunisiens*, Paris Mouton, 1977.
Vallin J., 'La nuptialité en Tunisie', *Population*, 1971, pp. 250—66.
Weekes R.V., ed., *Muslim Peoples. A World Ethnographic Survey*, Westport New York), London, Greenwood Press, 1978.

Central Asia: Turkey, Iran, Afghanistan, Pakistan and Bangladesh, Soviet Central Asia.

Ahmed A.S., *Millennium and Charisma among Pathans. A Critical Essay in Social Anthropology*, London, Routledge and Kegan Paul, 1976.

Bennigsen A. and Lemercier-Quelquejay C., *L'Islam en Union soviétique*, Paris, Payot, 1968.

Blanc J.-C., *L'Afghanistan et ses populations*, Brussels, Éditions Complexe, 1976.

Dirks S., *La Famille musulmane turque*, Paris, Mouton, 1969.

Karpath K.H., *The Gecekondu: Rural Migration and Urbanization*, Cambridge, Cambridge University Press, 1976 (Turkey).

Keyser J.M.B., 'The middle eastern case. Is there a marriage rule?' *Ethnology*, XIII, 1974, pp. 293–309.

Mac Pastern C., 'Cousin marriage amoung the Zikri Baluch of coastal Pakistan', *Ethnology*, xviii, 1979, pp. 31–47.

Magnarella P.J., *Tradition and Change in a Turkish Town*, New York, Wiley, 1974.

The Population of Turkey, CICRED, World Population Year 1974.

Poulton M. and R., *L'Afghanistan*, Paris, PUF, 1981.

Stirling P., *Turkish Village*, London, Weidenfeld and Nicholson, 1965.

Weekes R.V., ed., *Muslim Peoples. A World Ethnographic Survey*, Westport (New York), London, Greenwood Press, 1978.

Asymmetrical community family

India

Ahmad I., *Family, Kinship, and Marriage among Muslims in India*, New Delhi, Manohar, 1976.

Alam I. and Cleland J., *Illustrative Analysis: Recent Fertility Trends in Sri Lanka*, World Fertility Survey, no. 25, London, November 1981.

Behura N.F., *Peasant Potters of Orissa*, New Dehli, Sterling Publishers, 1978.

Brow J., *Vedda Villages of Anurdhapura*, Washington, University of Washington Press, 1978.

Census of India, 1971. Pocket Book of Population Statitics, New Delhi, 1972.

Census of India, 1971. Social and Cultural Tables, New Delhi, 1st ser., part II–C(II).

Davis M., 'The politics of family life in rural west Bengal', *Ethnology*, xv, 1976, pp. 189–200.

Dumont L., *Une sous-caste de l'Inde du Sud*, Paris, Mouton, 1957.

Giri Raj Gupta, *Marriage, Religion and Society. Pattern of Change in an Indian Village*, London, Curzon Press, 1974.

Kapadia K.M., *Marriage and Family in India*, Calcutta, Oxford University Press 1981.

Kumar J., 'Family structure in the Hindu society of rural India', in G. Kuriam, ed., *The Family in India, a regional view*, Paris — La Haye, Mouton, 1974.

Leach E.R., 'Polyandry, inheritance and the definition of marriage', pp. 151—62, in J. Goody, *Kinship*, London, Penguin Books, 1971.

Leach E.R., *Pul Eliya, A village in Ceylon*, Cambridge, Cambridge University Press, 1961.

Mencher J.P., 'Changing familial roles among south Malabar Nayars', *Southwestern Journal of Anthropology*, 18, 1962, pp. 230—45.

Narain D., 'Interpersonal relationships in the Hindu family', *FEW*, pp. 454—80.

Parry J.P., *Caste and Kinship in Kangra*, London, Routledge and Kegan Paul, 1979.

The Population of Sri Lanka, CICRED, World Population Year 1974.

Punit A.E., *Social Systems in Rural India*, New Dehli, Sterling Publishers, 1978.

Puthenkalam Père J., 'Marriage and family in Kerala', *Journal of Comparative Family Studies*, Calgary, Canada, 1977.

Shah A.M., *The Household Dimension of the Family in India*, California, University of California Press, 1974.

Srinivas M.N., ed., *India's Villages*, Bombay, MPP, 1955.

Tambiah S.J., 'Polyandry in Ceylon, with special reference to the Laggala region', in Von Fürer-Haimendorf C., *Caste and Kin in Nepal, India and Ceylon*, London, Asia Publishing House, 1966.

Indians of Chile

Faron L.C., *The Mapuche Indians of Chile*, New York, Holt, Rinehart and Winston, 1968.

Faron L.C., *Mapuche Social Structure*, Illinois Studies in Anthropology, no. 1, 1961.

Stuchlik M., *Life on a Half-Share. Mechanisms of Social Recruitment among the Mapuche of Southern Chile*, London, C. Hurst, 1976.

Anomic family

South-East Asia — general

Blayo Y., 'Les premiers mariages féminins en Asie', *Population*, 1978, pp. 951—86.

Brown D.E., *Principles of Social Structure — Southeast Asia*, London, Duckworth, 1976.

Condominas G., *L'Espace social. A propos de l'Asie du Sud-Est*, Paris, Flammarion, 1980.

Smith D.P., *Age at First Marriage*, Comparative series, no. 7, World Fertility Survey, London, April 1980.

Burma

Haas M.R., 'Sibling terms as used by marriage partners', *Southwestern Journal of Anthropology*, 1969, no. 25, pp. 228—35.

Henderson J.W. et al., *Area Handbook for Burma*, Washington, American University, 1971.

Nash J. and M., 'Marriage, family and population growth in Upper Burma', *Southwestern Journal of Anthropology*, 19, 1963, pp. 251–66.

Spiro M.E., *Kinship and Marriage in Burma*, California, University of California Press, 1977.

Thailand

Annuaire statistique de Thaïlande 1974–1975 (2517–2518), Bangkok, pp. 48–51 (average household size by district).

Embree J.F., 'Thaïland. A loosely-structured social system', *American Anthropologist*, 1950, vol. 52.

Evers H.D., ed., *Loosely Structured Social Systems: Thaïland in Comparative Perspective*, 'Southeast Asia Studies', Cultural report series, no. 17, Yale University.

Hamburger L., 'Fragmentierte Gesellschaft. Die Struktur der Thaï Familie', *Köln Zeitschrifte fur Soziologie und Sozialpsychologie*, 17, 1965.

Kaufman H.K., *Bangkhuad. A Community Study in Thaïland*, Locust Valley, New York, Association for Asian Studies, 1960.

Kingshill K., *Kudaeng. The Red Tomb. A Village Study in Northern Thaïland*, Chiangmai, Thaïland, The Prince's Royal College, 1960.

The Population of Thailand, CICRED, World Population Year 1974.

Potter S.H., *Family Life in a Northern Thaï Village*, California, University of California Press, 1977.

Rural Abortion in Thaïland: A National Survey of Practitioners, Research and Evaluation. National Family Planning Program, Bangkok, January 1979.

Laos

Levy P., *Histoire du Laos*, Paris, PUF, 1974.

Taillard C., 'L'espace social: quelques réflexions à propos de deux exemples au Laos', *Asie du Sud-Est et Monde insulindien*, vol. 8, no. 2, Paris, 1977, pp. 81–103.

Philippines

Dozier E.P., *The Kalinga of Northern Luzon, Philippines*, New York, Holt, Rinehart and Winston, 1967.

Philippines, 1970. Census of Population and Housing, National Census and Statistics Office, Manila, Philippines.

The Population of the Philippines, CICRED, World Population Year 1974.

Quisumbing L.R., *Marriage Customs in Rural Cebu*, Cebu City, University of San Carlos, 1967.

Reyes F., *Evaluation of the Republic of the Philippines Fertility Survey 1978*, World Fertility Survey, no. 19, London, March 1981.

Takanashi A., *Land and Peasants in Central Luzon*, Honolulu, East-West Center Press, 1969.

Cambodia

Delvert J., *Le Paysan cambodgien*, Paris, Mouton, 1973.
Ea Meng-Try, *Histoire de la population khmère*, unpublished thesis, Université René-Descartes, Paris V, 1980.
Martel G *Lovea, village des environs d'Angkor*, Paris, École française d'Extrême-Orient, 1975.

Malaysia

Djamour J., *Malay Kinship and Marriage in Singapore*, London, Athlone Press, 1959.
Firth R., *Housekeeping among Malay Peasants*, London, Athlone Press, 1966.
Husin Ali S., *Malay Peasant Society and Leadership*, East Asia Social Science Monographs, Oxford University Press, 1975.
Jones G.W., 'Malay marriage and divorce in peninsular Malaysia' *Population and Development Review*, vol. 7, no. 2, June 1981, pp. 255–78.
The Population of Malaysia, CICRED, World Population Year 1974.
Tey Nai Peng Abdurahman I., *Factors Affecting Contraceptive use in Peninsular Malaysia*, World Fertility Survey, no. 23, London, November 1981.
Veron J., 'Appartenance ethnique et comportement des populations de Malaisie et de Singapour', *Population*, 1978, pp. 937–50.

Indonesia

Freeman J.D., 'The family system of the Iban of Borneo', in J. Goody, ed., *The Developmental Cycle in Domestic Groups*, Cambridge, Cambridge University Press, 1969, pp. 15–52.
Guermonprez J.F., 'L'organisation villageoise à Bali', in *Cheminements. Écrits offerts à Georges Condominas, Asie du Sud-Est et Monde insulindien*, Paris, 1982, pp. 37–53.
Koentjaraningrat R.M., *A Preliminary Description of the Javanese Kinship System*, Yale University, Southeast Asia Studies, 1957.
Loeb E., 'Patrilineal and matrilineal organization in Sumatra. Part 2. The Minangkabau', *American Anthropologist*, 1936, vol. 36, pp. 26–56.
Pelras C., 'Culture, ethnie, espace social. Quelques réflexions autour du cas Bugis', *Asie du Sud-Est et Monde insulindien*, vol. 8, no. 2, Paris, 1977, pp. 57–79.
Polak A., 'Some conflicts over the bride-price in an Indonesian peasant community', *Tropical Man*, IV, 1971, pp. 117–48.
The Population of Indonesia, CICRED, World Population Year 1974.
Population and Manpower Statistics, Jakarta, Penduduk Jawa-Madura, 1978.
Subandrio H., *Javanese Peasant Life. Villages in East Java*, unpublished thesis, London University, 1951.

Madagascar

Bloch M., *Placing the Dead. Tombs, Ancestral Villages and Kinship Organization in Madagascar*, London, Seminar Press, 1971.
Nelson H.D. et al., *Area Handbook for the Malagasy Republic*, Washington, 1973.
Raminosoa N., 'Recherche sur l'organisation sociale des Vakinankaratra', *Asie du Sud-Est et Monde insulindien*, vol. 7, no. 4, Paris, 1976, pp. 197–202.

Indians of the Andes

Clastres P., *La Société contre l'État*, Paris, Minuit, 1974.
Labarre W., *The Aymara Indians of the Lake Titicaca Plateau, Bolivia*, American Anthropological Association, 1948.
Korb G.M., *Ticaco. An Aymara Indian Community*, New York, Cornell University Press, 1966.
McEwen W.J., *Changing Rural Society. A Study of Communities in Bolivia*, Oxford, Oxford University Press, 1975.
Mason J.S., *The Ancient Civilizations of Peru*, London, Pelican, 1968.
Necker L., *Indiens guaranis et Chamanes franciscains, 1580–1800*, Paris, Antropos, 1979.
Reichel-Dolmatoff G. et A., *The People of Aritama. The Cultural Personality of a Columbian Mestizo Village*, Chicago, University of Chicago Press, 1961.
Steward J.H., *Handbook of South American Indians*, vol. 2, *The Andean Civilizations*, Washington, 1944.
Steward J.H., *Handbook of South American Indians*, vol. 3, *The Tropical Forest Tribes*, Washington, 1948.
Weil T.E., *Area Handbook for Bolivia*, 2nd edn. Washington, 1974.
Weil T.E., *Area Handbook for Paraguay*, Washington, 1972.
Von Hagen V.W., *The Aztec. Man and Tribe*, New York, New American Library, 1961.
Wolf E.R., *Sons of the Shaking Earth*, Chicago, University of Chicago Press, 1959.

African systems

Clignet R., 'Determinants of African Polygyny', pp. 163–80, in J. Goody, ed., *Kinship*, London, Penguin Books, 1971.
Dupire M., 'Matériaux pour l'étude de l'endogamie des Peuls du Cercle de Kedouja', *Cahiers du Centre de recherches anthropologiques*, no. 2, 1963, pp. 223–8.
Girling F.K., *The Acholi of Uganda*, London, Her Majesty's Stationery Office, 1960.
Goody J. and Buckley J., 'Inheritance and women's labour in Africa', *Africa*, 43, 1973, pp. 108–21.

Goody J. and Goody E., 'Cross-cousin marriage in northern Ghana', *Man*, 1, 1966, pp. 343–55.

Goody J. and Goody E., 'The fission of domestic groups among the Lo Dagaba', in J. Goody, ed. *The Developmental Cycle in Domestic Groups*, Cambridge, Cambridge University Press, 1969, pp. 53–91.

Goody J. and Goody E., 'Sideways or downwards. Lateral and vertical succession. Inheritance and descent in Africa and Eurasia', *Man*, New series, 5, 1970, pp. 627–38.

Gutman H.G., 'La composition de la famille et du foyer noirs après la guerre de Sécession', *Annales ESC*, 27, 1972, pp. 1197–218.

Gutman H.G., 'Famille et groupe de parenté chez les Afro-américains en esclavage dans la plantation de Good Hope (Caroline du Sud) 1760–1860', in S. Mintz., ed., *Esclave = Facteur de production*, Paris, Dunod, 1981.

Henderson R.N., *The King in Every Man. Evolutionary trends in Onitsha Ibo Society and Culture*, New Haven, Yale University Press, 1972.

Holy L., *Neighbours and Kinsmen. A Study of the Berti People of Darfur*, London, Hurst, 1974.

Huber H., *Marriage and the Family in Rural Bukwaya*, Studia Ethnographia Friburgensia, Friboug, The University Press, 1970.

Hurault J., 'Éleveurs et cultivateurs des hauts plateaux de l'Adamawa', *Population*, no. 5, 1970, pp. 1039–84.

Kennedy J.G., *Struggle for Change in a Nubian Community*, Palo Alto, Mayfield, 1977.

Krige E.J., 'Asymmetrical matrilateral cross-cousin marriage. The Lovedu case', *African Studies*, vol. 34, no. 4, 1975, pp. 231–57.

Kyewalyanga F.X., *Marriage Customs in East Africa*, Fribourg, Renner Publications, 1978.

Lawrance J.C.D., *The Iteso. Fifty years of Change in a Nilohamitic Tribe of Uganda*, Oxford, Oxford University Press, 1957.

Mair L., *African Marriage and Social Change*, London, Frank Cass & Co. 1960.

Mair L., *Native Marriage in Baganda*, Oxford, Oxford University Press, 1940.

Marris P., 'African families in the process of change', *FEW*, pp. 397–409.

Martin Révérend père V., 'Structure de la famille chez les Sérères et les Ouolofs au Sénégal', *Population*, pp. 77–96.

Mogey J.M., 'The Negro family system in the United States', *FEW*, pp. 442–53.

Nadel S.F., *The Nuba*, Oxford, Oxford University Press, 1947.

N'Diaye B., *Les Castes au Mali*, Bamako, Éditions populaires, 1970.

Phillips A. and Morris H.F., *Marriage Laws in Africa*, Oxford, Oxford University Press, 1971.

The Population of Ghana, CICRED, World Population Year 1974.

The Population of Liberia, CICRED, World Population Year 1974.

Richards A.I., *The Changing Structure of a Ganda Village*, Nairobi, East Africa Publishing House, 1966.

Rose E.J.B., *Colour and Citizenship. A Report on British Race Relations*, Oxford, Oxford University Press, 1969.

Stenning D.J., 'Household viability among the pastoral Fulani', in J. Goody, ed., *The Developmental Cycle in Domestic Groups*, Cambridge, Cambridge University Press, 1969, pp. 92–119.

Wane Y., *Les Toucouleurs du Fouta Tooro (Sénégal). Stratification sociale et structure familiale*, (thesis), Dakar, 1967.

Antiquity

Brehier L., *La Civilisation byzantine*, Paris, Albin Michel, 1950.

César, *La Guerre des Gaules*, Paris, Garnier-Flammarion, 1964.

Ducellier A., *Le Drame de Byzance*, Paris, Hachette, 1976.

Erman A. and Ranke H., *La Civilisation égyptienne*, Paris, Payot, 1980.

Gaudemet J., *Le Droit privé romain*, Paris, Armand Colin, 1974.

Glotz G., *La Cité grecque*, Paris, La renaissance du livre, 1928.

Grimal P., *L'Amour à Rome*, Paris, Les Belles Lettres, 1979.

Hubert H., *Les Celtes et la civilisation celtique*, Paris, Albin Michel, 1974.

Flacelière R., *La Vie quotidienne en Grèce au siècle de Périclès*, Paris, Hachette, 1959.

Fustel de Coulanges, *La Cité antique*, Paris, Hachette, 1927.

Tacite, *La Germanie*, Paris, Les Belles Lettres, 1967.

Villers R., *Rome et le droit privé*, Paris, Albin Michel, 1977.

RESEARCH ON ANTHROPOLOGY AND CULTURE
IN EUROPE AND THE WORLD

Anderson M., ed., *Sociology of the Family*, London, Penguin Books, 1971.

Baechler J., *Les Suicides*, Paris, Calmann-Lévy, 1975.

Barnes J.A., 'The frequency of divorce', pp. 47–99, in A.L. Epstein, ed., *The Craft of Social Anthropology*, London, Tavistock, 1967.

Bertillon J., *Les Naissances illégitimes en France et dans quelques pays d'Europe*, Vienna, IVe Congrès de démographie, 1887.

Bunle H., *Le Mouvement naturel de la population dans le monde de 1906 à 1936*, Paris, Institut national d'études démographiques, 1954.

Chesnais J.-C., *Histoire de la violence*, Paris, Laffont, 1981.

Chesnais J.-C., *Les Morts violentes en France depuis 1826. Comparaisons internationales*, Paris, PUF, 1976.

Clyde-Mitchell J., 'On quantification in social anthropology', pp. 17–45, in A.L. Epstein, ed., *The Craft of Social Anthropology*, London, Tavistock, 1967.

Devereux E.C., 'Socialization in cross-cultural perspective: comparative study of England, Germany and the United States', *FEW*, pp. 72–106.

Douglas J.D., *The Social Meanings of Suicide*, Princeton, Princeton University Press, 1970.

Festy P., *La Fécondité des pays occidentaux de 1870 à 1970*, Paris, PUF, 1979, (Cahiers de l'INED, no. 85).

Flandrin J.-L., *Familles, parenté, maison. Sexualité dans l'ancienne société* Paris, Hachette, 1976.

Fox R., *Kinship and Marriage*, London, Penguin Books, 1967.

Furet F. et Ozouf J., *Lire et écrire: l'alphabétisation des Français de Calvin à Jules Ferry*, Paris, Éditions de Minuit, 1977.

Coode W.J., *World Revolution and Family Patterns*, London, Macmillan, 1963.

Goody J. et al., *Literacy in Traditional Societies*, Cambridge, Cambridge University Press, 1968.

Goody J., Thirsk J., Thompson E.P., eds., *Family and Inheritance in Rural Western Europe*, Cambridge, Cambridge University Press, 1976.

Hajnal J., 'European marriage patterns in perspective', pp. 140–48, in J. Goody, ed., *Kinship*, London, Penguin Books, 1971.

Hartley S.F., *Illegitimacy*, California, University of California Press, 1975.

Huth A.H., *The Marriage of Near Kin*, London, 1887.

Kiev A., *Transcultural Psychiatry*, London, Penguin Books, 1972.

Laslett P. and R. Wall, eds., *Household and Family in Past Time*, Cambridge, Cambridge University Press, 1972.

Laslett P., *Family Life and Illicit Love in Earlier Generations*, Cambridge, Cambridge University Press, 1977.

Laslett P., Oostervenn K., Smith R.M., *Bastardy and its Comparative History*, London, Edward Arnold, 1980.

Le Bras H., *L'Enfant et la Famille dans les pays de l'OCDE. Analyse démographique*, Paris, OECD (Organisation for Economic Co-operation and Development), 1979.

Le Play F., *L'Organisation de la famille*, Tours, Mame, 1875.

Le Play F., *L'Organisation du travail*, Tours, Mame, 1870.

Le Play F., *Les Ouvriers européens*, 6 vols., Tours, Mame, 1879.

Lévi-Strauss C., *Les Structures élémentaires de la parenté*, Paris, Mouton, 2nd edn, 1967.

McEvedy C. and Jones R., *Atlas of World Population History*, London, Penguin Books, 1978.

Mair L., *Marriage*, London, Penguin Books, 1971.

Maisch H., *L'Inceste*, Paris, Laffont, 1970.

Mattila H.E.S., *Les Successions agricoles et la Structure de la société. Une étude en droit comparé*, Helsinki, Juridica, 1979.

Morgan L.H., *Ancient Society*, New York, H. Holt, 1877.

United Nations, *Compendium of Housing Statistics*. New York, 1980.

OCDE, *Perspectives économiques, décembre 1981* (30), Paris.

World Health Organisation *La schizophrénie: étude multinationale*, Geneva, 1977.

World Health Organisation *Le Suicide et les Tentatives de suicide*, Geneva, 1975.

Office statistique des communautés européennes, *Enquête par sondage sur les forces de travail*, Luxemburg, 1981.

Quetelet A. and Heuschling X., *Statistique internationale (population) publiée avec la collaboration des différents états de l'Europe et des Etats-Unis d'Amérique*, Brussels, Hayez, 1865.

Sabean D., 'Aspects of kinship behaviour in rural Western Europe before 1800', in J. Goody, J. Thirsk, E.P. Thompson, eds, *Family and Inheritance in Rural Western Europe*, Cambridge, Cambridge University Press, 1976, pp. 96—111.

Stahl P.H., *Ethnologie de l'Europe de Sud-Est. Une anthologie*, Paris, Mouton, 1974.

Statistical Abstract of the United States, 1978, Bureau of the Census, Washington.

Statistique internationale du mouvement de la population, Ministère du Travail et de la Prévoyance sociale, Paris, Imprimerie Nationale, 1907.

Tapinos G., Piotrow P.T., *Six Billion People, Demographic Dilemmas and World Politics*, New York, McGraw-Hill, 1980.

Thirsk J., 'The European debate on customs of inheritance 1500—1700', in J. Goody, J. Thirsk, E.P. Thompson, eds., *Family and Inheritance in Rural Western Europe*, Cambridge, Cambridge University Press, 1976, pp. 177—91.

IDEOLOGY

Almond G.A and Verba S., *The Civic Culture. Political Attitudes and Democracy in Five Nations*, Boston, Little, Brown and Company, 1965.

André R. and M.-L., *Avec Jésus vers le père* (pour les enfants de 6 à 8 ans), Lyon, Éditions Robert, 1952.

Arrighi G. and Saul J.S., *Essays on the Political Economy of Africa*, New York, Monthly Review Press, 1973.

Arvon H., *L'Anarchisme au xxe siècle*. Paris, PUF, 1979.

Arvon H., *Le Bouddhisme*, Paris, PUF, 1951.

Augustine (Saint), *City of God*, ed. David Knowles, London, Penguin Books, 1972.

Balazs E., *La Bureaucratie céleste*, Paris, Gallimard, 1968.

Baroja J.-C., *Les Sorcières et leur monde*, Paris, Gallimard, 1972.

Bechtold P.K., *Politics in the Sudan*, New York, Praeger, 1976.

Bennassar B., *L'Inquisition espagnole xv—xix siècle*, Paris, Hachette, 1979.

Bernstein E., *Les Présupposés du socialisme*, Paris Éditions du Seuil, 1974 (translation of German edition of 1899).

Blaker M.K., *Japan at the Polls. The House of Councillors Election of 1974*, Washington, American Enterprise Institue for Public Policy Research, 1976.

Bloodworth D., *An Eye for the Dragon. South-east Asia Observed 1954—1973*, London, Penguin Books, 1975.

Bougle C., *Essais sur le régime des castes*, Paris, PUF, 1935.

Blum J., *Lord and Peasant in Russia from the Ninth to the Nineteenth Century*, Princeton, Princeton University Press, 1961.

Buron T. and Gauchon P., *Les Fascismes*, Paris, PUF, 1979.

Butler D. and Kavanagh D., *The British General Election of 1979*, London, Macmillan, 1980.

Castellan G., *L'Allemagne de Weimar 1918—1933*, Paris, Armand Colin, 1972.

Catéchisme à l'usage des diocèses de France, Bourges, Tardy, 1947.

Caviedes C., *The Politics of Chile: A Sociogeographical Assessment*, Boulder, Colorado, Westview Press, 1974.

Cayrac-Blanchard F., *Le Parti communiste indonésien*, Cahier de la Fondation nationale des sciences politiques, no. 26, Paris, 1973.

Cerny K.H., *Germany at the Polls, The Bundestag Election of 1976*, Washington, American Enterprise Institute for Public Policy Research, 1978.

Cerny K.H., *Scandinavia at the Polls*, Washington 1977.

Chaliand G., *L'Enjeu africain*, Paris, Éditions du Seuil, 1980.

Conze E., *Le Bouddhisme*, Paris, Payot, 1971.

Coutrot A. and Dreyfus F., *Les Forces religieuses dans la société française*, Paris, Armand Colin, 1965.

Coverdale J.F., *The Political Transformation of Spain after Franco*, New York, Praeger, 1979.

De Testa F., *Le Pakistan*, Paris, PUF, 1962.

Dickens A.G., *The German Nation and Martin Luther*, London, Edward Arnold, 1974.

Dumont L., *Homo hierarchicus*, Paris, Gallimard, 1966.

Dupont-Bouchat M.-S., Fijhoff W., Muchembled R., *Prophètes et Sorciers dans les Pays-Bas xvie—xviiie siècles*, Paris, Hachette, 1978.

Duverger M., *Les Partis politiques*, Paris, Armand Colin, 1957.

Engels F., *The Origin of the Family*, trans. A. West and D. Torr, London, Lawrence and Wishart 1943.

Fejtö F., *Le Coup de Prague 1948*, Paris, Éditions du Seuil, 1976.

Fejtö F., *La Social-démocratie quand même*, Paris, Laffont, 1980.

Fischer S.L., *The Minor Parties of the Federal Republic of Germany*. The Hague,Nijhoff, 1974.

Fistie P., *La Thaïlande*, Paris, PUF, 1980.

Fol J.-J., *Les Pays nordiques aux xixe et xxe siècles*, Paris, PUF, 1978.

Freud S., *The Future of an Illusion*, London, Hogarth Press, 1973.

Freud S., *Totem and Taboo*, trans. J. Strachley, New York, Norton, 1950.

Front de Libération national, *Charte nationale 1976*, République algérienne démocratique et populaire.

Garaud M. and Szramkiewicz R., *La Révolution française et la Famille*, Paris, PUF, 1978.

Gernet J., *Chine et Christianisme*, Paris, Gallimard, 1982.

Ginzburg C., *Les Batailles nocturnes. Sorcellerie et rituels agraires en Frioul, xvie—xviie siècles*, Verdier, Lagrusse, 1980.

Gonin D., *Thaïlande*, Paris, Éditions du Seuil, 1976.

Graff V., *Les Partis communistes indiens*, Paris, Presses de la Fondation nationale des Sciences politiques, 1974.

Hermet G., *Les Catholiques dans l'Espagne franquiste*, tome 1, *Les Acteurs du jeu politique*, Paris, Presses de la Fondation nationale des Sciences politiques, 1980.

Hermet G., *L'Espagne de Franco*, Paris, Armand Colin, 1974.

Hobsbawm E.J., *Primitive Rebels*, Manchester, Manchester University Press, 1959.

Ib Khaldûn, *Discours sur l'histoire universelle*, (Al-Muqaddima) trans., preface and notes by Vincent Monteil, Paris, Sindbab, 1968.

Isambert F.-A., *Atlas de la pratique religieuse des catholiques en France*, Paris, CNRS, Presses de la Fondation nationale des sciences politiques. 1980.

July R.W., *A History of the African People*, New York, Scribner, 1970.

Ken Ling, *La Vengeance du ciel. Un jeune Chinois dans la Révolution culturelle*, Paris, Laffont, 1981.

Kitzinger U., 'The Austrian election of 1959', *Political Studies*, 9, 1961, pp. 119–40.

Küng H., *Infallible?*, Paris, Desclée de Brouwer, 1971.

Lacouture J., *Survive le peuple cambodgien*, Paris Éditions du Seuil, 1978.

Laveissière M., *Contes du Vietnam*, Pierru, Coubron, 1968.

Lefort R., *Éthiopie, la révolution hérétique*, Paris, Maspero, 1982.

Larner C., *Enemies of God*, London, Chatto and Windus, 1981.

Lerner D., *The Passing of Traditional Society*, New York, The Free Press, 1958.

Lewin L., Jansson B., Sörborn D., *The Swedish Electorate (1887–1968)*, Uppsala, 1972.

Li O., *Histoire de la Corée*, Paris, PUF, 1969.

Lijphart A., *The Politics of Accommodation. Pluralism and Democracy in the Netherlands*, California, University of California Press, 1975.

Lubeigt G., *La Birmanie*, Paris, PUF, 1975.

Mabro R., *The Egyptian Economy 1952–1972*, Oxford, Oxford University Press, 1974.

Macfarlane A., *Witchcraft in Tudor and Stuart England. A Regional and Comparative study*, London, Routledge and Kegan Paul, 1970.

Mahomet, *Le Coran*, Paris, Garnier, 1960.

Mandrou R., *Magistrats et Sorciers en France au xviie siècle*, Paris, Éditions du Seuil, 1980.

Marx K., *Pre-capitalist Economic Formations*, London, Lawrence and Wishart, 1964.

Meyer E., *Ceylon – Sri Lanka*, Paris, PUF, 1977.

Milet J., *Dieu ou le Christ? Les conséquences du christocentrisme dans l'Église catholique du xviie siècle à nos jours*, Paris, Trévise, 1980.

Milza P. and Berstein S., *Le Fascisme italien (1919–1945)*, Paris, Éditions du Seuil, 1980.

Monteil V., *Indonésie*, Paris Éditions du Seuil, 1972.

Myrdal G., *Le Drame de l'Asie*, Paris, Éditions du Seuil, 1976.

Naipaul V.S., *An Area of Darkness*, London, André Deutsch, 1964.

Niedergang M., *Les Vingt Amériques latines*, Paris, Éditions du Seuil, 1969.

Penniman H.R., *Australia at the Polls. The National Election of 1979*, Washington, American Enterprise Institute for Public Policy Research, 1980.

Penniman H.R., *Ireland at the Polls. The Dail Election of 1977*, Washington, American Enterprise Institute for Public Policy Research, 1978.

Penniman H.R., *New Zealand at the Polls. The General Election of 1978*, Washington, American Enterprise Institute for Public Policy Research, 1979.

Penniman H.R., ed., *France at the Polls*, American Enterprise Institute for Public Policy Research, Washington, 1975.

Pin Yathay, *L'Utopie meurtrière* (Cambodia), Paris, Laffont, 1980.

Pons P., *Japon*, Paris, Éditions du Seuil, 1981.

Portal R., *Les Slaves, peuples et nations*, Paris, Armand Colin, 1965.

Raeff M., *Comprendre l'ancien régime russe*, Paris, Éditions du Seuil, 1982.

Robert J., *Le Japon*, Paris, Librairie générale de droit et de jurisprudence, 1969.

Rose R., *Electoral Behaviour. A Comparative Handbook*, New York, The Free Press, 1973.

Rousseau J.-J., The Social Contract, trans. M. Cranston, Penguin Books, 1968.

Rovan J., *Histoire de la social-démocratie allemande*, Paris, Éditions du Seuil, 1978.

Rupnik J., *Histoire de parti communiste tchécoslovaque*, Paris, Presses de la Fondation nationale des Sciences politiques, 1981.

Russell B., *A History of Western Philosophy*, London, Allen and Unwin, 1946.

Saint François d'Assise, *Œuvres*, Paris, Albin Michel, 1959.

Schœnbaum D., *La Révolution brune, la société allemande sous le IIIe Reich*, Paris, Laffont, 1979.

Seal A., *The Emergence of Indian Nationalism*, Cambridge, Cambridge University Press, 1971.

Siegfried A., *Tableau politique de la France de l'Ouest*, Geneva-Paris, Slatkine Reprints, 1980.

Slicher Van Bath B.H., *The Agrarian History of Western Europe*, London, Edward Arnold, 1963.

Spengler O., *Le Déclin de l'Occident*, Paris, Gallimard, 1948.

Thapar R., *A History of India*, London, Penguin Books, 1966.

Thousand and One Nights, The, trans. B.W. Lane, London Chatto and Windus, 1912.

Tocqueville A., *De la démocratie en Amérique*, Paris, Gallimard, 1961.

Trevor-Roper H.R., *The European Witch-Craze of the Sixteenth and Seventeenth Centuries*, London, Penguin Books, 1969.

Tsebelis G., *Analyse de correspondance: application à la géographie électorale de la Grèce (1958–1977)* (thesis) Institut d'études politiques de Paris, 1979.

Vié M., *Le Japon contemporain*, Paris, PUF, 1971.

Warburg G., *Islam, Nationalism and Communism in a Traditional Society. The Case of Sudan*, London, Frank Cass, 1978.

Watt W.M., *Mahomet*, Paris, Payot, 1980.

Weber M., *Economy and Society*, California, University of California Press, 1978.

L'Éthique protestante et l'esprit du capitalisme, Paris, Plon, 1964 (German edn, 1920).

Weil R, ed., *Politique d'Aristote*, selected texts, Paris, Armand Colin, 1966.

Wilson A.J., *Electoral Politics in an Emergent State. The Ceylon General Election of May 1970*, Cambridge, Cambridge University Press, 1975.

Wittogel K., *Le Despotisme oriental*, Paris, Éditions de Minuit, 1964–77.

Wolf E.R., *Peasant Wars of the Twentieth Century*, London, Faber, 1969.

Wolf E.R., *Peasants*, Englewood Cliffs, Prentice-Hall, 1966.

Index

absolute nuclear family
and agriculture, concentration of 62
in Britain 15
and Catholicism 80
and communism, support for 50—3
definition and characteristics of 10, 99
and equality, attitude to 28
and government changes 69
and incest taboo 20
incidence of 31, 127
suicide rate in 41
see also nuclear family
Africa
anthropological data on 191
inheritance patterns in 192, 193
Islam in 138, 139
literacy in 193, 194
matrilineal system in 166
military regimes in 194, 195
African family systems 25, 26, 191—5
characteristics of 25, 26, 191, 192
husband/wife age difference in 192
incidence of 31
American Civil War 131
amok
anthropological origins of 183—5
in politics 185—7
AMP (Asiatic mode of production) 176,
177
anarchy 104, 105
anomic family 171—90
age at marriage in 178, 180
amok 183—5
and Buddhism 184, 185
in Ceylon 170
and class endogamy 174, 175
common household form in 23
cultural dynamism in 178—80
definition and characteristics of 20,
24, 171, 183
distribution of 24, 173, 174
and equality, attitude to 28
and incest 23, 24, 116, 171—3, 177
incidence of 31
in Latin America 115, 116
and marriage partner, choice of 27
and neutralism 182, 183
and political ambivalence 180—2
religions in 173, 174

and state structure, fragility of 175—8
anti-semitism 61, 89, 90, 131
origin of 58, 59
see also Nazism
anthropology
and ideology, relationship of 13
social, definition of 6
asymmetrical community family 22, 24,
155—70
characteristics of 155, 159, 160
and equality, attitude to 28
ideological manifestations of see
caste system
incidence of 31
atheism 5, 38, 39
Austria
elections in 72
marriage age in 83, 85
authoritarian family 55—98
and communism, support for 50—3
definition and characteristics of 11, 55
distribution and incidence of 31, 55,
56, 66, 127
and education 93
and equality, attitude to 28
ideological manifestation of see
authoritarian societies
illegitimacy in 90
and incest taboos 20, 22, 23
marriage age in 82, 83
and physical violence 64
and socialism and Catholicism in
Europe 67
suicide rate in 41
and witch-hunts see separate entry
women, role and status of, in 64,
65, 112, 113
authoritarian societies 55—98
asymmetry and anarchy in 59, 60
asymmetrical pluralism and elections
in 69—73
contradictions in 65, 66
economic aspects of 61—3, 107, 108
electoral rigidity in 68, 69
government changes in 69
ideological manifestations of 66—8,
73, 76
particularism of 75
political parties in 71